M000009253

To my mother, with love

And in memory of
Fatima Hamid
and
Lalla Kiltum, "Tagullizt"
ad tnt iṛḥm ṛbbi

Additional praise for *We Share Walls*

"A beautiful and deeply researched ethnography that elucidates how performance genres like talk, song, and poetry create a sense of place and a particularly Berber (and gendered) response to modernity."

Deborah Kapchan, The Tisch School of the Arts at New York University

"At last we have an account of Berber Morocco that probes space, culture, and people in a highly sensitive and eloquent style. Hoffman brings to the forefront a long marginalized language and an almost forgotten community. This is indeed ethnography at its best. Readers will be inspired by the breadth and depth of Hoffman's treatment."

Enam Al-Wer, University of Essex

"With compassion and intellectual acuity, Hoffman's study of the Berber-speaking Ishelhin of Southern Morocco evokes a society where the spoken word has molded a deep attachment to place. Her observations glow with the intensity of lived experience, distilled from a total immersion in the land, language, and people of this remote region. Using speech, poetry, and song as keys to understanding social process, *We Share Walls* represents a major contribution to contemporary Moroccan Studies and to the wider field of ethnolinguistics."

Susan Gilson Miller, Harvard University

"An excellent in-depth study of the gender and language dynamics in Berber communities. A highly readable and timely addition to the emerging and promising scholarship on language, gender, and women in Morocco."

Fatima Sadiqi, Harvard University

Linguistic anthropology evolved in the 20th century in an environment that tended to reify language and culture. A recognition of the dynamics of discourse as a sociocultural process has since emerged as researchers have used new methods and theories to examine the reproduction and transformation of people, institutions, and communities through linguistic practices. This transformation of linguistic anthropology itself heralds a new era for publishing as well. **Blackwell Studies in Discourse and Culture** aims to represent and foster this new approach to discourse and culture by producing books that focus on the dynamics that can be obscured by such broad and diffuse terms as "language." This series is committed to the ethnographic approach to language and discourse: ethnographic works deeply informed by theory, as well as more theoretical works that are deeply grounded in ethnography. The books are aimed at scholars in the sociology and anthropology of language, anthropological linguistics, sociolinguistics and socioculturally informed psycholinguistics. It is our hope that all books in the series will be widely adopted for a variety of courses.

Series Editor

James M. Wilce (PhD University of California, Los Angeles) is Professor of Anthropology at Northern Arizona University, where he is currently Director of Asian Studies. He serves on the editorial board of *American Anthropologist* and the *Journal of Linguistic Anthropology*. He has published a number of articles and is the author of *Eloquence in Trouble: The Poetics and Politics of Complaint in Rural Bangladesh* (1998) and *Language and Emotion* (forthcoming) and the editor of *Social and Cultural Lives of Immune Systems* (2003).

Editorial Board:

Richard Bauman – Indiana University
Eve Danziger – University of Virginia
Patrick Eisenlohr – Washington University
Per-Anders Forstorp – Royal Institute of Technology, Stockholm
Elizabeth Keating – UT Austin
Paul Kroskrity – UCLA
Norma Mendoza-Denton – University of Arizona
Susan Philips – University of Arizona
Bambi Schieffelin – NYU
Lukas Tsitsipis – University of Thessaloniki, Greece

In the Series:

1. *The Hidden Life of Girls*, by Marjorie Harness Goodwin
2. *We Share Walls: Language, Land, and Gender in Berber Morocco*, by Katherine E. Hoffman

Forthcoming:

- *Living Memory*, by Jillian R. Cavanaugh
- *The Language of White Racism in the United States*, by Jane Hill

We Share Walls

Language, Land, and Gender in Berber Morocco

Katherine E. Hoffman

Blackwell
Publishing

© 2008 by Katherine E. Hoffman

BLACKWELL PUBLISHING
350 Main Street, Malden, MA 02148-5020, USA
9600 Garsington Road, Oxford OX4 2DQ, UK
550 Swanston Street, Carlton, Victoria 3053, Australia

The right of Katherine E. Hoffman to be identified as the Author of this Work has been asserted in accordance with the UK Copyright, Designs, and Patents Act 1988.

All rights reserved. No part of this publication may be reproduced, stored in a retrieval system, or transmitted, in any form or by any means, electronic, mechanical, photocopying, recording or otherwise, except as permitted by the UK Copyright, Designs, and Patents Act 1988, without the prior permission of the publisher.

Designations used by companies to distinguish their products are often claimed as trademarks. All brand names and product names used in this book are trade names, service marks, trademarks, or registered trademarks of their respective owners. The publisher is not associated with any product or vendor mentioned in this book.

This publication is designed to provide accurate and authoritative information in regard to the subject matter covered. It is sold on the understanding that the publisher is not engaged in rendering professional services. If professional advice or other expert assistance is required, the services of a competent professional should be sought.

First published 2008 by Blackwell Publishing Ltd

2 2008

Library of Congress Cataloging-in-Publication Data

Hoffman, Katherine E.
We share walls : language, land, and gender in Berber Morocco / Katherine E. Hoffman.
p. cm.—(Blackwell studies in discourse and culture)
Includes bibliographical references and index.
ISBN 978-1-4051-5420-8 (hardcover : alk. paper)—ISBN 978-1-4051-5421-5 (pbk.: alk. paper) 1. Berbers—Morocco—Social life and customs. 2. Berbers—Morocco—Social conditions. 3. Women—Morocco. 4. Acculturation—Morocco. 5. Morocco—Ethnic relations. I. Title.

DT313.2.H64 2007
305.89′33064—dc22

2007018980

A catalogue record for this title is available from the British Library.

Set in 11.5 on 13.5pt Bembo
by SNP Best-set Typesetter Ltd., Hong Kong

For further information on
Blackwell Publishing, visit our website:
www.blackwellpublishing.com

Contents

Figures, Tables and Transcripts

Figures

Tables

Transcripts

Series Preface

Blackwell Studies in Discourse and Culture was launched in 2005, committed to publish new titles with an ethnographic approach to language and discourse, and ethnographic works deeply informed by theory. *We Share Walls* by Katherine Hoffman is just such a work, illuminating precisely the issues outlined in the call.

The series books foreground the dynamics of discourse by illuminating issues such as:

- the global and local dynamics of the production, reception, circulation, and contextualization of discourse;
- the discursive production of social collectivities;
- the dynamic relation of speech acts to agents, social roles, and identities;
- the emergent relation of ideologies to linguistic structure and the social lives of linguistic forms; and
- the dialectic relations of local speech events to larger social formations and centers of power.

As Hoffman explains in the first chapter, her title derives from one of the performance forms that helps to constitute Ashelhi social life – a particular *tazrrart* or "sung poem" about "sharing boundaries" and "being one." The original poem is particularly apt as a source for the title, for it expresses the effort – part of which is expended in the very performance of such expressive forms – that "being one" entails. The agents Hoffman describes, including the poet in this case, are often Ishelhin women – singing, socializing their children, defying stereotypes by living their Tashelhit-speaking lives even in the Sous plains, and actively consuming media (radio in particular) while producing intelligent commentary thereupon.

Katherine Hoffman is an ethnographer's ethnographer. Spending three and a half years in the field (unusual for a dissertation project) has yielded a remarkable richness, with many layers to every experience, many methods to support every claim, many sites to illustrate each tendency, and three relevant field languages – Tashelhit, Arabic, and French – on which she draws to lend each translation its nuance. We find here both self-deprecating *self*-reflexivity and documentation of the reflexivity of Tashelhit actors busily engaged in producing goods for circulation. Included in these are, of course, goods such as Modern Standard Tashelhit, or MST. Though the actors here, producing their neologisms, are mostly elite urban radio personalities far removed from those with whom Hoffman spent most of her time in the mountains and on the plains, we should not think that the latter groups labored only to produce subsistence goods. Hoffman demonstrates again and again that ordinary women and men are the crucial producers and circulators of the genres in which Tashelhit has its life.

Each time we follow Hoffman, we meet with surprise – whether we accompany her on the discursive pathways that trace Ashelhi identity and the purity of the Tashelhit language to the mountain homeland or *tamazirt,* or we squeeze with her into a crowded taxi whose passengers – including the author – debate gendered visions of responsibility for various threats to Tashelhit; or we land in the midst of parties in the mountains or wedding songfests in the plains; or we listen in as urban Ashelhi radio personalities surprise some listeners with the latest MST coinage. The surprises result from the very things that make this book a fine exemplar of the series – Hoffman's constant attention to the *dynamics* of social, cultural, and linguistic processes. Thus, for example, the *tamazirt* is built, and gendered – and Tashelhit preserved – through performance, which Hoffman envisions as combining "manual labor practices alongside discursive practices" (compare Irvine 1989 on Wolof *griots*). The surprises in Hoffman's account of the informal party in Chapter Three are several – it is a mixed-sex gathering of unmarried adolescents in which, as Hoffman puts it, "rural and (returned) urban youths fashion each other" by exchanging the symbolic goods associated with mountain and city life. In this and many other ways Hoffman enriches us. Given the manifold forms of active engagement Ishelhin have with Tashelhit ways of speaking, *We Share Walls* is a unique contribution on many fronts, telling complex stories about culture and metaculture, gender, performance, language shift and maintenance.

Thus, it gives me great pleasure to introduce this exquisite ethnography, and with it, *Blackwell Studies in Discourse and Culture.*

Jim Wilce
Series Editor

Acknowledgments

This book was made possible by the women and men of Ida ou Zeddout, Arazan, Tazzemourt, Tiout, Touraght, Indouzal, and Taroudant, many of whom are given pseudonyms in this work. I sincerely hope that my affection and respect for them come through in these pages, and that readers will come to care about these people who have been sometimes exoticized and other times disregarded, but rarely taken at their word.

Without the people who helped me to learn to speak and understand Tashelhit, and then to transcribe, transliterate and translate it, this book never would have been written. Thanks go to Ahmed Boukous and Mohamed Najmi for their initial lessons in Tashelhit. Latifa Asseffar had an enviable attention to detail, taste for hard work, and calm disposition that made the years of transcribing together a joy. The mutual intellectual and emotional growth our friendship fostered has enriched my life immeasurably; I am thankful as well to her mother Zayna and sister Samira for their hospitality. My neighbors in Taroudant not only taught me Tashelhit but became my surrogate family: gentle Fatima Mhammd ("Little Fatima") and outgoing Fatima Hamid ("Big Fatima") took me into their lives as a beloved equal with their sons Omar, Mustafa, Mohamed and Kemal; they taught me to bargain in the markets, stand up for myself, preserve lemons, make couscous, and be patient. Mina Alahyane from Ida ou Zeddout brought me to her mountains, endured my persistent questions about life there, shared festive times, and steadfastly bore witness to my character when it was under fire. She enthusiastically took on the role of the critical insider-outsider on whom many of us anthropologists depend. I am deeply touched by her dedication to this research and her abiding friendship.

For support, encouragement, suggestions for improvement, and corrections of errors I am grateful to innumerable friends and colleagues, and ask forgiveness from those I fail to mention here. In Morocco, I am thankful for the warm collegiality and assistance of Ahmed Aassid, Lhaj Hmed Ahamayti and his wife Fadila, Fatima Agnaou, Omar Amarir, Ahmed

Amrani, Abdelmajid Araaman, Ahmed Boukous, Ahmed Bouzid, Hmed El Harim, Mohamed Elmedlaoui, Abdallah El Mountassir, Mhand El Moussaoui, Abdessalem Id Belkassm, Rachid Laabdelaoui, Saadia Maski, Mohammed Mhemdi, Mbarka Mrat Lhaj, Mohammed Ounougo, Ismael Khattouch, Omar Shatar, Fatima Taki, Mina Z. and her mother-in-law Tafqirt, and Hmed ou Hmou. I benefited immeasurably from stimulating discussions with fellow researchers Shana Cohen, Diana Davis, Susan Schaefer Davis, Ramzy Kanaan, Oren Kosansky, Geoff Porter, and especially David Crawford; with graduate students in Ahmed Boukous' sociolinguistics seminar at Mohamed V University, Rabat (1996); and with Meghan Donahue, Molly James, and Chris Ormsby. I have been fortunate to work with exceptional colleagues at the University of California at Los Angeles, University of Illinois at Chicago, and Northwestern University, several of whom provided useful critique and support for this project, among them Alessandro Duranti, Candy Goodwin, Charles Goodwin, Elinor Ochs, Paul Kroskrity, Robert Launay, Micaela di Leonardo, Bill Leonard, and Bill Murphy. Many undergraduates and graduate students at these institutions have forced me to link the particulars with the bigger picture; Devon Liddell was particularly inspiring in this regard. A chance encounter with Ted Levin in Morocco not only led to a raucous party for his students with local performers at my house in Taroudant, but also introduced me to ethnomusicology and got me thinking about the relationship between speech and song. Miriam Rovsing Olsen and Claude Lefebure have generously shared their vast knowledge of Berber music and poetry and provided a French check on my analyses. Christopher Bradley's help in notating field recordings allowed for more in-depth understanding of musical code-switching and variation than did the song texts alone. The staff at the Division de la Statistique and the Ministère de la Prévision Economique in Rabat were most helpful in providing statistics. Jilali Kouainso, then with the Division of Economic and Social Affairs, Province of Taroudant, offered his unpublished, detailed manuscript on the province. I am grateful to all of them.

This book started as a doctoral dissertation at Columbia University, and I am indebted to teachers there and elsewhere who guided me. M. Elaine Combs-Schilling helped me to place this work in a trajectory of historical shifts in Morocco, considering the contingency of ethnicity and language allegiances, and emboldened me to look for radical alternatives to dominant discourses from strong women. She coaxed me, as she often put it with her students, to "consider other realities, just for a moment," an approach I have retained as a teacher as well as researcher. David Koester meticulously and diplomatically intervened at key moments and pushed me to justify my attention to language in this cultural project. Brinkley Messick provided useful insight into this project in the *longue durée* of Moroccanist scholarship. Philip Schuyler still generously shares his appreciation and vast knowledge of Berber music as well as his field contacts; he has been indispensable to my development as a Berberist scholar. My deepest intellectual debt and greatest admiration goes to Bambi B. Schieffelin, mentor, friend, and traveling companion. She asks the hard questions and remains confident that I will answer them, and she has always looked one step ahead of me in my scholarly development. I deeply respect her work, appreciate her trust in my abilities, and treasure her friendship. Thank you.

Several colleagues read and generously commented on parts of one or more chapters: Jillian Cavanaugh, Judith Irvine, John Jackson, Alexandra Jaffe, Kathleen Riley, and Paul Silverstein. It is my great fortune that one of the few other American Berberists is Jane Goodman; it has been a pleasure to learn from her on conference panels, review each other's work, and share insights and resolve translation problems. Richard Bauman and Deborah Kapchan read the entire manuscript and provided encouragement and helpful insights for improvement. I have tremendous respect for their scholarship and am humbled by their interest in my own. This book has been enthusiastically supported by the editorial board of Blackwell's Discourse and Culture series. Series Editor James Wilce thoughtfully worked through each sentence in this text, offered crucial suggestions for revision, and helped buoy my spirits when they flagged. At Blackwell, I wish to thank former editor Jane Huber for her support of this book, as well as her successor Rosalie Robertson and editorial assistant Deirdre Ilkson for their attention to detail and good cheer. Mohammed Lahnin, Katie McKeown, and Julia Fraser provided helpful bibliographic assistance. I am grateful to them and to Ana Croegaert and Aurélien Mauxion who meticulously proofed the book.

Generous grants for field research (1995–9) and write-up came from the Wenner-Gren Foundation for Anthropological Research, the Program for the Near and Middle East and the International Predissertation Fellowship Program of the Social Science Research Council, the Fulbright IIE program administered through the Moroccan-American Commission in Rabat, the National Endowment for the Humanities, the Institute for the Humanities and the Office of the Vice Chancellor for Research at the University of Illinois at Chicago, the American Institute for Maghrib Studies, and the Northwestern University Research Grants Committee. Northwestern generously provided the publication subvention that returned the radio chapter to this book.

I want to thank several people for their companionship and intellectual stimulation at different stages of this project: Aicha Azzaoui, Greta Austin, Susan Bronson, Alex Costley, Neal Durando, Mokhtar Ghambou, and Mei Lin Kwan-Gett. Frederick Ilchman, then in Venice, encouraged me to describe all the sights, smells, tastes and sounds of Morocco; I cherish those airmail letters and the friendship that inspired them. Mike Kanovitz opined, at a crucial juncture, that surely there must be a connection between drought and language. During the book revisions, Sheldon Lutte and Helen Thompson provided welcome social diversions and unfailing support. Carlos Hurtado applied his poetic good sense and sensibility in helping to finalize translations. In Cruzy le Châtel, Burgundy, Flo and Jean-Louis Yvon fed and housed me and helped me to keep a sense of humor; Geneviève and Lounis Ibouadilène, Pascal Herbaut, and Marie-Thérèse and Jean-Paul Boucher also provided social and gustatory nourishment across several years of revisions. Jean-Yves Boucher's passion for every last corner of his rainfed, rocky fields instilled in me – *enfin* – a visceral sense of what it means to be anchored in ancestral lands. Thank you – *ou plutôt merci* – to all of you.

Most of all, I want to thank my mother, Sonja Kay Hoffman, who enthusiastically nurtured my early fascination with language. She helped me to apply for a Rotary exchange scholarship, which led to a high school junior year abroad in a working class neighborhood of Brussels where many of my friends were of Moroccan and Algerian descent. That year set the stage for a life-long commitment to understanding linguistic and cultural diversity and change as well as marginalization. Over a decade later, my mother delighted in my Moroccan adventures both through her two visits and extensive letter-writing; she jogged my memory about things learned in the field and then forgotten, and she handled the subletters, mail, pet care, and logistical support over many years. She is now tired of my frequent departures, but she is fundamentally responsible for sparking my anthropological curiosity.

I also owe a serious debt to *larzaq*, fate or luck. My Soussi friends and consultants reasoned that I was among them because it was my larzaq to like the *amarg n tmazirt*, the mood or music of the countryside. They were right, and what I learned from them transformed my mind, my heart, and my soul for the better. To all of you, *ad iyi isamḥ ṛbbi*. As for the errors in hearing, understanding, and interpretation that remain in this book, I accept sole responsibility.

* * *

Earlier formulations of some of the material in Chapters Four and Five appeared in *American Ethnologist* (2002) 294:928–62.

Lines from the work of W.B. Yeats ("The Second Coming," 1921 and "Easter 1916," 1924) are reprinted in the US with the permission of Scribner, an imprint of Simon & Schuster Adult Publishing Group, from *The Collected Works for W.B. Yeats, Volume I: The Poems*, revised and edited by Richard J. Finneran. Copyright © 1924 by The Macmillan company; copyright renewed © 1952 by Bertha Georgie Yeats. All rights reserved. In the UK, these are by the permission of A.P. Watt Ltd on behalf of Gráinne Yeats, Executrix of the Estate of Michael Butler Yeats.

"Older Women," from *The Great Fires Poems 1982–1992* by Jack Gilbert, is copyright © 1994 by Jack Gilbert. Used by permission of Alfred A. Knopf, a division of Random House, Inc.

Note on Transcription and Transliteration

Abbreviations in this text include CA for Classical Arabic, SA for Standard Arabic, and MA for Moroccan Arabic.

On first use, Tashelhit is italicized, Arabic is underlined; bivalent terms and phrases (equally integrated in both Tashelhit and Arabic) are italicized and underlined. French terms are italicized. I take a Tashelhit speaker's perspective in marking lexical items as Tashelhit, MA, or bivalent. For this reason, terms with Arabic or French origins that are fully assimilated into Tashelhit are marked in italics (e.g. *sukkar* "sugar," *laṣl* "roots"). Both Tashelhit and MA are characterized by consonant clusters such as s+h, s+ḥ, š+t. I transcribe with one grapheme per phoneme.

Common sounds shared by Tashelhit and MA, and not found in English, include emphatics marked with subscript dots ḍ, ḥ, ṣ, ẓ, ṭ, and ṛ and the following:

ġ	(voiced uvular fricative, like a nasal pronunciation of the French r)
q	(glottal stop deep in the throat)
r	(once-rolled r, as in the Spanish "pero")
x	(voiceless uvular fricative, often transcribed from Arabic as /kh/ as in makhzen, central government)
ε	(in Tashelhit, a softened Arabic 'ayn)
^{w}	(particular to Tashelhit; a high rounded and extended ooo sound typically preceded by a doubled (labiovelarized) consonant)

Other transcription conventions here include:

š	(as in "shoe")
ay	(a dipthong, as in "eye")
i	(long vowel often transcribed as ī, as in "sheet")
j	(initial consonant in the French "Jacques")
g	(as in "gas")

Tashelhit has three vowels: a (as in "ah"), i (as in "East"), and u (as in "boot"). Moroccan Arabic also has e (as in "end").

The ġ has often been transcribed as gh in Anglophone and Francophone scholarship; colonial French texts also transcribed with ṙ. In many contemporary works, the ġ is transcribed with the gamma (γ). In Morocco, the gamma was long associated with Amazigh activism, and its use indexed a political pan-Amazigh stance with an intellectual core in neighboring Algerian Kabylia. I have retained ġ as a more neutral convention and to increase accessibility to non-Berberists.

The definite article /l/ preceding Tashelhit nouns usually indicates assimilated borrowings from Arabic, as in *lmdrst*, school (Ar. madrasa).

Additional transcription conventions include : to indicate a lengthening of the preceding sound and [to mark overlap between speakers.

Place names and common nouns are conventionally spelled without diacritical marks: e.g. Ishelhin (*išlḥiyn*), Tashelhit (*tšlḥiyt*), makhzen (maxzn), Sous (*sus*), Ait Ida ou Zeddout (*ayt idaw zddut*), Quran (*qur'an*).

I recorded all the sung poetry in this book between 1996 and 1999 unless otherwise noted. The recordings were transcribed into Tashelhit using a system of Arabic script I developed with Latifa Asseffar. Mina Alahyane generously helped to transcribe the tizrrarin sung poetry from her native Ait Musi section of Ida ou Zeddout. Both of them preferred working with me in the Arabic script; subsequent transliteration from Arabic to Latin script was then necessary. Linguist Rachid Laabdelaoui of IRCAM (Royal Institute of Moroccan Amazigh Culture) carefully assisted with this task using recently standardized word segmentation principles. All translations from Tashelhit, Arabic, and French into English are my own unless otherwise noted.

Part I

Prelude

Et nous osons espérer que si nous nous sommes éloignés du vrai,
nous sommes tout au moins resté dans le vraisemblable.
We dare to hope that if we have strayed from the truth,
we have at least remained in the plausible.

– Officier Interprète Rabia (1935),
"La coutume Ait Tayia"

iġ ilkum yan imi n tmazirt imiyys iqqiys
anna d salan ayt tmazirt lhun d isn
If you arrive at the edge of a land, watch discreetly
Whatever the people of that land do, follow their lead

– Anti-Atlas tazrrart

Chapter 1

Introduction: Staying Put

Things fall apart; the center cannot hold
– W.B. Yeats, "The Second Coming" (1921)

When rain falls in the winter in the Anti-Atlas mountains of southwestern Morocco, almond and wild pistachio trees bloom in the spring, their foliage dusted with dirt as the heat increases in summer. Juniper bushes dot the mountainside. In the summer the heat obscures the height of Adrar Tisfane (Mount Tisfane) to the west and Adrar Toubqal to the north. In the dead of winter, the peaks punctuate the bright blue sky, and the late afternoon light tinges the walls and earth a deep salmon. Most years, in both the Anti-Atlas mountains and the Sous Valley, rain is scarce or absent altogether, heat is dense, and dust covers everything. Brushing off the dust – from floors, tea glasses, clothes – is constant and instinctual, like waving at a fly on your lip, but just as futile. Some areas of the mountains are blessed with scattered almond or argan trees, and when it rains, fields of barley sprout bright green in the spring. Most years, however, drought prevents even a modest harvest, and everything in sight is the color of parched earth. Resident women curse global warming, believing what they have heard on the radio about the earth getting hotter as evidence of their wretched lot and fuel for their desire to leave for the city.

You scan the dry landscape for flora, and notice the telephone and electricity poles that pass through the countryside without servicing it, en route to the towns. You notice the pink and yellow-painted cinder block houses, the half-constructed villas that encircle the stone villages. Then you wonder where the men are. Boys leave for the cities by the time they reach adolescence, joining the men who did the same in their youth. Women are alone with each other, their daughters, their young sons, and their daughters-in-law in these dry mountains. In the mornings, they collect fodder and wood, dressed in ankle-length navy wraps (*tamlḥaft*-s) over layers of colorful dresses, skirts, and pants, their heads wrapped in more color or in the traditional black. In the late afternoon sun, they perch like multicolored birds on the door stoops, chatting in the long shadows of their stone houses. Children scamper about or cling to their mothers' backs if they are too young to play.

The omnipresent mountain woman at the end of the twentieth century was iconic of the Ashelhi Berber ethnolinguistic group, an entity for whom both language and land have become contested terrain in this postnationalist phase of the post-Independence period following the French Protectorate (1912–56). For both emigrant men in the cities and the broader Moroccan citizenry, the Berber woman came to personify the rugged, stoic, yet vulnerable homeland and its inseparable twin: the persistent, ancient, hearty, yet threatened language. In this set of associations, women effectively acted not only for themselves and their families, but also for the whole of the ethnolinguistic group. Women bore both the material and symbolic responsibilities for maintaining the land and the Tashelhit Berber language so closely associated with it. Emigrant men leaving the mountains for the cities, in particular, demonstrated to me that they considered the Tashelhit language as key to a moral universe whose values were expressed in talk, song, and non-verbal behavior, attesting to men's continued relevance despite their infrequent presence in the *tamazirt* (homeland, countryside or rural place; pl. *timizar*). Through their native language, emigrant men maintained authority over family and community affairs, marked group boundaries, and delimited a geographical space in which the social and linguistic hierarchies favored them, a sharp contrast with the cities where Arabic held symbolic capital. This order of things entailed both responsibilities and privileges for women, as it became apparent to me during three and a half years of residence in Morocco (1995–9), three of them based in the market town of Taroudant from which I moved into the Anti-Atlas mountains and Sous plains for research and participated in national and religious rituals, agricultural cycles, school years, and life-cycle events such as engagements, weddings, circumcisions, and funerals.

This book aims to understand how expressive culture mediated constructions of place, personhood, and community among a marginalized yet fetishized indigenous group of Berber language speakers in the late twentieth century, and where the effects of these practices took hold in people's lives. For outsiders to these communities, there was a taken-for-granted association between rurality, Tashelhit language, and the cultural distinctiveness that set Ishelhin apart from urban residents and others generally called Arabs. Within these rural communities, in contrast, the link between language and land was frequently debated and actively nurtured. A gendered vigilance, both in terms of practices and boundary maintenance, countered an imagined atrophy that was believed, if left unchecked, to turn Ishelhin into Arabs, dissolve the Tashelhit language, and erase their as-yet mostly unwritten histories. Things fall apart. The center must constantly be renewed if it is to hold. Efforts to prevent the Ashelhi tamazirt and the Tashelhit language from "falling apart" – by repairing a pocked asphalt road, adorning one's head with silver for a wedding, or purging one's Tashelhit speech of Arabic and French borrowings – instantiated intentional, deliberate efforts at rejuvenation, not a mere maintenance of the status quo.

With massive rural–urban migration throughout the twentieth century, these indigenous people were intimately familiar with the discourses of authenticity, linguistic purity, and morality that made their homelands a distinctive material and symbolic core for the Ashelhi ethnolinguistic group. I propose that we conceive of mobility and movement not as indicative of the decay of the community, culture, or language, but as constitutive of its growth, in this case building the homeland, thereby maintaining a location and a nexus of social relations in which other practices consolidate Ashelhi identity as idiosyncratic, stigmatized, or defiant. Such an approach requires that we strive to understand the homeland and Tashelhit language from its residents' contested and situated perspectives, rather than relying on judgmental or romantic urban perspectives of their Other.

Many outsiders presume that Moroccan mountains are Berber spaces in Lefebvre's (1991) sense of spaces as pre-modern, natural terrains distinct from places that, in contrast, are shaped by historical and global forces. Yet from the inside looking out, rural places are as much historically shaped as are towns and cities. For their inhabitants, the presumed association between rurality and ethnolinguistic identity is passionately and constantly negotiated. How are bundles of associations – like the central one considered in this book, linking Tashelhit language, rural lands, and women – consolidated and reproduced, and under which conditions and by whom are they negotiated and contested? Such matters are by no means taken for granted in rural areas, as attested by rich discourses of both contestation and affirmation. Material and discursive practices together make Berber places meaningful and Berber language appropriate. Both practices and discourses are gendered, and plains and mountain communities operate in relation to different political economies.

We Share Walls

> *a yan a nga nkki dun yan nšrk*
> *nšrk didk iwtta d lɛyun nswa ukan*
> *ula targ*^{w}*a nġ nsswa nssu winnun*
> We are one, you (pl.) and me, we share walls
> Our fields share boundaries and springs
> and from our channels we water yours
> – Eastern Anti-Atlas tazrrart, Ida ou Zeddout

Hajja, a grandmother who produced this sung poem (*tazrrart*, pl. *tizrrarin*), married into Ida ou Zeddout, where I worked, from her native Ida ou Naḍif near Igherm. She sang this song at a wedding I attended with her and her children. In the verse, being "one" means sharing land and water, the most basic elements, even though in practice the community relies heavily on remittances and external goods to survive. The symbolic importance of tending the land emerges in this verse in no small part because of the community that people forge through the land. But the verse suggests as well that "being one" means sharing boundaries, markers that divide. "We are one" not because we are from the same lineage, village, tribe, or ethnic group, or because we are fond of each other, but because our plots share demarcations. I gloss these borders here as "walls" to evoke the simultaneously material and symbolic facets of such divisions. Moreover, the phrase "we share walls" metaphorically evokes the barriers many Berber women told me they sensed in terms of their access to linguistic and material resources. Taken in the context of the mountain wedding in which Hajja sang the verse, "we" are self-sufficient yet interdependent in maintaining connectedness and delineation by, for instance, assuring that the stones dividing field plots remain as they were. Instead of naming the entity entailed in "we," the verse describes conditions of attachment. "Being one" requires vigilance and maintenance; it is active, not a natural or inherent state of affairs, and thus vulnerable to shifts in a neighbor's good will.

At this wedding, female guests from the bride's village and their children sat in one section of the courtyard, and those from the groom's village sat in another. Each group sang a series of tizrrarin, alternating between vocalists while stringing them together. When the women from one village tired, those from the other took over, ensuring a smooth succession of verse production during the hours waiting for the evening meal, and later in the evening, for the collective dance entertainment. Given the context, Hajja addressed the women of the other village. Their fields literally shared neither borders nor water sources. Instead, the interdependence to which Hajja referred was more symbolic than material, an attempt to nurture good relations with female guests who were largely strangers brought together through the families of the bride and groom.

Hajja's song contains an ambiguous referent that is suggestive of the marginalization these women experienced. When rural Ishelhin in the 1990s talked about group solidarity, they rarely did so according to urban intellectual concepts like identity (Ar. huwiyya) or ethnicity (Fr. *ethnie*). There are Tashelhit terms for "our talk" (*awal nġ*) and "our people" (*ayt darnġ*), as well as gender- and number-specific derivations of the latter (*ult darnġ*, our sister and *gu darnġ*, our brother) for a female or male from one's own community. Ishelhin from the Anti-Atlas spoke also of the tribe (*taqbilt*, Ar. qbila), and in town people referred to *aqbayl*, dear ones, meaning biological or fictive kin.

Yet in the midst of these generalities, Ishelhin were attentive to the "pleasures of microdifferentiation" (Tsing 1993:61), among individuals and between groups. Differentiating practices emerged when women gathered in public festivities and inquired into each others' laboring and cultural practices: "Who plows in your lands, men or women?" "What grows in your fields?" "Who is your saint?" "Where is your market?" Women were the tradition-bearers; once married, women perpetuated their husbands' traditions rather than their patriline's traditions. For an older generation of Sous plains Arab women, this could even mean learning Tashelhit. Yet by the late 1990s, Arab women rarely married into Tashelhit-speaking families; Arabic speakers generally viewed Tashelhit as hindering economic and social opportunities. Berber cultural heritage has often been written about as though it were singular, or unified within a geographical mountain range (the Rif, the Eastern High Atlas/Middle Atlas, and the Western High Atlas/Anti-Atlas) by its dialectal variety. From the perspective of Ishelhin I knew, however, verbal expressive practices were highly variegated by subgroup in ways that were openly discussed, debated, yet agreed to be "just the way things are" (*lqaɛida*). It made little sense to village women to talk about preserving cultural practices, including language. Intentionality came up short against God's will.

Language as Knowledge, Knowledge as Capital: Ideologies of Language

The value of language in encoding sets of knowledge was apparent in my interactions with Ishelhin in which my presence provided a counterpoint for people to reflect on their own subjectivities. A particularly illustrative encounter took place during Ramadan, the Muslim month of fasting, in January–February 1997. I spent most of it among the Ida ou Zeddout people and in the town of Igherm in the Eastern Anti-Atlas. Whereas the town had electric heat and gas-powered water heaters, in the mountains no comforts mediated the winter chill. Without the distraction of the harvest cycle, village women warded off hunger and thirst by sleeping late in the morning. They greeted each other outside their homes with the question "Ramadan's not too much for you?" (*izd ur am iḥawl Rmdan?*). Women bundled in layers of colorful floral and striped polyester blouses and skirts, acrylic and wool leggings, and socks. Their days were full of domestic chores and visiting, unlike years in which Ramadan fell during the busy plowing, planting, or harvesting seasons. Eager to make the time pass convivially, Hajja and her teenaged daughter Ftuma offered to make me a rug. Hajja's high school-aged daughter Mina and I set off to buy weaving supplies in Igherm, now a market town but built as a fortress by the French in 1927 and named accordingly. With its elevation and vantage point, Igherm stood at the French Protectorate frontier between the *tribus soumis* (pacified tribes) in the general direction of Taroudant and the *tribus dissidents* (dissident tribes) due south and southeast. Igherm remained a harsh frontier town where women left their homes to walk the dry dirt paths only when absolutely necessary. Men crowded the public squares where buses departed for towns and cities, and buses and collective taxis forged deeper into the mountains. Purveyors of household staples stocked up in Igherm at unmarked warehouses; the town center boasted a public phone shop, stationary store, and a few tea houses that also sold hard-boiled eggs and packaged cakes to men in transit. There were no cell phones yet, so news from family and friends in distant cities was infrequent, and their visits were anxiously anticipated yet rarely materialized.

It was the wrong time of year to buy weaving supplies, since women spun and dyed their wool in the warmer months, and the vegetable-dyed spools had sold quickly. All that remained was *ṣuf ṛṛumi*, Christian wool: chemically dyed, soft synthetic yarn in bright colors like yellow and green. Mina and I chose more subdued navy, burgundy, and royal blue yarn, as well as some white for accent; these were far from the earthy, vegetable-dyed tans, rusts, sages, dusty roses, salmons, and mustards of the rugs that lined mountain sitting rooms. Upon our return, Hajja barely concealed her disgust at our color selection, but she promised to do her best. With the help of the other village grandmothers, she set up the loom, passing onion over it to ward off the evil eye (Figure 1.1). Soon after she started into the first *ifassn* (lit. hands) or stripes, neighbors came to inspect the progress, took turns weaving, and added to the chorus of dismay at the color scheme. Some set off to find brightly colored yarn from their own storerooms, and soon enlivened the rug with a hand of grass green next to one that was fire-engine red. The women were clearly delighted with their resourcefulness and the vibrant colors. My own aesthetic sense was appalled: these were tacky Christmas colors. I tried to temper my disappointment, given their generosity, and acclimated to their good humor in carrying on despite

Figure 1.1 Ida ou Zeddout women prepare loom and pass onion over it before weaving

the substandard materials with which I had furnished them. Village women took turns weaving in pairs. The young women with whom I socialized most were conspicuously absent. Later I learned that few young women knew spindle weaving techniques, although some made rag rugs from scraps of fabric on their mothers' looms. The elaborate rugs on which young women slept had been passed down for generations, but not the skills to replace the rugs when they wore thin.

As the older women whiled away the Ramadan hours at the loom, they talked. They talked about talk. They talked about silence too, especially my periodic silence as I sulked guiltily over the colors, and about their incomprehension of my silence. One glanced at me and uttered, "God gave us so much to talk about!" suggesting that my silence was intentional and strategic, perhaps "an expression of power, a refusal to enter into the intercourse that a social inferior is demanding" (Harvey 1994:52). Surely the women did not consider themselves inferior given that they repeatedly alluded to the inferiority of non-Muslims and to my bizarre status as an unmarried woman in her late twenties of unknown *laṣl* (Ar. a̱ṣl, roots or origins). Yet my silence was roundly interpreted not as the resistance I was experiencing, but as a failure to show solidarity, the preferred mode of interaction between Tashelhit women that reinforced the density of their social networks (Milroy 1987). In contrast, I experienced my own silence as submission and awkwardness, denoting what Quechua-speaking women of Ocongate, Bolivia see as "recognition of another's superiority and a simultaneous sense of shame (*verguenza*) in one's own inferior position. An extreme of this meaning is silence as stupidity, silence as indication that a potential speaker can think of nothing to say" (Harvey 1994:53). I would learn over the years of working with the Ida ou Zeddout and other Tashelhit-speaking women that speaking wisely and appropriately – but amply – when among women ensured a woman's status, her perceived intelligence, and her commitment to solidarity. The silence of respect was reserved for mixed-sex settings. Despite my silence during the rug-weaving, women caught up on news of their sons and husbands in the cities and expressed their desires for men's return for the *Id Imẓẓin* or Little Feast (Ar. 'Id Al Fiṭr) soon to mark the end of Ramadan.

Unavoidably, conversation periodically turned to the Westerner in their midst. Fadma, one of the village mothers who had not spent time with me before, looked my way and remarked to the others, "Ah, she speaks Tashelhit." From behind the loom, Hajja's daughter Ftuma elaborated: "She knows Tashelhit, she knows Arabic, she knows French." To this, Fadma retorted, "Well, I know *tafullust* (chicken), I know *taġyult* (donkey), I know *tagant* (forest). These are my Arabic, my French, my English." By equating chickens, donkeys, and forests with Arabic, French, and English, Fadma suggested that each comprised a body of knowledge – and thus wielded power. Languages, in this view, are skill sets, what a person "knows," resources to attain one's livelihood – a view that is shared equally often by advocates of both multilingualism and monolingualism worldwide. In the mountains, chickens provide eggs and meat; a donkey is only good when it eases labors such as hauling water and carrying wood from the forest, but is otherwise scorned as stupid and stubborn, its name a common insult. In Fadma's view, languages were useful only when they achieved some end; languages were (as the villagers believed) what students learned in schools. Knowledge, then, did not include rural women's material and expressive skills, because "their knowledge is not codified: it is oral, practical, and experiential" and thus outside of "the only sanctioned process of knowing in contemporary mainstream epistemology" (Sadiqi 2003:257). "Languages," not including what was then called the Tashelhit lahja (Ar. dialect or Tash. *awal*, talk), were forms of codified knowledge that were sanctioned and promoted by schools and powerful outsiders. Village children entered school as monolingual Tashelhit speakers, but became conversant in Moroccan Arabic (MA; darija) within a few years, since this was the language their teachers – usually Arabs from northern cities – used with them, rather than the Classical Arabic (CA, fuṣḥa) mandated by the curriculum. It was thus unsurprising that unschooled villagers believed schools taught "the [Arabic] language" (al luġa) and "writing" (*tiġri*) rather than subjects like history or arithmetic. Perhaps it also should not have been surprising to hear school-aged children in the mountains who had never stepped foot in town nonetheless speaking in halting MA to the outsider in their midst.

Planting, harvesting, gathering wood, and food preparation all involved bodies of knowledge that the village women shared and valued for their life-sustaining character – but they were well aware that individuals with authority did not need that knowledge. Outsiders and emigrant men relied on markets to provide them with consumables and material goods, and on women to process wool and homegrown barley into household goods. Moreover, powerful outsiders used Arabic, French, and increasingly English – not the contracting (so-called "endangered") Tashelhit language. For monolingual Tashelhit-speaking village women, languages were powerful resources they lacked. This was in part because it was God's will, they often told me, but in part because many husbands, fathers, and sons saw women's monolingualism – and their presence in the village – as critical to the socialization of children, the maintenance of patrimony, and the upholding of reputations. Women maintained the cultivatable land, practiced local religious and secular traditions, and socialized children into the Tashelhit language that linked the countryside's population. They did this despite the national and global processes that increasingly rendered their land, heritage, and language unprofitable, untenable, and undervalued.

My presence among monolingual Tashelhit women commonly enough elicited similar metaphors to indicate that these language ideologies were not altogether idiosyncratic. Following Schieffelin and Woolard (1994), Woolard (1998b), and Silverstein (1979, 1998), I use "ideologies" here rather than "attitudes" to draw attention to the social and power dynamics involved in language use. As Schieffelin and Woolard state, ideologies of languages "are not only about language. Rather, such ideologies envision and enact links of language to group and personal identity, to aesthetics, to morality, and to epistemology" (1994:55–6). They are "representations, whether explicit or implicit, that construe the intersection of language and human beings in a social world" (Woolard 1998b:3). While mountain women understood their monolingualism as further impeding them from joining the march towards prosperity that they thought everyone but them enjoyed, they were paradoxically crucial agents in the maintenance of Tashelhit, a role that most educated, urbanized, and polyglot Amazigh activists could not occupy. Many women I knew in the Anti-Atlas told me that their monolingualism trapped them in the mountains. Yet to men, this further increased women's purity and value, especially for those men familiar with linguistic discrimination who found solace in Tashelhit-dominant mountain spaces. That solace came at a price for the women who maintained the language, the homelands, and the moral economy.

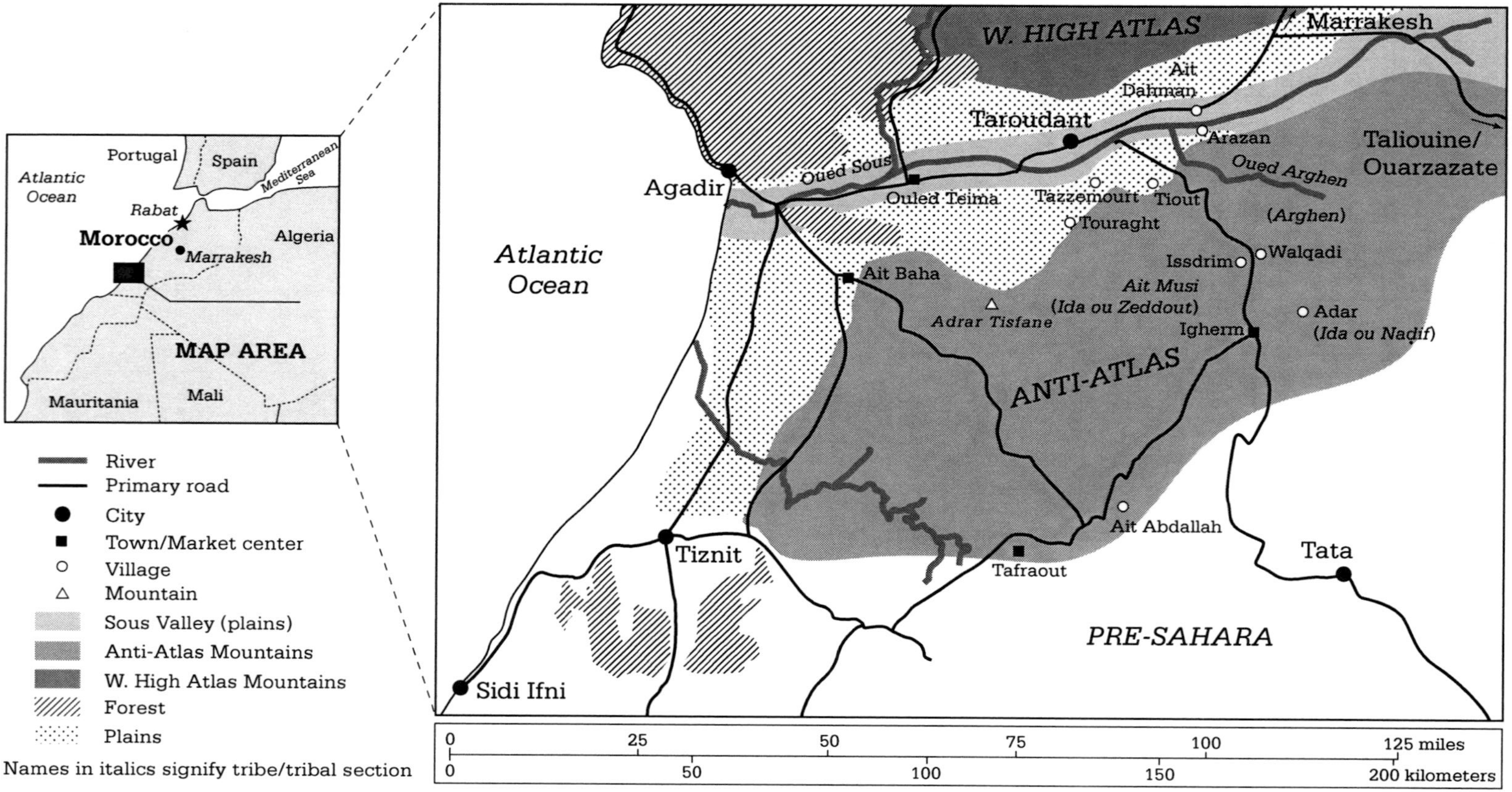

Figure 1.2 Map of Sous Valley and Anti-Atlas mountains, southwestern Morocco

Instead of approaching language as a unitary whole, then, we might approach it as sets of simultaneously communicative and identificatory practices that map onto genres, contexts, and historical moments (Friedrich 1989; Hill and Hill 1986; Irvine 1989; Irvine and Gal 2000), as a prism that refracts, reflects, and propels changing understandings of individual and collective subjectivities. I focus in this book on a range of Ashelhi expressive practices, and map their diversity onto political economic histories and structures. Land tenure systems and the spread of commercial agriculture in formerly subsistence communities have led to language shifts and an overall decline in the use of the marginalized Berber vernaculars. The postnationalist moment requires that we transcend the flawed dichotomies of nationalist rhetoric that developed in contradistinction to colonial concerns.[1] What the French colonizers called *les indigènes* – a category including all "natives" – distilled in the post-Independence period into a perceived unified Arabo-Islamic population. Yet the persistence of the indigenous person disrupts the homogeneity implied by the nationalist model.

Language and Ethnicity in Morocco

> sukkan al maġreb al aqdamun humu al barabera abnā'u maziġ jā'u min al yemen ɛibra al ḥabaša wa miṣr
> The first inhabitants of Morocco were the Berbers. The descendants of Mazigh came from Yemen via the Horn of Africa and Egypt.
> – Moroccan primary school history textbook

As in other contemporary nation-states undergoing social change, language in Morocco reflects and in part shapes its social context. Most everyday speech takes place in the vernacular MA or one of the geolects (regional vernaculars) of Tamazight, the umbrella term for the Berber language. Tashelhit is the geolect spoken in the southwest; Tarifit is spoken in the northern Rif region on the Mediterranean; and the variety locally (and confusingly) called Tamazight is spoken in the Middle and Eastern High Atlas regions.[2] About 80 percent of Moroccans speak MA, although only about half are native speakers. Standard Arabic (SA) is the language of the televised and print media, and is based on CA, the language of literature, and the Quran. French is the other literacy language. Spanish is better known than French in the former Spanish zones of the Rif and pockets of the south (including Sidi Ifni). English is making inroads in business and education sectors. Western languages do not have a presence in the rural Sous outside of the restricted contexts of the tourist industry – most notably hotels, restaurants, and guided tours – and aside from assimilated borrowings into MA and Tashelhit. In Morocco, speaking competence in SA and French is generally acquired through the educational system, although unschooled individuals often understand some SA and even Egyptian Arabic from televised films and soap operas. As in other Arabic-speaking countries, the Arabic of the home and streets is mutually unintelligible with the SA/CA of radio, television, and texts.

Contrary to the depiction of Imazighen as emigrants from Yemen, as the nationalistic history lessons taught Moroccan children from 1966 to 1975, it is now generally accepted that Imazighen or Berbers, and among them the Ishelhin of southwestern Morocco, are North Africa's indigenous people. For contemporary Ishelhin, both Imazighen and Berber constitute what Baumann calls "alien summary label[s]" (1987:9). I generally refer to this umbrella group as Berber, to the Berber language in general as Tamazight, and to the language of Ishelhin specifically as Tashelhit. As Goodman (2005) has argued persuasively, the term Imazighen is more appropriately reserved for references to Berber *militants*, the activists whose concept of a united Amazigh nation in northern and western Africa (Tamazgha) is politically charged, although I would qualify that the terms Imazighen and Tamazight are increasingly used by Moroccan laypeople, not just activists and diasporic members. By no means should my use of the term Berber in this book be construed as perpetuating an essentializing, nineteenth-century French idea of a non-Arab North African *race berbère* with phenotypical, cultural, legal, and religious qualities proximate to those of Europeans (cf. Lorcin 1999).

In the nationalist and post-Independence periods, Berbers were tagged by intellectual and political elites as the Other in their midst, worthy of tolerance and assimilation – but not accommodation. In a sense, "Berber" identity has long been formulated from the outside, and has usually been derogatory (Brett and Fentress 1996). The recent Amazigh movement has reclaimed a collective identity and has striven to put a positive valence on Amazigh identity and heritage (Crawford and Hoffman 2000; Goodman 1996; Lafuente 1999; El Aissati 1993). The term Berber originally meant "babble" or "nonsense," and was used by Romans to refer to non-Romans whose speech they found unintelligible. The root b-r-b-r in MA means to boil up, to come up, like heated water or the sun on a scorching day. For the Romans, a *barbarus* was a barbarian – one unlike and inferior to them. The early sociologist, historian, and historiographer Ibn Khaldûn, in his fourteenth-century work on Berber empires, identified three regional Berber subgroups (Ibn Khaldûn 1968 in B. Hoffman 1967:20). Beyond these, the tribe, tribal fraction and village are the most common classifications. The question remains open whether speakers of the varieties of spoken Berber felt what Ibn Khaldûn called ɛaṣabiyya or social solidarity.

Today Berbers comprise a heterogeneous ethnolinguistic group that stretches from Morocco, Algeria, Tunisia, and Libya down to Mali, Burkina Faso, and Niger. Almost all Moroccan Berbers today, including Ishelhin, are Muslim.[3] Ishelhin are one of the three main subgroups of Berbers in Morocco who together comprise a sociocultural and linguistic group whose members refer to themselves with a variety of ethnolinguistic, tribal, and regional names (Hart 2000; Hoffman 2000b). Collectively, Tamazight speakers and their (in many cases) Arabic-speaking children make up less than half of the Moroccan population, although there are no official statistics. Scholarly estimates for Berbers in Morocco have ranged from 30 to 60 percent; massive urbanization (and resultant linguistic Arabicization) of the 1970s leads me to put the number on the lower end. It remains unclear whether such numbers reflect Berber ancestry or familiarity with Tamazight language. My attempts to gather language statistics from the 1996–7 census – in which household language was a line item – were dismissed by provincial and national officials, and were even met with hostility and suspicion. Unlike data from the other census questions, the aggregate numbers were not made public. One Taroudant province official, responding to my query about province-level numbers of Arabic and Tashelhit speakers, tartly remarked that linguistic differences were superficial since it was the French who made a false distinction between Arabs and Berbers. When I clarified that my question concerned home language and not ethnic group, he instructed me to simply add the populations of mountain villages to arrive at the number of Tashelhit speakers, and to combine the populations of the plains and towns for the number of Arabic speakers. Participant observation discredited that oversimplification: this ethnography is full of Ashelhi voices from plains and towns. In this and countless other interactions with officials and laypeople clearly annoyed by the non-Arabic speakers in their midst, it was clear that Tashelhit language itself, and Tamazight more generally, had become iconic of rurality *tout court.*

The ancestors of today's rural Arabs in southwestern Morocco arrived with the Beni Hilal mercenaries hired from Egypt in the eleventh century for military support for the Sultan. As early as the seventh century, Arabs from the Arabian peninsula had settled and built cities in the northern areas of the empire with the early westward military expansion of Islam. During the second wave of invasions into Morocco, Arabs displaced Berbers from the plains and towns. In most mountain villages, Arabic is not a native vernacular – but even this has been changing since the dramatic Arabicization that began in the 1970s with massive rural–urban migration. This is especially apparent in the low-lying mountains and plains around market centers-turned-cities such as Marrakesh (Fernea 1976; Peets 1988), Beni Mellal (Kapchan 1996), and Taroudant (D. Dwyer 1978; K. Dwyer 1982; Hoffman 2006). Other Moroccan Arabs, especially in the Imperial cities of Fes, Marrakesh, Rabat and Tangier, claim descent from Andalusia, the southern region of Spain ruled by the Moroccan Almoravid and Almohad empires from the late seventh to the late fifteenth century. The expansion of Islam from urban Morocco to the hinterlands in the eighth century had little effect on the language spoken in rural areas until the Beni Hilal Bedouin invaders from Egypt in the mid-eleventh century brought about extensive linguistic Arabization. The argument placing Amazigh roots in the Arabian peninsula dates to Ibn Khaldûn's fourteenth-century writings, but this genealogy reflects a desire to legitimate Berber membership either in the international umma of Muslim believers via proximity to the Prophet Mohammed and the early Islamic community (Shatzmiller 2000), or relative to Arab nobility (McDougall 2004). Another origin myth places Amazigh ancestry on the European continent, mapping as evidence apparent phonological and morphological similarities between Tamazight, Celtic, and Breton languages. Dark-skinned Moroccans, found throughout Morocco today and including many Berber communities from Marrakesh south to the Sahara, trace their roots to Senegal and Guinea in particular, whose ancestors arrived as slaves or as students of Islamic sciences and law in Fes's prestigious Al Quarawayn University.

Since Independence, Moroccan and Western scholars have tended to characterize Morocco as "mixed": part Arab, part Mediterranean, part African, part Amazigh. Leaving the matter there suggests that ethnolinguistic mixing is politically unproblematic and regionally undifferentiated, simply a colorful mélange of historical, cultural, and linguistic traditions to be celebrated at an historical moment when attention to "ethnicity" smacks of folklorization at best and racism at worst. The melting pot claim is akin to characterizing Americans as an unvariegated jumble of Native American, Latino, Anglo, African, and Asian heritage, disregarding the historically situated struggles around ethnicity, language, and economic difference, and the political economic factors that shape them. This raises the question of what "mixed" and "pure" mean on the ground, in people's everyday lives. Dominant discourse around mixing and hybridity in Morocco largely holds that ethnicity is temporally grounded in a distant past, and its only vestiges are shared by all Moroccans in an undifferentiated amalgam of cultural practices. Yet this shared Moroccan-ness has, until recently, required that Berbers assimilate culturally and linguistically. Beginning with the Protectorate period but accelerating in the post-Independence years, Berbers essentially were encouraged to leave their quaint customs and language in the countryside in order to integrate into the national public through a process that "is intrinsically biased towards the whole which it presupposes" (Baumann 1987:1). That whole – the contemporary nation-state – remains static in this discursive construction. In Morocco, with the rise in awareness of Berber matters since the 1990s, Amazigh activists and scholars proposed an alternative to integration that more closely matches what Baumann terms redintegration. Local redintegration, as he uses the term in reference to the Nuba people of Sudan, refers to processes oriented towards "preserving, restoring or renewing [a] community's sense of wholeness, however it is locally defined" (Baumann 1987:3). Such redintegration actually precludes integration or assimilation, Baumann posits; it is "the converse of national integration" for it prevents focus on the national "whole." While seemingly inclusive, the nation-state "whole" more commonly permeates minority communities in ways that are ideologically discordant with local moral economies, supplanting minority cultural practices and social organizational principles. Many Moroccans, however, especially in the towns and cities, remark that they are neither Arab nor Berber/Amazigh/Ashelhi/Arrifi, but instead are a mixture of both. In the view of yet other Moroccans, particularly the urbanized, Arabic-speaking elite, an Arab-Berber distinction is irrelevant at best, spurious at worst. For those whose urbanity is predominant to their personal and collective subjectivities, this dismissal is understandable. Comments about the insignificance of ethnic heritage are prevalent in part because until recently, claiming Amazigh ancestry was the marked position, meaning that it was seen by governmental officials and nationalists as a threat to a unified Moroccan nation and, by a deeply engrained and naturalized leap of logic, to the legitimacy of the monarchy. An Arab emphasis in state rhetoric was long justified by the centuries-old genealogy linking the Alawi dynasty to the Prophet Mohammed, a primary source of the monarchy's political legitimacy (Combs-Schilling 1989).

At the broadest level, the Tashelhit language itself, as a variety of the Tamazight language, has long been iconic of rurality, grounded in a social history in which "Berbers" and "Arabs" were geographically distinct populations in the countryside and cities, respectively. The persistence of this essentialized topographical dichotomy is striking, given massive urbanization since the 1970s, the sizable presence of Berber speakers in the cities since as early as the 1920s, and the Eastern Arab roots of many rural communities. The icon (Tamazight = rurality) obfuscates more subtle distinctions between rural dwellers themselves – since both Arabic and Tashelhit speakers live in rural areas, and given the differences in verbal expressive culture between plains and mountains Ishelhin. Rurality can be invested with either positive or negative moral valence. While its complement, urbanity, is similarly multivalent, the Arabic language that Moroccans associate with urbanity suggests piety, knowledge, worldliness. Many Moroccans I knew did not conceive of Islam as antithetical to the Tashelhit language or Ashelhi identity, although among unschooled Ishelhin, there was significant conflation of classical and colloquial Arabic varieties. In Muslim societies with no indigenous Arabic vernacular-speaking population (e.g. Afghanistan, Indonesia, India), spoken Arabic vernaculars are not invested with piety. More often, the written Arabic word is considered sacred, and this belief underlies a range of practices involving the ingestion or dissolution of paper containing Arabic writing. Moroccan Arabs tended to regard spoken Tashelhit indifferently at best or negatively at worst, as a heritage language for those with Ashelhi roots, but almost quaint and unnecessary for the country as a whole, if not an impediment to national unity. In the late 1990s, given the associations of these Tashelhit and Arabic icons, and in an environment of government-sponsored hostility towards the Berber vernaculars, many Moroccans had difficulty endowing Berber with positive, forward-oriented qualities that might have raised the esteem and profile of native Tamazight speakers within Moroccan society.

Ishelhin among whom I lived engaged in ethnic and linguistic differentiating practices that drew on the cultural, expressive, and economic practices they encountered in their immediate surroundings, and that shaped their choice of spouse, their expectations of themselves and their neighbors, the places they lived, the labor they performed, the language they used to communicate with children and neighbors, and their collective ritual practices. Their choices were influenced by convention and socialization, to be sure, but also by new messages about morality and modernity that arrived via the radio, audio cassettes, television, school teachers, political leaders, human rights groups, migrant workers, and even resident social scientists.

A southwestern Moroccan's self-classification as Ashelhi or Arab may shift over the course of a lifetime, or from one generation to the next, and an individual can claim to "be" Arab and Ashelhi simultaneously or alternately between interactions (Rosen 1984) just as patron-client or master and disciple roles can be occupied by the same person in different contexts (Hammoudi 1997). Ishelhin shared a sense of Moroccan nationhood with those they called Arabs (Crawford and Hoffman 2000). With the concurrent urbanization and Arabization trends of the 1970s and 1980s, Moroccan towns increasingly became places where Tashelhit speakers metamorphosed into bilinguals or monolingual Arabic speakers. The countryside increased in value in many male emigrants' eyes for it lacked the stigma associated with Ishelhin in the ethnically mixed (*xlḍn*) cities.

Any variant of Berber identity – whether forwarded by urban male pan-Amazigh rights activists, or practiced by unschooled rural women themselves – challenges the Arabo-Islamic narrative of innocuously colorful, regionally variegated Morocco. During both fieldwork and archival research, I found it impossible to overlook linguistic, cultural, and agricultural practices that seemed "mixed" to my informants: a village with a Berber name whose residents spoke Arabic; a wedding where the bride self-consciously chose "traditional" or "modern" practices and ornaments (Hoffman 2006); a holiday in the mountains where young emigrant men spoke Arabic to each other while monolingual young women urged them to speak Tashelhit; young women's revitalization of *tiwizi* (Ar. twiza), collective work projects, fallen out of favor.[4]

There was a concerted effort from the rise of the nationalist movement in the 1920s until the early twenty-first century to relegate the Berber component of Moroccan heritage to a footnote in the evolution of the modern nation. Today, scholarship is recovering the histories of marginalized communities largely absent from the scholarly record (e.g. Aouchar 2002). In the late twentieth century, to counter stereotypes of Ishelhin as provincial, some of the Imazighen who wrote, spoke, and sang in mass mediated formats attempted to imbue previously denigrated places and cultural practices with positive content. Teachers, poets, traditional musicians, and historians of local history and lore formed the core of Tashelhit radio programming, for instance, and became local celebrities as a result, further bolstering their authority and increasing the sale of their essays, proverbs, and verbal art printed in Casablanca, Marrakesh, and Agadir. These purveyors of Berber culture, language, and history found a receptive audience among literate rural agriculturalists as well as high school boys boarding in the market towns of Taroudant and Igherm.

Talk accompanied almost every aspect of life in the Sous, and the level of sociability there ensured that talk was not peripheral to activities but rather part and parcel of social action. Talk preceded, organized, and followed manual laboring. Talk distinguished between different kinds of work, whether manual labor – *tawwuri* for cyclical manual labor and *tammara* for physically stressful labor – or the "clean" work of offices and schools (*lxdmt*; Ar. xedma).[5] Talk provided pleasure in everyday activities, and everyday interactions were recounted in dramatic he-said-she-said (Goodwin 1990) reenactments. In these rural lands where little seemed to happen during lulls in ritual and agricultural cycles, Tashelhit women's performative flair transformed mundane activities into discrete events. Arguably, Berber women have long been depicted as powerful relative to their Arab counterparts. Given the recent public visibility for the Tamazight language, however, methods of language maintenance are increasingly scrutinized. Here, too, the mountain village and its women residents would seem to have heightened social value. They have been, after all, almost single-handedly responsible for socializing children into the Tashelhit language. Despite the emergence of scholarly and policy-oriented language and cultural institutes like IRCAM (Institut Royal de la Culture Amazigh) in the nation's capital, Rabat – a significant victory for advocates of Amazigh inclusion – the rural homelands remain the core language institutes. There, native speakers transmitted, debated, reformed, and fashioned expressive culture both intentionally and inadvertently in ways that accommodated changing social desires, a massive influx of market goods, and shifting aspirations and self-images. The Ishelhin among whom I worked, in the Eastern Anti-Atlas mountains and Sous Valley, granted an importance to language not only as a medium of communication, but also as an index of commitment to a geographically dispersed subjectivity – marginalized from the outside as insufficiently Islamic, yet sometimes celebrated from within as adaptive and resistant.

Language is a crucial component of Berber identity today in the view of many Berbers themselves – although what this "language" is, precisely, is not always immediately apparent. Equally importantly, native language has been crucial to teachers, intellectuals, activists, and those laypeople in regular contact with native speakers of other languages. Language professionals have gained visibility in their efforts to encourage state recognition of Berber language and heritage in Moroccan public domains, and more modestly, to open public discussion about the challenges native language poses for national development, especially in terms of education and training. Yet "language" is not just code choice and does not just concern the polyglot and the urbane. Even monoglot rural women hold language ideologies about the relationships that obtain among individuals, communities, and expressive cultures. Language ideologies shape their understandings of the inherent properties of various languages, their aesthetic qualities, and their appropriate uses. Here is where participant observation is crucial; the fieldworker must speak and understand the field languages well enough to grasp what people say to each other and how speech operates as social performance as well as referential tool for relaying information. For all the rhetoric about language's role in Moroccan individual and collective identities, we still have few empirical qualitative data grounded in recordings of actual instances of verbal expression *in situ*, particularly for Berberophone groups. Kapchan's beautifully detailed account of Arab women's genres in and around the Moroccan marketplace is an inspiring model for future work (1996). More commonly, however, we have composites from memory, just-so generalizations, and elicited genres like poetry, narrative, and proverbs. In contrast, this book situates some aspects of language use among minority Berber speakers in one part of one region at the end of the twentieth century, complementing recent Anglophone publications on the circulation of culture and identity among Kabyle Berbers in both Algeria and the diaspora in France (Goodman 2005; Silverstein 2004). By expanding our familiarity with Berbers, we can better understand the complexities and richness of language, culture, and society in North Africa, and begin to work against the Arabocentric bias in Anglophone scholarship on the region.

Rhetorically, advocates for Tamazight linguistic and cultural rights increasingly compare their lot to that of other endangered and minority groups worldwide, simultaneously emphasizing their indigeneity and rightful occupation of the land. Like other indigenous rights movements increasing in visibility since the mid-1980s, the Amazigh rights movement "involves reinvigoration of the comfort and color of local traditions with the safety-in-numbers effect of a global movement" (Niezen 2003:13). Yet as recently as ten years ago, maintenance programs for endangered languages did not appear to serve as viable models for sustaining Moroccan Tamazight and its regional varieties. It would be folly to compare Tamazight speakers' predicament to that of Native American groups with only a few hundred or a few dozen speakers, or a single speaker (Nettle and Romaine 2000). Despite a lack of official statistics on the number of Tamazight, Tashelhit, and Tarifit speakers, we can estimate that they number around 10 million of the over 30 million Moroccans. The proportion of speakers and legal status of Tamazight are more comparable to indigenous languages of South America, notably Quechua in Peru and Ecuador (Harvey 1994; King 2001; Rindstedt and Aronsson 2001; Saroli 2004).

Despite rhetorical references to international discourses, and even the occasional international involvement on behalf of the Moroccan Amazigh rights movement, this – like other minority and indigenous rights movements – remains first and foremost a struggle *within* the nation and *with* the state. Its implications are international, and its outcome still uncertain – most particularly whether the fate of Tamazight will follow that of significant minority languages such as Catalon or Basque, or the linguicide of Australian Aboriginals. There are two facets to this struggle. One is with the majority of Moroccans, now native Arabic speakers, who do not necessarily value Berber language and heritage. A second is with government institutions. *De jure* political acceptance of Tamazight does not imply *de facto* practice. The Amazigh movement has been more concerned with governmental recognition and policies than with popular support, motivated by an underlying conviction that the masses, especially in a tightly controlled police state, follow authorities' cues. Of particular interest are King Mohamed VI's efforts at inserting the Tamazight language into public spheres, a move initiated with his father Hassan II's 1994 call for Tamazight in primary schools. A pilot program began with the 2003–4 academic year, and by spring 2004 manuals were available for distribution and teachers were being trained, albeit for a short two-week period in the already inadequate pedagogical and language training of newly minted Moroccan teachers who are usually assigned to the countryside.

Future research will have to assess the success or failure of recent language policy reforms that have brought Tamazight into national public domains. My goal in the pages that follow is to sketch the parameters of rural Tashelhit verbal expressive practices and language ideologies that preceded the significant early twenty-first century shifts in governmental policy, particularly the gendered forms they took, and trace their relationships to the different political economies operating in southwestern Morocco's plains and mountains. I use the phrase "verbal expressive" rather than "linguistic" in many instances to highlight how the matter goes beyond formal linguistic characteristics of colloquial speech, such as lexicon, syntax, phonetics, and prosody, to expressive genres like song, religious chant, proverbial speech, and oratory. Competing hegemonies come together in these collective displays, and through them plains Ishelhin both challenge and reproduce their marginal structural position vis-à-vis the state and its presumed Arab citizenry with regard to privileged access to political, cultural, and economic capital.

A gap is likely to widen between assimilationist Ishelhin and those attempting to establish Tamazight's place in Moroccan public domains along the lines of Catalan in Spain, but without an insistence on territorial and political autonomy from the state. Already in Morocco, an Amazigh intellectual group has emerged whose tone differs markedly from that of the late 1990s (Silverstein and Crawford 2004). Most striking is the current leaders' insistence on secularism (personal communication, Silverstein 2004), a continuity with certain strains of the Amazigh movement, but in notable contrast to that of the religious or moderate Swasa (Sous residents, sing. Soussi) figuring centrally in the 1990s. Given political Islam's increased visibility since 2001, the Moroccan Amazigh cultural elite take their cues more from their Kabyle counterparts in Algeria than from the historically religious moderates of the Moroccan South.

Shifting Language Hierarchies

Historically, linguistic influence appears to have gone both from Berber to Arabic and from Arabic to Berber. Colloquial MA displays grammatical, lexical, and syntactic features shaped by the Tamazight language, and each variety of Tamazight contains Arabic borrowings in the form of lexical items and phrases. As Chtatou has noted (1997), MA contains lexical and grammatical features of CA that originated in Eastern Arabic but fell into disuse long ago and are unknown to Eastern Arabs who consider these elements as resulting from Tamazight influence when they were instead archaic Arab Peninsula characteristics. Plains MA contains Tashelhit borrowings and phonetic influences, and plains Tashelhit borrows extensively from colloquial Arabic. The speech of those Arabic speakers who did not speak Tashelhit was distinguishable as "Soussi" by northerners for its distinctive phonetic and lexical features. Individuals who were raised speaking Arabic used to marry into Tashelhit-speaking families and become

Pre-Protectorate and Protectorate (1912–1956) Periods:

CLASSICAL ARABIC (fuṣḥa)
[FRENCH]

Moroccan Arabic (darija) | Tamazight Varieties (Tashelhit, Tamazight, Tarifit)

Post-Independence Period (1956 to present):

"ARABIC" (ɛrabiyya)
(Classical / Standard Arabic + Moroccan Arabic)
|
[FRENCH]
|
Tamazight Varieties

Figure 1.3 Language hierarchies in Morocco

Tashelhit-dominant just as the opposite was true. Yet by the late 1990s, it was rare to find a native Arabic speaker who became Tashelhit dominant in adulthood. The symbolic capital associated with Arabic greatly exceeded that associated with Tashelhit. In sum, language shift in the Sous largely went from Tashelhit to Arabic in the post-Independence period.

Over the twentieth century, the symbolic importance of Arabic increased to the point where many Moroccans associated Arabic language, even in its vernacular form, with religious piety. MA and the Berber varieties were once hierarchically equal and inferior to CA and, under the Protectorate, to French. Prior to Independence in 1956, before the generalization of schooling and the expansion of the French-initiated state bureaucracy, rural communities and tribes in many respects shared the same structural position vis-à-vis the state. In the Sous, any given community had a predominantly MA- or Tashelhit-speaking population, with male tâlib-s (religiously trained scholars) and *imġarn* (elected village leaders) serving as language brokers when necessary with makhzen (governmental) officials and trading partners. A negligible number of Moroccans had basic literacy skills prior to Independence. The rural religious schools (*timzgida*, mosque) taught the Arabic alphabet and some Quranic verses to boys who developed rudimentary literacy skills (Spratt et al. 1991; Wagner 1993). Lay people had few pretensions to literacy; specialists handled reading and writing.

From the French Protectorate through Independence, two concurrent processes were responsible for shifts in the language hierarchy. First, the expansion of infrastructure and road-building under the French stimulated the development of a market economy that encouraged male migration to the urban centers. Second, the independent state generalized education; non-specialists (and non-elites) had access to literacy training. Yet as Bourdieu and Passeron (1970) found for France, Moroccan schools favored the existing social class structure and helped to reproduce it as well by consolidating material and symbolic capital among the urban, Arabic-speaking elite. In more intimate spheres, Tashelhit speakers continued to anchor their origins (laṣl) in a rural homeland (tamazirt) where Tashelhit remained the *lingua franca* and MA was associated with outsider bureaucrats.

Yet increasingly, lay people accorded higher status to MA, the vernacular of the Moroccan elites (but also many non-elites), than to the Tamazight vernaculars. Non-elite MA speakers and Berber speakers found themselves jockeying for economic, political, and social symbolic resources under the newly independent Moroccan state. The ideological elision between SA and MA meant, and continues to mean, tolerance for MA in the media and institutions like schools, either with or at the expense of SA. In classrooms, for instance, where oral communication was supposed to take place in the official SA that few mastered, MA became an accessible proxy. Despite an ideological preference for SA in the media, Moroccan television and radio interviews that open in SA eventually shift to MA, at least until a ritualized formula initiates a resumption of SA particularly by the program's close.[6] In urban contexts, MA was the unmarked vernacular; the Berber vernaculars were marked. An eventual elision in the popular imagination between vernacular MA and formalized SA (cf. Boukous 1995) meant that the linguistic hierarchy came to favor MA relative to Berber, at least in shared, urban, public domains, and MA now occupies domains once exclusively reserved for SA or CA (Boukous 1995) (Figure 1.3). Standard/classical Arabic has cultural capital not only because of its links to Islam and the sacred (Haeri 2003), but also because of its aesthetic, political, and cultural links to the Eastern Arab world that serve as more of a metropole to many Moroccans than does Europe, especially for popular cultural productions such as music, film, and television (Ossman 1994, 2002), as well as religious philosophy, politics, and literary aesthetics.

The Tamazight language varieties became increasingly viewed as undesirable relics of an internally fractious past. With the generalization of education in an Arab nationalist period came an unfavorable political climate that discouraged overt references to Amazigh identification. In the plains, Arabicization of the everyday vernacular resulted from subtle, non-coercive forces as well as economic and land tenure transformations. Once an arid grazing land, the Sous Valley became one of the most fertile commercial agricultural regions in Morocco. Massive farms brought together Arabic and Tashelhit-speaking laborers whose families intermarried and increasingly saw their fates as intertwined.

After years of resisting homogenization, Ishelhin and other Berbers are now facing a different governmental approach: inclusion. As late as the late 1990s, Ishelhin resisted state efforts to literally track their numbers through the agricultural census and the identity card registration campaign, although many women in particular weighed the costs and benefits before participating (Hoffman 2000b). Under Mohamed VI, neighboring Algeria's domestic politics, particularly in the Kabylia Berber region, have led the Moroccan government to watch its own Amazigh activists more closely. In conversations with educated young people in the Anti-Atlas in August 2001, men and women demonstrated their awareness of police abuses and the demonstrations that had been taking place in the previous four months in Kabylia, Algeria. In hushed whispers, youths told me that Kabylia was the real reason Mohamed VI was creating an Amazigh institute. The popular pan-Mediterranean, bilingual (French-Arabic) radio station out of Tangier and other North African hubs, Médi 1, offered updates on Kabylia beyond the state-controlled media that previously controlled this flow of information more closely. Moreover, inexpensive public Internet access became widespread in towns and cities from 1995 as entrepreneurs modeled their services after the *téléboutiques* that offered telephones and faxes for hire and served as meeting places for youths.

Emplacement and Mobility

Land has been as central as language to Berber understandings of subjectivity. Co-presence, like talk, renders geographical space meaningful. Place-making, like talk, engages negotiations over morality, community, social change, and human nature. The designation of in-between places, languages, and cultural forms seldom arises from within. "Mixed" cultures hint at movements; it is analytically difficult to ground heterogeneity in a single place when its composite elements are more easily locatable here or there. Culture, Malkki explains, is "a profoundly territorialized (quasi-ecological) concept in many settings":

> Violated, broken roots signal an ailing cultural identity and a damaged nationality . . . And in uprooting, a metamorphosis occurs: The territorializing metaphors of identity – roots, soils, trees, seeds – are washed away in human floodtides, waves, flows, streams, and rivers. These liquid names of the uprooted reflect the sedentarist bias in dominant modes of imagining homes and homelands, identities and nationalities. (Malkki 1995:15–16)

The "sedantarist bias" pertains both to internal and external characterizations. People render rural cultural practices meaningful in contrast to perceived urban practices. The city becomes the antithesis of the homeland, its own antidote (Williams 1973). In Protectorate discourse, Berbers tended to appear entrenched in their deeply loved lands as "France's sequoias"

(Berque 1967:219) – yet they and their social networks spread far and wide, attaching like ivy to stones in their paths, their roots digging down into the ground beneath the rivers that pass over them, as Fatima Tabaamrant (1998) sings. Contemporary popular depictions, too, portray Berbers as heroic autochthonous peoples. Malkki argues that such depictions of indigenous groups justify efforts to preserve indigenous life ways (Malkki 1995). Contemporary state rhetoric represents Moroccan identity in terms of a colorful quilt of discrete, codifiable regional traditions, essentialized in reenactments for folklore festivals.

Yet the rooted sequoia was only one half of contemporary identity formation among Ishelhin among whom I worked. For Anti-Atlas Ishelhin, in particular, at the end of the twentieth century, migration complemented rootedness. Together, male moving and female dwelling created and sustained the tamazirt. Indeed, a fundamental characteristic of being an Ashelhi or Tashelhit person was an active relationship with a tamazirt. Such places were arguably the core of the Ashelhi social group, albeit the periphery of Moroccan society. This alternative core was a material one for residents who worked the land and a discursive one for emigrants who did not. Its perceived proximity to the "intermediate zone" (B. Hoffman 1967:40) of the Sous plains was in constant flux.

Ashelhi identity in the late 1990s, and for at least the previous three-quarters of a century, was anchored neither exclusively in rural lands, nor in migration to the cities, but instead in the tension between mobility and emplacement, between moving and dwelling. This anchoring might suggest instability, as Tsing claims for the Meratus of Indonesia:

> Instability might be interpreted, for example, as the inevitable product of "assimilation" and "change" as "tradition" is threatened. This view presupposes a site of intact tradition somewhere up in the hills or, at least, somewhere in the recent past. But, what if tradition itself is always negotiated in relation to state demands and local concerns about regional and ethnic status? (1993:105)

Instability and mobility, that is, may be integral to stability; tradition is never inherent, but relative. For the Meratus, relegated discursively, materially, and politically to the periphery of the modern state, Tsing writes that "Mobility over a diversified landscape fosters a proliferating appreciation of differences; Meratus note minute distinctions of taste, language, and style between themselves and their neighbors, even between housemates." From their perspective, Tsing argues, "mobility and microdifferentiation offer the pleasures of autonomy as well as the stigma of disorder" (1993:61).

While scholars have documented Soussi merchants in Casablanca and their social networks (Adam 1972; Waterbury 1972a and 1972b), I focus here instead on those who stayed in the Anti-Atlas and Sous plains to examine what it meant to be Ashelhi for those whose lives were shaped, in part, by the comings and goings of loved ones and neighbors. A deeply gendered spatial distinction among Ishelhin in the Anti-Atlas – with emigrant men working in cities most of the year, and mountain-dwelling women working the land – had led men to associate the countryside with longing, experienced through nostalgia, whereas women associated it with hard labor. Both agreed that a close relationship with the land was crucial to maintaining the language, yet emigrant men remained the strongest supporters of Tashelhit language maintenance, although they were least able to participate in it.

Men's presence was constant despite their absence, however, due to women's pervasive uncertainty about men's movements and their impending return, as well as the uncertainty around men's financial contributions to the household. Before the arrival of cell phones in 2000, women rarely heard from their husbands, fathers, and sons in the cities. They did, however, receive periodic shipments of goods: household staples like tea, sugar, and soap, and clothes like socks and navy nylon wraps (tamlḥafts). The wraps served both practical and indexical functions: they marked women's ethnicity and local affiliation, they protected women from the elements, they doubled as storage for fodder, and the excess material in the front formed a pouch in which, like the pouches of Pakistani Kalashi women's dress, "all manner of good and useful things can be carried and hidden" (Maggi 2001:98). Thus even before she spoke, a Tashelhit woman was readily distinguishable from an Arab and from Tashelhit women in other tribes and tribal sections. She could not pass as Arab due to her language and dress, beautiful according to internal standards but provincial, backward, and defiant in the view of many urbanites (Durham 1999; Maggi 2001). An entrenched moral code circumscribed women's emplacement in their husbands' homes, the immediately surrounding villages, and occasionally further afield for a visit to female relatives. Women expressed their anxiety as entrapment by their Tashelhit monolingualism and their illiteracy. The linguistic and pragmatic modifications advocated by language activists were inconceivable to women who could not imagine Tashelhit written, orthography standardized, or lexicon enhanced to suit modern purposes. How could Tashelhit be the language of schools and state institutions when it wasn't written, they asked me; *taɛrabt* (Arabic) already served that purpose. How could Tashelhit possibly become the language of the street, when only mountain folk spoke it, and Arabs scoffed at it? How could Tashelhit become the language of upward mobility, they asked rhetorically, when the world's wealthy people spoke French? Such language ideologies encouraged language shift, for Ishelhin were particularly resistant to the idea of using Tashelhit outside of intimate circles. Few Arabs bothered to learn to speak it, and there was seemingly little reason for them to do so. Linguistic accommodation consequently went one way, and many emigrant Ishelhin who accommodated

Arabs end up abandoning Tashelhit altogether. It is unclear how such patterns of accommodation and resistance may shift among the next generation given that, as people increasingly remark, Berber is no longer taboo.[7]

Organization of the Book

Language and gender are always emplaced. This ethnography is organized around two zones that are less topographical locations and more indexes of political-economic systems. Political economies have shaped not only different Amazigh groups' economic capital and access to it, but also cultural and symbolic capital that similarly are produced, circulated, consumed, and discarded. What I am calling the tamazirt would conventionally be conceived as a satellite of the cities, supplying the metropole with foodstuffs and labor and ensuring the functioning and well-being of its inhabitants. An alternative analysis, however, takes seriously the symbolic aspect of political economies, especially the quasi-mythical yet utterly unromantic rural mountain village and its residents, especially women. This homeland differs in important respects from the villages of Tamazight-speaking Kabylia, Algeria (Goodman 2005). In a reversal of world systems theory and historical revisionists' rightful identification of the "people without history" (Wolf 1982), my ethnography positions the Ashelhi (Tashelhit "Berber" or Amazigh) homeland in the Anti-Atlas mountains as the civilizational pole around which Ashelhi identity is oriented, and rural residents as central to the moral and symbolic economy of the indigenous Tamazight language group. The mountains emerge as central every time a Moroccan or an outsider claims that authentic Amazigh language and people are only found there. By calling the mountain homeland the civilizational pole for Ishelhin, and thus their inhabitants as central to the moral and symbolic economy of the language and ethnic group, I am evoking an alternative hegemony and organization, a pride of place that both rural and town dwellers found distinct from the "mixed" towns and plains. The mountain homeland's "periphery" then becomes the Sous Valley, or at least its Tashelhit-speaking villages, as well as the towns and cities to which Ishelhin emigrate, Taroudant and Casablanca among them. This periphery was characterized not by an economic dependence on the homeland but instead by its symbolic and discursive dependence on it. Women's and men's contemporary experiences of land and language disrupt fantasies of a pristine rural homeland, suggesting instead a more complex set of processes linking people, places, and cultural practices.

After a short Chapter Two on methods, Part II (Chapter Three) brings together mountains, plains, and towns to consider gender in late twentieth-century expressive cultural mediations of Ashelhi land and language through the production and consumption of metaculture (Urban 2001). The very women who have ensured the maintenance of Tashelhit language, despite decades of official disdain for the vernacular and the histories of their speakers, now compete with national narratives over the role of what used to be called the Tamazight dialects – and are now called languages – of Moroccan cultural heritage. Pervasive images of an idealized Tamazight woman iconize the ethnic group, but only as long as her self-presentation (through dress, bodily adornment, and speech) distinguishes her from Arabs. An authentic homeland affords spectacular views and is difficult to access, emigrant men told me. By this and other such criteria, Amazigh people, places, and practices were constantly ranked according to their authenticity or deviation from the ideal model, embodied in the mountain village. This fetish was encapsulated in the idea that one should go to the mountains to "get" the "real" Tashelhit, and that the "real" tamazirt was rugged and mountainous, far from roads and towns. Despite the almost mythical aura of the countryside in the view of many male emigrants, there was nothing ideal about it for the year-round resident women who worked their husbands' barren, rocky land and raised their children.

Chapters Four to Seven are the ethnographic heart of the book. Two chapters treat each of the topographical regions, the Eastern Anti-Atlas mountains (Part III) and the Sous Valley plains (Part IV). Each part contains one chapter on labor and the material construction of place, and a second on the discursive construction of those places and the social groups associated with them. The first chapter of each part (Chapters Four and Six) examines the local political economic histories and practices that have shaped ethnolinguistic differentiating practices and, by extension, ethnogenesis. Each provides a framework within which to understand intra-group differentiation in language practices and ideologies that are the subject of Chapters Five and Seven. These two chapters consider how community and marginality are created, maintained, and reproduced through language practices, not merely reflected in these practices (Friedrich 1989; Guneratne 2002; Hensel 1996; Kroskrity 1993). Chapters Four and Five position the Eastern Anti-Atlas mountain region of Ida ou Zeddout and surrounding *tiqbilin* ("tribes," sing. taqbilt) as the Ashelhi "homeland." Chapters Six and Seven explore the Sous Valley plains region of Arazan of the Arghen tribe and the Guettiaoua lands and surroundings as a "periphery" (see Figure 1.2). Chapter Five, on the mountains, argues that the talk and song allow for different expressions of the collective experiences of home and away, and that these are gendered due to the sharply gendered pattern of emigration. In Chapter Seven on discourse in the plains whose population is not heavily marked by emigration, I instead focus on the patterning of languages (Tashelhit and Arabic), across the modalities of speech and song and through a multi-sited engagement party. Here, too, language mediates political economy, and the central issue that gets negotiated in the plains is code choice (rather than gender) in discursive constructions of place and community.

Part V opens with Chapter Eight that examines reverberations of the political economy of Tashelhit language in the sometimes masterful, *bricoleur* discourse of Tashelhit radio. Radio discourse reflected a moment of Moroccan history in which political repression was fresh on the minds of Amazigh language professionals, yet an international receptiveness to indigenous demands and an impulse to self-expression encouraged broadcasting in the "dialects." The chapter analyses the form and substance of an increasingly objectified and standardized Tashelhit language in media collected in the years directly following the introduction of television news in the Tamazight varieties in 1994. Part V closes with a conclusion, Chapter Nine.

This ethnography is peppered with material from Protectorate archival documents with no attempt to cover a systematic chronology across the last century. I have written elsewhere on shifts away from tribal names (for places and people) and towards post-Independence administrative and market centers and loci of allegiance, discussing more extensively the period mostly glossed over here, between the mid-1950s and the mid-1990s (Hoffman 2000b). A fuller elaboration of French native policy (*politique indigène*) in the Sous and its implications will have to await a future manuscript (cf. Hoffman forthcoming 2008), although some of the seeds are here. Moroccan administrators after Independence continued the projects oriented towards the metropole (Wright 1991), ultimately to dissimilar ends – although Protectorate control and appropriation of the rural areas and local powerful rulers arguably continued in new forms after 1956. This is not a cynical suggestion that a conspiracy linked the nationalist elites to their former French "protectors," but rather a nod to the abiding practicality of Moroccans who, in many respects, are more likely to use the colonizers' tools for their own ends than reject them on principle. The *bricoleur* spirit that spurred a young Razani man I knew to build a *rbab* stringed musical instrument from a rusted oil can, Bic plastic razor safety guard, bicycle wire, and nails has its parallel in infrastructural planning. This was true in agricultural development after Independence, as Swearingen (1987) has painstakingly documented. For all of these reasons, the narratives in this book move between chronological periods in a sort of "dumbbell structure" (di Leonardo 1998:151), using colonial voices to illuminate late twentieth-century ethnographic concerns. I emphasize the centrality of colonial constructions of space and community, albeit resolutely not to fetishize colonial fantasies of Berbers and their cultural practices as seemingly distinct from those of Arabs (cf. Hammoudi 1993; Hannoum 2001).

Chapter 2

On Fieldwork Methods and Movements: "Song Is Good Speech"

ha iyyi fkiġ i tmizar ur xaliḍaġ
ur iyyi gis baba ula immi qnḍġ
ur iyyi gis dadda maġ immaln
Here I am, given to an unfamiliar land
My father isn't here, my mother isn't here, I'm lonely
There's no older brother to guide me
– Ida ou Zeddout tazrrart

At the outset of an investigation, it is not so much the intellectual faculty for making formulas and definitions that leads the way, but rather it is the eyes and hands attempting to get the feel of the actual presence of the subject matter.
– Vološinov (1973 [1929]:45)

On n'oublie rien de rien
On n'oublie rien de tout
On n'oublie rien de rien
On s'habitue – c'est tout
– Jacques Brel (1961)

Early in my extended research and residence in Morocco (1995–9), I was adamant about not focusing on fixed genres and only hesitantly wrote down proverbs, sayings, or even oral poetry that I encountered. These genres could be elicited, I reasoned, and I wanted instead to capture the texture of naturally occurring, everyday discourse. I came to realize the arbitrariness of the analytical boundary scholars place between everyday talk and seemingly "fixed" forms of expressive culture. When I was learning Tashelhit Berber, an oral language that was not taught in the classroom, I audiotaped naturally occurring speech, transcribed it with a native speaker, and learned to use the words, intonation, and conversational patterning I heard Ishelhin use with each other. There was some resistance to my taping, however, as some people were fearful that outsiders would judge them by what they considered their deficient speech. Although my method yielded results, Ishelhin often told me that I would be better off listening to the old *rways*, the singer-songwriters whose lyrics are full of artfully deployed proverbs, metaphors, allusions, and archaic lexicon. Poetry draws attention to itself, as Jakobson (1987 [1920]) points out, and I was more interested in how people used Tashelhit than in Tashelhit as a thing unto itself. Hirsch (1998:180–1) observes that poetic speech "indexes who has the right to use what kinds of speech in what circumstances." Tashelhit poets strive to resuscitate archaic Tashelhit terms that I would never hear reinforced in conversation, and so patterning my own speech after their lyrics did not ring true to my previous experiences in language learning. But in this advice was an instructive piece of language ideology about song as "good speech." Oral poetry, in this view, was purer and more complete than everyday "mixed" Tashelhit speech infused with Arabic borrowings and assimilated lexicon. "Mixed" things – whether gatherings, towns, dress styles, or languages – carried connotations of pollution and impurity (Douglas 1966). Yet Moroccans' verbal expressive practices displayed a subtlety, accommodation, and playfulness that belied purism.

From my home base in the crowded market town and provincial administrative center of Taroudant, I traveled southwestern Morocco with people whose paths often overlapped. There was nothing unusual about my travels, in the eyes of my consultants, except the frequency with which I undertook them; American fellowships provided more ample funds than my Moroccan friends could access. But I followed the rhythms and patterns of their movements, and with time learned the connections between places that appear unrelated on a Michelin road map. Through both moving and dwelling in the Sous, I came to understand something of how Swasa place themselves and each other on the social landscape, and what made a group of people a community. Taking my directed wanderings as a starting point allows me to draw on experience gained from numerous places without forcing me to claim expertise or absolute authority on a single community. Delimiting the ethnographic study to a single community has long been the traditional anthropological route, although it has been roundly challenged, for instance by Marcus (1998), who has advocated multi-sited ethnography. Delimiting the study as well to either mountains or plains would likewise be arbitrary, as Swasa have moved between them for as long as memory and records attest. Moreover, the people I knew imagined themselves as part of broader communities than those in which they spent their days. If I dwell longer here on the mountains than the plains, it is because I know them best and because they most captured my mind's eye. One incentive for spending time in the mountains initially was that I could be sure of a

Tashelhit-immersion environment. Plains-dwelling Swasa, many of whom were at least marginally bilingual with Arabic, were keen to accommodate their interlocutors and tended to speak to me in Arabic until I was fully capable in Tashelhit. While initially I was interested in the forms of talk, in the mountains I came to care deeply about the speakers themselves and the content of their talk. In this book, I explain my methodology at some length for the simple reason that my social identity was an integral part of the interactions in which I learned something about life in the Sous and Anti-Atlas. As Vološinov notes, "Any true understanding is dialogic in nature" (1973 [1929]:102). Such are the conditions of doing fieldwork; obscuring them would be dishonest.

The people whose voices fill these pages are located in three zones in the Sous: the Anti-Atlas mountains, the Sous plains, and the town of Taroudant. I draw most from the voices least heard outside their villages: residents of the Anti-Atlas mountains who speak almost exclusively Tashelhit and are idealized in Amazigh activist rhetoric. The means and circumstances in which I conducted fieldwork in each zone differed, and I use them to elaborate different parts of my overall argument about the crucial role of political economy in shaping relations to the land and expressive cultural practices. Intensive 24-hour interaction over days or weeks was possible in the mountain villages I frequented, while more casual, half-day or shorter visits to consultants' houses in Taroudant followed women's local visiting patterns. One to three-day visits to Sous plains villages with neighbors from Taroudant coincided with specific occasions such as weddings, baby naming ceremonies, or the one-year return of a bride to her parents' home. These plains visits originally broke up the intensity of fieldwork in the mountains and transcription in Taroudant, but over time they became part of the field research. Through this constant moving throughout the seasons of the year, I learned that while plains dwellers maintained strong ties to people and jobs in Taroudant, for mountain dwellers Taroudant served merely as a transportation hub on their way to the urban centers of Casablanca and Marrakesh. With time, I noticed the patterns of human movement between town and country, between rural villages in the same region, and between the plains and mountains.

My participant observation took several forms. I moved physically through the region to get a sense of geography, roads, human links, and similarities and differences between them. I listened to the linguistic codes people used (their styles of Tashelhit and/or MA) and discerned the factors governing variety in use and context. I lined up historical connections between places with their contemporary connections, assessing what happened when people from recognizably different communities gathered, how they talked to and about each other, and minding the role that my presence as foreign researcher had on a given situation. In all of these, I participated and observed, sometimes elicited oral histories and to some extent sung poetry, audiotaped and collected commercial recordings, and finally transcribed.

I insisted during fieldwork on focusing on the everyday and the heteroglossic (Bakhtin 1981) rather than ritual or idealized representations of the "here's-what-we-do" variety that informants sometimes offered me. Influenced by both practice theory and recent literature on language ideology in multilingual societies, I believed that attending to the verbal "give and take of everyday life" (Schieffelin 1990) would yield insights into the role of expressive culture in negotiations of self-presentation and evaluations of other people. Collecting spontaneous speech seemed to be the best avenue to pursue. All verbal practices are rule-governed, whether conversation or prepared speeches. However, I was resistant to include oral poetry and song in my study because I presumed that they were more rule-governed and formal than everyday talk. Besides, I figured, folklorists already study ritualized verbal expressive genres; anthropologists should study broader cultural systems and everyday practices. But as I learned to speak and listen in both Moroccan Arabic and Tashelhit, I began noting the formulaic, ritualized aspects of everyday communication and interaction, and began questioning the distinction I had presumed. My findings support Irvine's (1979) critique of Bloch's (1975) argument that oratory is formal whereas speech is not. That is, Irvine argues counter to Bloch, everyday speech can be "formal," and "formal" verbal expression can be spontaneous and informal. The particular contexts and social circumstances in which any kind of speech act (spoken or sung) takes place establish the ritualism or spontaneity of a given speech event. Table 2.1 maps out the verbal expressive genres to which I refer in the following chapters.

In addition to theoretical and data-generated motivations, my research methods were also spurred by my Ashelhi consultants' wishes and concerns. These concerns reflected three ideas: (1) song (especially old mountain song) is good Tashelhit; (2) informal conversation should not be recorded; and (3) asking questions is not an acceptable means of inquiry. I want to address each of these concerns in turn.

First, Ishelhin repeatedly told me that the best way to learn Tashelhit was to listen to older Tashelhit song. Tashelhit speakers in town told me that their mastery of Tashelhit was flawed and inadequate; proper Tashelhit, they told me, came in the form of proverbs and song, "good words" (*iwaliwn fulkinin*) and "meaningful words/sayings" (*lmεani*) that only the mountain dwellers knew. Mountain dwellers were to them the repository of "real" language, allegedly used by earlier generations and less influenced by urbanization and Moroccan Arabic. Similarly, Hirsch's Swahili Kenyan informants attempted to direct her queries towards ideals, in her case written rather than oral, noting more generally that "The

Table 2.1 Selected verbal expressive genres, southwestern Morocco

Modality	Genre	Gender	Language	Community or commercial	Accompaniment	Key and other characteristics
Talk (*awal* – al hadra)	*Ġir awal*	F/M	Tashelhit			Light; dishonest
	Lmεani/mεana	F/M	Tashelhit/ MA			Fixed forms
	Tajmmaεt	F/M	Tashelhit			Dialogue
	ṣalat εla nbi	F	MA		Ululations (*taġʷrit*)	Filler; fixed form
Song (*lġa* /laεb/ *lhawa*)	*Tizrrarin*		Tashelhit	Community	Chorus at refrain	
	Tinḍḍamin	F/M	Tashelhit	Community; commercial	Chorus at refrain; drum	Heavy; orig. or reworked rways
	Agwal	F	Tashelhit	Community	Drumming, clapping, group dance	Heavy, slow then fast; mixing of fixed forms
	Aḥwaš	Mostly M	Tashelhit	Community	Drumming, clapping, group dance	Heavy, slow then fast; accompanied by dance; mixing of fixed forms
	Rways	M	Tashelhit	Community	Rbab, vocals	Fast, light; original composition
	Rways	F/M	Tashelhit	Commercial	Rbab, backup vocals	Fast, light
	Lεab/*lhdṛt*	F/M	MA	Community	Drumming, clapping, group dance	Generic term for music-making
	Ganga/dqqa/ mizan	F/M	MA	Community	Drumming, nqas, clapping, group dance	Houara plains; fast

foreign anthropologist just arrived in a community is regularly directed toward the ideal – often toward textual sources that prescribe behavior rather than toward behavior itself" (Hirsch 1998:38). Swahili scholars suggested that to learn about marital court disputes, Hirsch should consult the law library for Islamic law sources and hypothetical divorce contexts, rather than record and observe in the courts. Maggi's Pakistani Kalashi informants pointed her in the direction of the local ritual expert whenever she asked "cultural" questions or just responded, "Here, cut up this onion" (Maggi 2001:45). Ishelhin likewise directed me towards unadulterated Tashelhit language and customs in the mountains. At first I noted such comments as instances of language ideology which favored a purified Tashelhit. I continued to insist that I would not focus on formal verbal practices because the folklore and French colonial literature on Berber poetry and song already tended to objectify these cultural forms as art forms, worthy of contemplation outside their social use. Yet my interest lay in how we might read social relations, culture, and politics *through* speakers' language practices. I found little sociological inspiration in detailed collections of sung poetry compiled by French linguists and ethnographers, nor those assembled by native Tashelhit-speaking local academics and journalists from their home regions. Goodman, in contrast, traced the historical trajectories of the production and circulation of Kabyle Berber poetry from colonial collections through contemporary activist poetry (Goodman 2005:97–119). That a similar textual document of oral culture exists in Morocco is interesting in itself, and the ways people interact with such literature are even more interesting. Indigenously produced literature may be seen as serving an archival purpose, preserving a decontextualized verbal art abstracted from the situations that brought it about, although Goodman argues that it reinterprets, thus simultaneously centering and decentering both "Berber" and "universal" culture. I was more interested during fieldwork in understanding the circumstances that bring about the desire to document, and the breaks between somewhat idealized representations of these communities and their more heterogeneous realities.

The second concern was that my consultants simply did not want me to tape much everyday conversation. Their reasons were primarily three: (a) everyday talk is not "good" talk, and they did not speak "well"; (b) people would get talked about and damage the speaker's reputation; and (c) I might have ulterior motives for using their words – I might be a spy or a journalist. The first reason could just have easily been uttered by people in my high school in Gas City, Indiana. The second reason is also not specific to the Sous, a recognition that people provide fascinating grist for conversation, and that words can make and break reputations. The third reason, however, felt (unreasonably, I realize retrospectively) more personal, and fortunately it lessened slightly over the course of fieldwork. My initial efforts to tape spontaneous speech were thwarted by sometimes playful, other times firmer suggestions that I had been sent by the CIA to spy on Ishelhin, or that I was a journalist looking to broadcast their silly chatter on Radio Agadir, humiliating those on tape in front of city and country listeners alike. At first when I asked questions about a task or event at hand, even when the others were talking amongst themselves, eventually someone would remark that I was "like [Hadda] Laâwich," a popular (female) Radio Agadir interviewer to whom program guests explained the customs of their homeland.

My presence, then, turned everyday conversation and metatalk in the mountains and plains into an opportunity for rural dwellers to consider the power dynamics of divulging information (*maɛlumat*) to an outsider or eliciting news (*laxbar*) from her. The anthropological literature had prepared me to know that my presence would shape any interaction in which I was present. I found that the researcher is not only a fly on the wall but rather, as one of Basso's consultants remarked, an annoying horsefly buzzing around the head (Basso 1996). Mountain women in particular reflected on the power inequalities inherent in the gathering of people from different social groups, economic classes and educational statuses (cf. Briggs 1986), informed in part by speech conventions they heard on Tashelhit radio. Radio, then, seemed to be an important source of outside information about language use and attitudes.

The third concern my consultants raised, at times explicitly and other times implicitly by refusing to comply with my requests, was that I needed to learn more culturally appropriate ways of "learning how to ask" (Briggs 1986). It took about a year of transcribing whatever informal and solicited talk I could capture on audiotape to realize that I rarely received a response to the question "Why?" and even less frequently received a simple response to requests for information about matters of anthropological interest like genealogies. Sometime during that first year in the field, during one of my bouts of inquiring about something that had happened that day, Hajja muttered under her breath, "Only the crazy ask questions." As people told me, though, this proverb had its opposite, as most proverbs do, here in the religious injunction from the Quran (Surat An-Anbiyā, ayah 7): "If you do not know, then ask the keepers of the oracles of God (ahl al dhikr)" (Ali 1984:275). I had been inquiring according to the latter principle, whereas for secular matters of everyday life that do not involve specialized training, the former proverb is more firmly in place. It is more for matters of religion that one should ask the learned, meaning the religiously learned. From this distinction it became apparent to me that transmission of different categories of knowledge was governed by different communicative conventions. Against Briggs' urging, I retreated from the informal interview as a research method and redoubled my efforts to be present in situations where people could address issues in their own terms and at their own pace.

Although villagers were scarcely enthusiastic about my taping everyday talk, they delighted in my taping their music. Community song is at once intimate and distancing since it is public. Rosaldo found a similar reaction among the Ilongot in the Philippines:

> Ceremony, song, and other formal aspects of a culture tend to be experienced by actors as having sense and significance independent of their particular situation; because they can be performed at different times by different people, they occasion understandings and response that are, like Ilongot talk of hearts and anger, reflective, and relatively speaking, context free. This is why, without instruction or previous experience, my Ilongot informants understood that song, magic, and formal speech were appropriate objects – in a way that casual talk was not – for tape-recording and transcription. (Rosaldo 1980:58)

Comfortable, then, with song as an appropriate object of recording and analysis, and convinced of the pervasiveness of song and music in everyday Soussi life, as well as the false distinction between formality and informality in verbal genres, I began to transcribe sung verse. In its production as well as literary content, song involves articulations of community boundaries and moral matters. The precise meanings were lost on me until well into my fieldwork, for lyrics rely on archaic lexicon, as well as metaphor, allusion, and word play. Villagers understood why I would want a tape of their music, since they enjoyed circulating tapes they recorded of male song. Yet they were puzzled by my fascination with women's tizrrarin, or short sung verses. People associated the genre with intimacy and, when produced by women, with a trivial amateurism – piquing my interest even further. While I have presented preliminary analyses of my field recordings in context (Hoffman 2002a), a more complete treatment of musical production in the Anti-Atlas and Sous Valley will have to await a future manuscript.

For many male villagers and interior ministry administrators, doubts remained throughout my fieldwork as to my real interests in life among Ishelhin.[1] They seemed hard-pressed to imagine why an outsider would be interested in words so intimately linked to a specific place. Some thought I might have a financial interest in learning Tashelhit song, like the only other light-haired Western woman they knew of who "spoke" Tashelhit (Raysa Kelly, the French sensation who made a fortune as a Tashelhit-singing commercial recording artist). Strangers sometimes confused us when I spoke Tashelhit; particularly at weddings, I sometimes heard women whisper to each other when they heard me speaking Tashelhit, "Is that Kelly?" Unlike strategies adopted by other linguistic anthropologists to learn expressive genre (Caton 1990), I intentionally did not sing out in front of people for fear of confirming rumors that I had a financial interest in Tashelhit oral culture.

My perceived social identity during fieldwork affected the material I could collect. As a woman, I spent the bulk of my fieldwork with girls and women, and it is from their section of any segregated event that I tape-recorded. Because I was an unmarried woman of unconfirmable roots (*laṣl*), women considered it inappropriate that I sit and discuss performances with older male singer-poets (*inḍḍamn*). One local amateur folklorist tried to thwart my research, objecting that regional "culture" should be recorded by insiders, and claiming – more dangerously – that I might be a spy. These challenges made my research harder than it would have been otherwise. A few lay men generously shared their reflections on Tashelhit song or dictated and explained lyrics to me. Young men who were more my peers also provided insight into how they perceived musical production and the issues song addresses. Older men expected that as a Tashelhit speaker, I would be familiar with classic poetry from rways like Lhaj Belaïd as well as the latest compositions. Their expectations surely sprung from their understandings of the kind of person who would solicit information (namely, men) and from an expectation that a Tashelhit speaker would have a certain expressive repertoire.

My attention to Tashelhit words and verse made more sense to rural women, but for many of their husbands and fathers, it did not sufficiently explain my presence in remote mountain villages. The proportion of time I spent with women in their daily chores, and my clear alliance with them, raised some eyebrows. Some men expressed anxiety that my presence would elicit women to embrace Western or urban values, even though we rarely discussed them. My affinity for rural women was obvious in my dress, for example, which varied by context but was explicitly designed to make women comfortable with me rather than announce my comparatively elevated socioeconomic status. I only wore skirts in the Sous, added a headscarf outside of town, and then a tamlḥaft wrap while in the mountains. Not many men were willing to talk to me about topics that women considered men's affairs: colonialism, markets, land tenure, rural political organization. Fortunately, this changed once I became a university professor, and probably because I continued to return to the Sous. The taped interviews and more informal discussions with the men who did help shaped my initial understanding of regional history, which I was later able to expand with archival research in Nantes and Vincennes. These men tended to have a personal interest in recording rural history, and a particular openness towards the possibility that a foreigner might try her hand at that task. I tried to explain my research as concerned with the history and society of the region, as well as the languages, but both men and women insisted that

I was there to study Tashelhit. Languages, after all, are what one learns in school; since I was then a student and already seemed to "know" Arabic, French, and English, I clearly had come to learn Tashelhit. These partial understandings complicated my efforts to inquire into non-linguistic matters. Yet the alternative scenario – to restrict my informants to urban educated men, to dress as a foreign professional – would not have been a feasible long-term research choice. It also would have impeded my Tashelhit acquisition, largely accomplished by keeping company with monolingual women and girls during chores and socializing.

Peoples' ideas about the importance or insignificance of Tashelhit as a social fact colored the ways in which they spoke Tashelhit with me or, instead, insisted on speaking colloquial Arabic in my presence. The fact of speaking Tashelhit rarely went unremarked, at least initially, since an interest in Tashelhit indexed a political stance towards Amazigh matters at a time when this was taboo. Many relationships I enjoyed with the Swasa among whom I worked were relaxed and marked by mutual trust and affection. I could not have remained in Morocco for three and a half years if they had not been. However, whenever a new person entered the social interaction (which was frequently), my outsider status spurred inquiry into the kinds of knowledge worth studying and documenting by foreigners or educated people. Islam should be studied, for example, but I was not studying religion. Literary Arabic should be studied too, as the vehicle of Islam; but I was engaged in writing down the spoken, the everyday – women's words, but not exclusively women's worlds.

For those without suspicions of my intentions, it made sense that if I liked Tashelhit and country ways, I would want to live among them as much as possible. My friends and acquaintances insisted that my own inclinations and personality figure into my research choices; this was especially important under trying circumstances in which the field-worker finds her/himself ignoring, trying to erase, or sensing a loss of personality, choice, and freedom. When my neighbor Fatima Mhammd told me my sore head looked as swollen as a pumpkin, and it turned out I had mumps, there was nothing to do but cry and accept her lovingly prepared meals for the week I spent in bed. Each of my actions and mishaps – a bad bicycle accident, one attempted courtship by the local butcher and another by an Islamist, a skin condition resulting from the evil eye at a wedding, the installation of a telephone line – made my life grist for stories and assessments. Soussi women demonstrated from the outset that they would not tolerate my presence as a mere observer, and they insisted that I allow them access to my personality, preferences, beliefs, and opinions. Since they knew I was not one of them, they wanted a sense of who I "was." In innumerable ways, their demands on my conduct during residence in the Sous shaped my experience of myself as both fieldworker and human being.

They required that I develop a social identity of my own, too, by forming friendships through which they made sense of my roots, since I appeared to have none; by visiting and reciprocating hospitality; by speaking my mind among peers and offering opinions; by laughing and making others laugh; and by working. At the same time, Swasa respected my relative autonomy. I housed with families when visiting villages, but retained my own rental home with electricity and running water as a base in Taroudant. Although this would have been unacceptable for one of their own, they reasoned that I was a foreigner with peculiar tastes. They respected the time I spent with my transcription assistant and my notebooks, although we sometimes disagreed about how much time was reasonable. They knew I had more money than they did and expected I would spend a portion of it to call my mother regularly from the public phone. They demanded that I articulate an individual identity that, given the new and novel contexts in Morocco, I was in the process of formulating and making sense of just to go about my days. This was not exceptional for the foreigner; among themselves, Swasa expect that individuals have personality quirks, tastes, inclinations and abilities, and within limits these differences are accommodated. I am forced to keep all of this in mind as I write about the collective, about group identity, and about how humans negotiate their ways through mixed discourses about themselves and others.

This book, like fieldwork itself, is "not so much the achieved consummation of that process [fieldwork]" but "a temporary truce among contending forces" (Smith 1983:24 in Lutz 1988:228). Much of the present text's unevenness results from the struggles and truces between at least three forces: (1) between myself and the fieldwork context, (2) between social scientific inquiry and the political and historical circumstances circumscribing relations between Moroccans and outsiders, and (3) between the realities and ideals of what is entailed in the experience of transcription from fieldwork to scholarly text. Unlike more text-based forms of research, "ethnography originates in orality and only makes the transition to writing with difficulty" (Marcus 1986:264–5). Writing ethnography is a solitary project, but the grist for writing is generated through fundamentally social interactions.

In telling a tale of my fieldwork, my intention is not simply to explain the methodology by which I collected research material. The research effort itself is a metaphor for the complexity of orientations that Ashelhi and Arab Swasa have to the production and dissemination of knowledge about people and places. Erasing the encounter between my consultants and me, in presenting what I learned from them, would sidestep an important opportunity to inquire into how inquiry itself engages conflicting valuations of knowledge. The roots of ideological valuation can be identified to some extent, categorized by variables such as gender, class, level and kind of education, relation to the urban versus rural, etc., and related to historical factors such as colonialism, tourism, and foreign aid. This complexity marks the encounter between researcher and researched. It affects what the researcher seeks to learn, how and whom she asks, and what consultants share with her. When I could not bear partaking in these power dynamics, I intentionally kept company with people who came to trust my motivations and character. Complementing the ethnographic research is archival material from the Protectorate period. It is necessarily one-sided, yet I try to balance it with oral histories whenever possible.

Much of my ethnographic material is from participant observation and conversation, either taped or transcribed from memory. Rural Moroccans living in a primarily oral society expected what they said to get repeated; word-of-mouth was how most information was conveyed. For this reason, I do not believe that the transcripts presented here violate any ethical principle. My tape recorder stood in the place of the keen memory for detail that my consultants shared but that I never developed, having spent too much of my life in books. At one level, then, I write about what my consultants wanted or allowed me to record. At another level, I analyze what their preferences and permissions imply. I recorded not only verbal expressive practices as windows onto social relations, but metalinguistic commentary as critiques of social identities, places, and fates. That said, in this book, I adopt a strategy that Ida ou Zeddout young women used when talking with young men from other villages. As one explained to me, "We don't divulge names . . . We trade them for other names." Similarly, Mills found by Afghan conversational standards, "Personal names are not usually volunteered" (Mills 1991:46). Here a few of my consultants have their real names because they preferred this; for the rest, I have switched names. Their narratives leave traces across multiple chapters, as it is difficult to confine a rich encounter to only one angle of analysis.

Historicizing Ethnography

> f lmaġrb la tstaġrb
> Don't be shocked when in Maroc.
> – Moroccan proverb

This book documents an historical moment that, at the time, seemed a continuation of four decades of Arabocentric governmental policies. No one I knew in the 1990s, whether illiterate agriculturalists or academics, imagined that the early twenty-first century Moroccan government would support the study, dissemination, and use of what francophones call *l'Amazighité*. Few predicted the political opening in 2002 that brought the Tamazight language into primary schools and founded a Royal Institute for Moroccan Amazigh Culture. In the final years of the twentieth century, governmental officials at the local, provincial, and national levels viewed the Amazigh language and cultural rights activism with suspicion, as potentially subversive and even anti-monarchical. From the present vantage point, linguistic self-determination, or at least the articulation of a majority-minority collective identity, may appear self-evident. Yet in Morocco, at least, a reversal of hegemony had to come about for these increasingly vocal discourses to be sanctioned and eventually absorbed. Both positions – the one considering the nationalist Arabic language as unifier and another advocating Berber difference – anchor their convictions in the Herderian paradigm that language, and especially poetic language, demonstrates a people's genius. Indigenous people – in their heterogeneous everyday practices, not in the purist discourses advocated by the intellectual vanguard – inherently compromise and challenge these frames. This book explores the same frames, the ideologies that support them and the discourses and practices through which they emerged. A prevailing language ideology in the period of my field research concerned the essential worth of the languages in play: it held that Arabic was a language (luġa), because it was written, whereas Berber was just a spoken dialect (lahja) or as it was simply called in Tashelhit, talk (*awal*). For this reason, common sense dictated, Berber had no place in public life and threatened the country's efforts to modernize and unify under a single language and a single religion. As one Ashelhi emigrant merchant asked me rhetorically, critiquing my efforts to learn Tashelhit, "How can you study a language that isn't written?" With Tamazight now being written and officially taught, the rug is pulled out from under this argument, and it would be surprising to hear, in the future, many of the disparaging comments about Tashelhit that pepper this book.

While any ethnographic insight should be historicized, the rapid social change affecting Berbers and language politics in Morocco only brings this imperative into relief. My decision to write in the past tense instead of the ethnographic present was largely made for me, and not only (but partially) spurred by Fabian's critique of the use of the ethnographic present to represent "the Other," as though only Western societies were subject to change, rather than simply deterioration in a kind of faux authenticity (Fabian 1983). His critique has shaken up anthropological writing – for the better – and influenced my own writing here, for all understanding is temporally locatable, even that of the ethnographer for whom "what we call our data are really our own construction of other people's constructions of what they and their compatriots are up to" (Geertz 1973:9). Yet I proceed with some trepidation, for using the past tense also implies a comparative or, worse, a contrast with a presumed present – and yet I plainly offer none. Inadvertently, then, my past tense may seem to suggest change even where there has been little. Still, I insist on rendering events and cultural meanings in the past tense, as well as events and conversations, for the simple reason that I cannot presume that individuals' structures of feeling (Williams 1977) have remained the same over the last decade, given the rapid clip of changes in Moroccan politics, technology, economics, and urbanization. Unless indicated otherwise, the ethnographic account here is intended to be illustrative of the time, place, and people encountered by one ethnographer, albeit one with a solid grasp of the field languages of Tashelhit, Moroccan Arabic, classical Arabic, and French; with several years of first-hand experience living among Soussi people, and familiarity with the whole of Morocco through media, education, and rural development projects continuing to the present; and steeped in the scholarship of cultural and linguistic anthropology, history, and ethnomusicology. The shame and marginalization I document here may be distant memories by the time the reader encounters this book. But there is no guarantee that they will dissolve entirely, or, if they do, that they will not reemerge at another historical moment, in a political atmosphere shaped by different international human rights pressures and internal regionalization policies. Most importantly, perhaps, marginalization shapes the lives of indigenous people in countless societies, only some of whose experiences are shared and acknowledged with the rise in consciousness about their shared lot vis-à-vis states, what Niezen calls indigenism (Niezen 2003; cf. Hoffman 2003).

Perhaps more than anything, current preoccupations remind us that ethnography has always been situated in time, place, and context and in the dialogic relationship between ethnographer and consultants (Fabian 1983; Rabinow 1977; Clifford and Marcus 1986; Wolf 1992), as has each reading (Boyarin 1993). Geertz was probably the best-known English-language ethnographer of Morocco who provided many pointed insights for anthropology as a whole. Yet I disagree on ethical grounds with his approach to cultural systems themselves as "texts." Ethnography captures verbal (and non-verbal) interaction in writing, translates and edits it, renders it as text for dissemination to scholars and students who could never have the conversations themselves. The interactive character of the dialogic encounter (Tedlock 1983; Dwyer 1982) must remain central to any account of verbal expression if it is to take seriously the sharp distinction between speech and text understood by many groups – including Ishelhin – as distinct, not at all interchangeable for those who do not write and read, such as most of the women in this book. Scholars ensconced simultaneously in books and dialogue tend to conflate text and talk, albeit inadvertently. Text cannot serve as a metaphor for talk/culture in societies where forms of authority map so disparately onto these modalities. Surely if "cultures" exist, a problematic thesis in itself (Abu-Lughod 1991; Eagleton 2000; Kuper 1999), "they" are something whose analysis needs to be grounded in situated fieldwork encounters, rather than as the representation of an abiding cultural essence. This approach usefully emphasizes the processual and emergent nature of the phenomena we study, here namely ethnolinguistic and gendered identities. Many other minority groups around the world are undergoing similar changes in their relationships to the state, shifting political economies responding to neoliberal policies and a flood of market goods, and shifting locations of cultural and symbolic capital (Balzer 1999; Bourdieu 1990; Colloredo-Mansfeld 1999; Frye 1996; Povinelli 2002; Tsing 1993; Turino 1993).

In retrospect, it appears that the late twentieth century I write about here was a turning point in Moroccan social history, nestled between, on the one hand, the didactic, widespread and only partially successful cultural Arabization and linguistic Arabicization efforts of the 1956–94 period, and on the other hand the increasingly vocal internationalization of human rights demands for indigenous people, including linguistic rights. Hassan II, an aging and infirm monarch who survived multiple coup attempts in the 1970s, died in late July 1999 during the final weeks of my extended residence. The news came through on Al-Jazeera while my hands were crusty with freshly applied henna while readying a friend for the wedding that had to be postponed due to the country's mandatory 40-day mourning period. Under Hassan II's rule, civil society began to play an increasing role and the Moroccan populace was gradually inserted into national decision-making. A dramatic demographic shift strengthened civil society: the generalization of education began only after Independence, in sharp contrast to the Algerian and Tunisian experiences. Rural–urban emigration intensified with the waves of drought that pushed agricultural workers from the lands where they worked as laborers, despite governmental plans that allowed some displaced Moroccans to purchase cultivatable land in agricultural collectives of the Sous plains, often nearby land usurped from their ancestors by Protectorate-era qayd-s (French-appointed regional Muslim rulers) and their families. A widespread and diffuse fear prevented open discussion on such topics during Hassan II's lifetime, a mood that began shifting almost immediately under the reign of his son Mohamed VI. A major national event thus closed the period of data collection for this book as well as the era I hope to evoke in the chapters that follow.

Part II

Dissonance: Gender

Language cannot properly be said to be handed down – it endures, but it endures as a continuous process of becoming.

– Vološinov (1973 [1929]:81)

Awal iġd iġli d idmarn
iġli s idrarn
When words leave your chest
They echo off the mountains
– Tashelhit proverb

Chapter 3

The Gender of Authenticity

Each farmer on the island conceals
his hive far up on the mountain,
knowing it will otherwise be plundered.
When they die, or can no longer make
the hard climb, the lost combs year
after year grow heavier with honey.
And the sweetness has more and more
acutely the taste of that wilderness.
– Jack Gilbert, "Older Women" (1994)

The proverbial old Berber woman in the mountains occupied what Foucault (1977) calls the panopticon, an elevated point from which one can monitor in a circumference, as from a prison watchtower. Yet while the Anti-Atlas mountain woman surveyed people and places around her, patrolling the boundaries of her fields and village, she – like her language – simultaneously was monitored. Subject to the wishes of her husband or father, the Tashelhit woman's subjectivity was conditional. Although certainly not inspired by the Anti-Atlas, the American poet Jack Gilbert captures one of its moods in "Older Women," hinting at the possible pervasiveness of this trope in other rural societies.[1] As with Gilbert's older women, the "sweetness" of Anti-Atlas women is heightened by their isolation in a sort of mountain island, evoking as well their desperation, here imagined as combs in a "hive" or home that each Anti-Atlas man "conceals . . . far up on the mountain." The Ida ou Zeddout women with whom I spent time feared the outrage of disappearing husbands and fathers who might encounter circulating photos of their wives. Women knew to avoid contact and conversation with unrelated men if they needed to be in their company; this was difficult in collective taxis and buses on mountain roads with hair-raising turns. Photos and conversations could "plunder" a woman by compromising her reputation, leaving her husband or father open to other men's critique*. Women,

*Images of women appear in this book with their consent.

like the "lost combs" that remain in the mountains, "grow heavier with honey." Both neglected and protected, women developed a "sweetness" tinged by "wilderness." Aptly enough, Ishelhin often characterized their native language as "sweet" because of its association with home, mountains, and safety from the dominant national moral system that denigrated Tamazight language speakers and their histories. Yet the pleasure was bittersweet for it came at the price of neglect and seclusion. Women safeguarded the "hive" in the homelands, and their estrangement from the outside world "sweetened them" when their keepers could "no longer make the hard climb," and they "grow heavier with honey." Like the metaphorical old woman in Gilbert's poem, the elderly Tashelhit woman was strangely eroticized, the object of men's longing despite her desexualized status. Men's absence enriched her desirability, at least in men's eyes; her maturity carried the sweet richness of her people's weighted history.

At the end of the twentieth century, Tashelhit women were their communities' repositories and the embodiment of its morality, purity, sensuality, vulnerability and stoicism. These are the women who, in both practice and shared language ideology, have "saved" Tashelhit language from "extinction," to appropriate a troubling biological metaphor common to both the language contraction literature and the advocacy organizations to preserve global linguistic diversity (cf. Hill 2002; Errington 2003). Rhetoric from both inside and outside of Morocco characterized mountain women and their language similarly: as spatially and intellectually circumscribed, precious, rugged, stoic, vulnerable, rich in cultural capital yet poor in symbolic capital. Through objectification, women become victims rather than agents of their circumstances and fates. Part of my task in this present chapter, as in those that follow, is to balance this lopsided imagery with narratives of women's agency.

To do this, I present several voicings of metaculture (Urban 2001), or culture about culture – meaning, more specifically, "judgments people make about similarities and differences" (Lee 2001:xi). These assessments compare different instances of purportedly the same cultural processes and products. The concept of metaculture helps us to understand how culture circulates between individuals and groups and over time and space, not simply how it is reproduced or socialized intact and wholesale. This approach imagines culture as more than "simply replications of specific antecedent[s]," in that "the new production makes reference to a range of prior and seemingly disparate cultural elements" (Urban 2001:5).

The voices here are dissonant, for there is no consensus on consciousness by those who share cultural practices. As such, they present alternative perspectives, not so much comparable as concomitant and synchronic. Cultural practices, relations to place, gendered practices and language ideologies are all situated in time and space. Often unwittingly, generation stands in for the elapsed time that we cannot witness firsthand unless we have had the luxury

Figure 3.1 Kiltum of Indouzal picking wildflowers from her summer barley fields

of a long life and repeated, prolonged exposure to a fieldsite. Generation comes to substitute for time in this respect, even though the fieldworker has no means to triangulate what she hears with the firsthand observation she uses for the present. We talk to the elderly to get a sense of change, allowing for their comparisons between "then" (or as the Berbers amorphously label the early days, *zikk*) and "now," even using indigenous categories such as "traditional" and "modern" to situate practices and people in time and space. From the elderly, we get an idea of how things were in an imaginary earlier time that always seems to have been more pure than the present, albeit whitewashed as memories fade. As fieldworkers, we look for patterns and their shifts. Just as often, we are left with dangling threads and frayed corners that resist finishing. I consider a few of them in the second half of this chapter. First, I turn to the feminization of Tashelhit that challenges recent activist and governmental attempts to mainstream the language's use.

The Feminization of Tashelhit

Anti-Atlas mountain discourse I collected during fieldwork gendered Tashelhit language as female and localized it in increasingly devalued rural lands. Berber more generally, according to Sadiqi, is "undergoing a conscious process of feminization on the part of the mainstream language ideology" (2003:225). This is because, she explains, "the situations in which

Berber is used are more and more women-linked than men-linked" (2003:225). However, here we might recall Ochs' (1992) injunction to consider the ways that language indexes certain features of social identity, such as gender, rather than directly stemming from them. Moreover, with the most recent emphasis on standardizing and teaching Tamazight language in the schools, a conventionally "male" domain – education – is opening to Tamazight language. It remains to be seen whether for this reason Berber's association with the feminine will decrease. Besides, the prominence of Berber in certain public domains, most importantly commerce with which only men are associated, compromises the argument that Berber is strictly a language of private domains. Regardless, Sadiqi's contention that women's orality/illiteracy "serves the general patriarchal need of keeping women under control" may be a red herring when indexing becomes our prism. Indeed, control of women involves what Silverstein (2003) has identified as second-order indexicality.

The feminization of Tashelhit fits within a broader pattern whereby rural women are expected to uphold "traditional Moroccan social structure" and to "channel these traditions and transmit them through female family networks" (Sadiqi 2003:169). The difficulty with this bundle of associations for Ishelhin was that it complicated both men's and women's abilities to imagine Tashelhit language as an urban and urbane vernacular, expressed through a textual medium, and employing a standard orthography – all markers of contemporary language revitalization efforts worldwide. Tashelhit thus has become rhetorically emplaced in rural spaces – especially in the mountains – in ways that both obscure its decline in use and perpetuate speakers' belief that the mountains will remain a Tashelhit-speaking homeland despite the demographic shift to urban areas. Women were ambivalent about their charge as the keepers of both Tashelhit language and the agricultural system closely associated with it.

Yet simultaneously, recent efforts to integrate Amazigh language and heritage into Moroccan public spheres (especially the schools) risk marginalizing those who have maintained Amazigh heritage – and erstwhile have been valued from inside their communities for doing so. As authoritative language forms shift from rural women's hands into those of highly educated urban male intellectuals and policymakers, we witness a gendered process in which "what is also displaced is the authority of women and their role as custodians of traditional knowledge and as agents of socialization" (Bauman and Briggs 2003:76).[2] Scholarly activism to this end is nothing new, as Bauman and Briggs detail, and indeed was part of the secularizing process. For the mid-seventeenth-century philosopher of language John Aubrey, as for others of his time, "antiquarian" or early folkloristic activities such as collecting women's tales provided grist for enlightened (male) conversation and reflection – if only to establish how far "we" had evolved as a people. In such associations, time becomes gendered in the sense that the past is associated with (lower class, poor, illiterate) women, and a more rational present/future is associated with (upper class, elite, schooled) men. For Henry Bourne, slightly later, the "vehicles for maintaining the old beliefs" consist of "legendary stories of nurses and old women," that is, vulgar, ignorant, rural, unrefined women who most closely guarded these traditions. Such characterizations forward the view that "authority is male, educated, literate, rational, persuasive" (Bauman and Briggs 2003:82). For indigenous people today, the stakes are different than they were for seventeenth-century Europeans. Yet a similar gendered process is underway that risks further marginalizing women and the ancestral keepers of indigenous languages such as Berber.

Voices in Metaculture

The secluded bride and the cassette

In the days leading up to her wedding, Saadia sat in her parents' home and prepared for her nuptials. Among the Ida ou Zeddout, this involved the bride's seclusion from men, restriction to her home, avoidance of the sun, and finally a steam bath where female relatives and friends would ritually cleanse her and apply purifying henna to her hair, hands and feet for protection during this liminal passage from virginity to womanhood. Before her body was cleaned and adorned, however, the future bride received girlfriends in her parent's home for entertainment. Usually, girlfriends sang slow tizrrarin poetic verses (Hoffman 2002a), one soloist at a time and each following on the heels of the last; tizrrarin tended to morph into the faster-paced agwal collective call and response musical genre, at which point the young women brought out improvised drums – any empty plastic or metal oil jug – to accompany their handclapping. These afternoons tended to be jolly but bittersweet as the lifelong friends joked, gossiped and told stories for hours on end, occasionally returning home for meals and chores, and otherwise biding time before the public wedding festivities.

I had been taping wedding tizrrarin for two years in Ida ou Zeddout before Saadia married, and had made a point of bringing back duplicates of the recordings for Mina to share with the village girls. Some of them, in turn, made copies of Mina's copies. My vague intention was one part fair play – why should I have their voices and they should not? – and one part archival. As we sat keeping Saadia company, I remarked aloud that no one was singing tizrrarin, thinking – selfishly, perhaps – this would be a safe, private place to further my own familiarity with the verses. Saadia turned towards the tape player just out of her reach and put in the cassette I had recorded one night in the *tamṣrit* of Hajja's old stone house, normally a sitting room for guests but in this case a storage room for grain, blankets, and dishes. The young women had assembled that night, at my request, to sing tizrrarin into my tape recorder, and the acoustics in the low-ceilinged room were excellent for this venture. The tape recorder caught the young women quickly shifting from melancholy verses to agwal, however, much to my disappointment at the time. Later I found this shift illustrative of the inseparability of the genres and the seamless way that a favorite tazrrart line got taken up in the faster, drum- and clap-accompanied agwal. Hearing the young women's voices on the future bride's cassette player, solicited and recorded over a year earlier, I asked Saadia why she had put on the cassette. She responded that there was no need to sing the tizrrarin any longer since they could play my recording.

I was horrified. Fieldworkers are aware of the Hawthorne principle, or observer's paradox, that posits that the act of observing something necessarily changes it. Yet it had never occurred to me that archiving metaculture could lead its practitioners to abandon the production of that same cultural practice. "What have I done?" was all I could ask myself. Ida ou Zeddout expressive culture suddenly seemed fragile. Urban suggests that the "thing" or cultural product – here, we might say either the sung verses or the cassette itself – allows for the dissemination of culture (Urban 2001:42). What then is the culture that is being transported by that vehicle? In the years of learning Tashelhit language, recording expressive culture, appreciating its subtleties and its centrality to the reproduction of cultural practices and social knowledge, I largely presumed that change mostly came in response to external factors. When Saadia played the recording, she instead demonstrated that she and her friends saw this indigenous musical genre as one among many genres of song, one among many modalities of expression, and interchangeably performable, recordable, repeatable, and ultimately discardable. She could play a commercial pop recording by a Tashelhit artist such as Fatima Tabaamrant or Oudadden. Or she could play a cassette of their own voices – exotic in its unfamiliarity, still titillating to the young women who previously had never heard the sound of their own voices so clearly, since the tizrrarin are sung solo and a cappella. To them, that moment did not necessarily signal a shift away from traditional expressive cultural practices; they were not acting either to maintain or to destroy Tashelhit language or expressive culture. I began to wonder whether a concept firmly held in the Tashelhit-speaking plains – namely, that public song performances were the domain of the professional – would soon take hold in the mountains and lead to the appropriation of Arabic-language song as it had in the plains. More immediately, I began to wonder whether this act signaled a willingness to accept that perhaps those in the younger cohort would not be able to sing the songs any longer. The younger girls present were deprived of an opportunity to practice their tizrrarin. They learned from the older girls that this was not a specialization that everyone could develop.

Lazy women and industrious others

Public transportation is often fruitful for social science research; travelers have a tendency towards reflection in semi-anonymous liminal spaces. During a particularly animated taxi ride from Taroudant to Igherm, the male passengers debated the difficulties of reconciling Tashelhit with state institutions and Arab dominance. As we drove southeast and neared Walqadi in Ida ou Zeddout, the taxi pulled over to pick up a slight man from the side of the road, wearing a light blue foqia robe over his pants and shirt, an index of mountain residence. The Ida ou Zeddout man started up a conversation with a man in his thirties sitting next to me, who in contrast to the slight new passenger had an ample belly and neck, and sported sunglasses and a fashionable plaid jacket. He had told me earlier that he led an Igherm-based rural development organization. The man we had just picked up complained that his daughter was failing her first year of school. Her teacher blamed the father, asking "How can you expect me to teach your girl Arabic when all you speak to her at home is Tashelhit?" The young activist responded to this provocation with agitation in his voice: "That's why we have to teach Tashelhit in the schools, put Arabic aside, teach our children in their own language!"

The father explained his daughter's dilemma as the result of rural–urban migration and the attendant linguistic shift towards Arabic. "Tashelhit is dying out," he said. "I give it fifty years before no one speaks it any more. Even now, our children don't want anything to do with Tashelhit anymore. It's all because of school and television. Tashelhit doesn't put food on the table" (*ur tšša aġrum*, lit. doesn't feed with bread).

While I had heard this observation dozens of times before, the activist's advocacy for education in Tashelhit was not common in the mountains. I hinted that the young activist's solution might be unfeasible given the uniform national curriculum. "Then they should do away with the curriculum!" the young man exclaimed. "Even the king himself said in 1994 that they were going to introduce the Berber dialects (al laḥajat al barbaria) into the schools," switching from Tashelhit into classical Arabic for this official (and officious) term. The father disagreed, saying, "Look, Arabic at least has writing, and French has writing. What does Tashelhit have? You can't learn Tashelhit through books; you learn it through speaking." He turned to me, the only non-native Tashelhit speaker present, and asked, "Isn't that right? You have to be with people who speak Tashelhit to learn it, like in our tamazirt." The association activist countered, "There are Tashelhit books in the bookstores. There are even books on how to learn Tashelhit!" All of this was true, despite the lack of Tamazight in the schools at that time.

The father refused to believe him, instead linking his daughter's school failure to urban influences on the countryside:

> Look even now, the children of Ishelhin (*tarwa n* šluḥ) don't even speak it! Look at the women in our village. They sit around all day staring at the television. With the satellite dish there's everything you want to watch, Egyptian and Lebanese and Algerian and French. That's all they see. They don't want Tashelhit any more.

I suggested that Egyptian films alone would not lead women to abandon their own language, which may be dear to them (or practical) for other reasons, and may be the only language they speak anyway. I offered myself up as an example, saying "No matter what other languages I hear on television, I cannot imagine abandoning my parents' language." "But it's different for you," the father retorted:

> With English (*tinglizit*) you can earn your bread well *and* speak your parents' language. But here, kids here go to school in Arabic. They watch television in Arabic. The boys come back from Casablanca and they don't speak Tashelhit. You speak it to them and they won't speak it back. You're forced to speak Arabic with them. If there are eight people in a room and only one person doesn't speak Tashelhit, you're forced to speak Arabic. Otherwise the Arab says, "What are you saying? Are you talking about me?" And you're just talking about nothing, but they get suspicious. Tashelhit won't last.

He was right, of course, that languages have unequal value in the linguistic market (Bourdieu 1991; Eckert and McConnell-Ginet 2003). With a wave of his arm towards the rocky fields we passed, he continued: "Look at all the timizar that are clearing out. Even the people who used to come back, they come back less and less. Soon they won't come back at all. They build their houses and they stay in the Gharb [Ar. West; Atlantic coast cities]. The women here have nothing to do. They don't even embroider and weave anymore, just watch TV." I objected that Tashelhit women never had embroidered; that was what city women did. The father responded, "Yes, but they need something to do with their time." I said that they filled their time fetching water and wood, and working the fields. He responded, "What, maybe an hour getting water, then they sit around. They don't do anything." The association president corrected him, saying, "More like four hours, in some places."

Ultimately, again, the burden returned to women. Not only did women prefer watching Egyptian Arabic films to speaking Tashelhit, although these two activities were not mutually exclusive; women no longer spent sufficient time on subsistence tasks. The father did not directly identify women as the perpetrators of language death, but he still placed them centrally in a linguistic shift that seemed inevitably to accompany economic change and migration.

After hearing the father's complaint, I wondered aloud what he considered a solution, and asked him what he thought would happen in the future given the significant number of city-dwelling Ishelhin; wouldn't they speak Tashelhit together? The father asked, "You mean if they are there together you think they'll band together? It's not like that. Everyone looks out for their own store, their own household, and that's all. They don't help each other in the cities, just because they're šluḥ. They may as well be Arabs." The rural development leader disagreed, naming a small market town further southwest with significant male emigration to Casablanca and a reputation for substantial remittances: "Look at Tafraout n Ammeln,[3] have you ever been there? There they teach their girls embroidery, and they teach their children to write in Tashelhit, to write Tifinagh,[4] the Tashelhit writing. The [Amazigh and local development] associations are active there. They don't want Tashelhit to die." The father did not concur that this countered his point, insisting that "Different timizar aren't the same. We're not like Ait Tafraout. Šluḥ aren't all one. Just like we're not like the Izayanin [Middle Atlas Berbers]: you can't understand their awal (talk/language)."

We might compare these taxi passengers' views with that of Hajja who sang "we share walls," a concept of "we" as a face-to-face entity. In the rural father's view as well, the community was visible, tangible, face-to-face, and performed; its members were in contact, under constant scrutiny, and this contact strengthened networks of interests. His view echoed that of Hajja, for whom individuals "are one" by sharing resources and boundaries between lands that ensured mutual reliance. Several other remarks in the taxi were iconic of commonplace language ideologies among Ishelhin in that they focused on one small aspect of a phenomenon as though it represented the whole. Most striking was the particular insistence on the abiding vigilance required to perpetuate Tashelhit. None of the participants took for granted that Tashelhit would continue to be spoken in the future. They saw threats from many sides. Young (impetuous) Ashelhi men in the cities preferred to speak Arabic over Tashelhit amongst themselves. Economic markets devalued Tashelhit. Writing Tashelhit seemed impossible. Ishelhin from different parts of the same region (like the Ida ou Zeddout and Ammeln in the Sous) lacked solidarity and tended towards household autonomy. In the view of both the father and the association leader, individuals needed to strictly monitor their behavior – both linguistic and social – to ensure their language's survival. Speakers guarded against using Arabic unless required, and against the impurity of Arabic and French loan words. But the young activist in the taxi went further, stating that Tashelhit should be used even for school instruction, because the educational system favored native Arabic speakers. Yet Tashelhit faced threats even from television entertainment and women's lack of "traditional" activities, according to one passenger.

The conversation was ostensibly about language, but the participants signaled that more was at stake than a communicative code: Ishelhin risked assimilation into a national Arabic-speaking citizenry that did not acknowledge the value of either their ancestral language or the traditions it reproduced. The men found themselves beaten in a contest of wills. Not "wanting" Tashelhit indicated disrespect, laziness, and weakness.

These taxi passengers blamed everyone but mature men for the decline of Tashelhit. Each individual ideally shouldered the responsibility for the group; many among them had failed. Further southwest in Ammeln, in contrast, the development groups encouraged industriousness: they offered embroidery classes to young women and Tifinagh classes to young men. Once again, the perpetuation of Tashelhit language and community required gendered labor, with the hard labor falling on the women, illiterate and thus unable to garner the symbolic capital of the Tifinagh script. When I pointed this out on occasion to men, they acknowledged that it was true, but that it was simply custom (*lɛada*) for women to labor in the countryside, not be concerned with schooling, and uphold the man's homestead. Custom was inherently indisputable, unchangeable – at least until it *did* change, at which point it was assessed and compared in the ever-shifting dichotomy of traditional (taqlidi) and modern (ɛṣri) practices.

The association leader conceived of community as held together by common language and the experiences that speaking Tashelhit entailed with Arabic speakers, without reference to place. In this view, the community was imagined, structured not only by a common heritage, origin, and language, but also by similar structural positions relative to the state and to those in positions of authority.

For both of these men, the "Other" that demarcated "us" was the Arab. Arabs, for the development leader, were the country's decision-makers, a structural position as much as an ethnic group. Since one identity tended to map onto another, Arabs included those who mandated that a Tashelhit girl could only be instructed in Arabic. For the father, Arabs were individuals one encountered who either mandated that everyone speak Arabic or persuaded them, through television or national imagery, that the shared national culture had no room for regional, rural, Berber ways. The activist and the father concurred that Tashelhit speakers were disadvantaged in communicative situations where Arabic speakers were present. Yet their positions signaled conflicting and deeper formulations of identity: on the one hand, individual identity as innate and located in a person's geographic origin; on the other hand, identity as performed, reinforced and monitored between people with shared material and social interests in specific homelands. While what separated "us" from "them" in the conversation was clear, what bonded "us," apart from being not-Arab, was less clear. Urban residence, in the father's view, further exacerbated latent individualism; the father evoked an abandoned moral universe in which Ishelhin banded together. The development leader's experience in urban settings was in schools and in the marketplace of ideas; the rural merchant traded in the marketplace of dry goods. Each contributed to the political economy of Tashelhit language and Ashelhi identity. A Moroccan who did not speak Tashelhit or one of the other Tamazight varieties, in this discourse, blended into the Arab majority.

The discussion continued, and the vocalist on the pop cassette sang of "my liver" (*tasa nu*), the Berber repository of affect that operates indexically in Tashelhit song as does the contemporary Arabic "heart" (galb/qalb in MA; *ul* in Tashelhit).[5] As we neared our destination in the early evening, the roadside hills steepened. The land was terraced into narrow foot-width plots; yellowish-green barley sprouted between the rocks. Piles of stacked, white-painted stones marked the field borders. In the fields, women bent over and used the excess material of their ample tamlḥafts to gather stacks of yellow fodder flowers on their backs. The women had hand-plowed virtually every inch of land; the already-narrow terraces thinned as the soil became increasingly rocky, until the fields faded into a solid rock terrain. These were clearly Ashelhi lands where men's authority was secure albeit contingent on women's hard labor, integrity, and resourcefulness.

The annual return: rural and urban youths fashion one another

ati tugl as i lġnbaz sul imẓẓikn	He picked the yellow flower while still a bud
iɛššaqn ad t ur yujjin ard ikmml	its admirers wouldn't wait for it to blossom

– Ida ou Zeddout tazzrart

The bi-annual returns of migrant workers to the tamazirt were moments when estranged emigrant males and village-locked females temporarily overlapped. For unmarried youths in their teens and twenties, the return was particularly portentous. For young men, it was the opportunity to renew friendships with other young men they might need to call on during hard times in the northern cities. Some of them had decided to marry, and were eager to hear about suitable brides from their families and friends. For young women, the young men they considered like brothers afforded the opportunity to practice interacting with the opposite sex, through teasing (Ar. tfliyya), friendly banter (*tajmmaɛt*), and more serious male–female conversational dyads (*imsqarn*). Young emigrants brought the unmarried women news of city life, fashion, adventure, gossip, and perhaps most importantly the hope that they, too, would one day leave the countryside. The level of trust between these young men and their female peers was unparalleled in mixed-sex encounters elsewhere in Morocco. While unmarried young Moroccan men have been characterized in the scholarly literature as seekers of alcohol, sexual pleasure, and other "deviations" (e.g. Hammoudi 1993:46; Davis and Davis 1989; Bennani-Chraibi 1994, 2000; Guessous 1996), and indeed sexual harassment is commonplace in Moroccan towns and even at times in the plains, in the mountain village setting young men behaved respectfully toward unmarried women, myself included, without the slightest hint of sexual innuendo or impropriety. Instead, a childish naïveté often prevailed. The mountain setting seemed to play a strong moralizing role in this regard; young people relaxed in mixed company, in contrast to the strict sexual segregation, or at least its norm, exerted outside the tamazirt and in rural ritual domains. For the young men, part of what characterized the tamazirt was the potential for mixed-gender activities: group dinners, evening conversations under the night stars, and musical performances, all absent from these young men's lives in the cities. Young migrant men and mountain-dwelling young women brought together the different worlds in which they grew up when they met up in the tamazirt. Yet both sets of peers claimed familiarity with the others' world while seeking more news (laxbar) from it.

A half-dozen mixed-sex *zerda*-s (informal dinner and dance parties), took place during my fieldwork in the Ida ou Zeddout village where I worked, as well as several female-only zerdas during the winter months while the young men were absent. Ideas circulated in the moments of encounter when both parts of the Ashelhi community negotiated their way through mixed messages to form visions of the collective. For young women, the preservers of Tashelhit language, zerdas brought negotiations over shared cultural capital into relief when young emigrants returned for brief visits to the village. Given the monotony and difficulty of daily life in the mountains, women constantly searched for stories that departed from the mundane, weaving events out of the constant stream of movement, assessing and evaluating human behavior. Zerdas thus provide insight into the collaborative vision of the homeland that young village women co-constructed with young emigrant men from the cities.

Summers were full of nightly socializing, sitting, talking, game-playing, and singing under the vast starry sky. In mixed-sex gatherings, young people discursively and physically negotiated and performed their normative beliefs about tamazirt and about Ashelhi society. As an unmarried woman myself, whom Moroccans frequently mistook for being younger than I was, I was typically age-segregated with the unmarried teenagers, rather than with the mothers who were closer to my age at the time. As a result, I was privy to a glimpse of rural Moroccan youth culture in the late twentieth century, largely absent from the scholarly literature.

One zerda in particular illustrates the youthful co-construction of Ashelhi community that characterized mixed-gender social events. The narrative here is extracted from an extended field notes entry from Ida ou Zeddout in January 1998. I intend it to convey the complexity of a set of interactions and negotiations that unfolded over the course of a single evening. All ethnographic writing involves multiple levels of translation and selection (Clifford and Marcus 1986), over and above the editing involved in fieldnote-taking. In analyzing a single event, I attend to the multiple discourses and practices that youths used to enact their understandings of tamazirt ways in contradistinction to urban life, and gendered participation in both. It is through such practices that meaning is construed and confirmed.

Practices come in many forms: they can be active, things that people do, or discursive, "doing things with words" (Austin 1962). People perform, interpret, and react to practices according to certain sets of expectations and understandings about what those practices signify. While a practice itself is empty of meaning, like a sign, the interpretation and understanding of one's own and others' practices result from expectations of human interaction informed by previous practices, ideologies, and beliefs. Since each individual's historical experience varies from the next, however, interpretations differ. There are moments in which interpretations come into relief when people gather. As I emphasize in this book, people do not gather in a vacuum, but rather in places they already endow with meaning and expectations of continuity with the past. When people gather, not all the elements individuals initiate get taken up by the collective; "a people's own analysis of its social order is intrinsic to the emergence of a central situational focus" (Irvine 1979:779). Dwelling in festive times provides a crucial counterpoint to the laboring that characterizes the balance of the year. The zerda described here contains several dimensions of this identity-building as the "situational focus" shifted through an afternoon into night.

It was the day after the Id n Ramadan marking the close of the month of fasting. There were enough young men back from Casablanca for a zerda, and several planned to leave the day after the Id. We sat scheming in Hajja's cement sitting room in the late afternoon; it was cold enough to see our breath. The young women and mothers were bundled up conventionally in navy tamlḥaft wraps over their skirts and sweaters, except for Mina, who was then a high school boarder in Taroudant, and who wore a pair of jeans borrowed from her brother the previous day. The jeans were her fifth layer of clothing, and she insisted on wearing them despite the order her mother delivered at the top of her lungs: "Get dressed, put on your tamlḥaft, you're my daughter and you aren't going to bring shame on me by going out among people dressed like that." Mina set herself apart from other young village women by refusing to wear a tamlḥaft, claiming that she was cold and wanted to wear her sweater (which ostensibly she could have worn under the tamlḥaft as did the others). Her hair fell loose on her neck; the other women tied their hair under scarves. She wore black platform slip-on sandals; the other young women wore the more rugged, red mountain slippers (*idukan*) then common in winter. Mina's logic, unlike that of her mother, was that since she was among intimates, she did not need to display modesty. Additionally, she liked wearing the jeans with her hair loose; the high school's administrators compelled her to wear the hijab (head scarf). While she positioned herself as male by skirting domestic chores and moving between town and village, her mother implored her to dress appropriately for the zerda.

Some of the young migrant men wore typical male village dress: a heavy woolen jellaba (hooded robe) over sweaters and slacks. Others wore polyester warm-up suits associated with a style called "speed" that otherwise included sunglasses, mopeds, baseball caps, tennis shoes, and Arabic language. Young men and women valued what the other brought to the interaction: the young men returned to the village to maintain ties, and they appreciated the confirmation that young women maintained village ways through dress, speech, and values. In turn, the young women sought the "news" and the prestige the young men brought back to the village from the city.

I remark on dress here because Ida ou Zeddout youth were conscious of the indexical power of dress to mark residence, local affiliation, and socioeconomic class. The tamlḥaft was required outerwear for all females in the village – the anthropologist included – regardless of age, origin, or marital status. Girls and women wrapped it over long skirts and long-sleeved blouses whenever they left their homes, and always in the company of non-family members. Leaving the house without a tamlḥaft even to visit the fields signaled immodesty and disrespect. Women's habitus led them to feel naked without it; when I first visited the village in July 1996, my hosts insisted that I immediately wrap a tamlḥaft over my long skirt and long-sleeved blouses. From then on, I wore a jellaba and headscarf to the mountains, changing upon arrival into a tamlḥaft. Villagers carefully monitored the boundaries between home and public through physical appearance. Young girls in the village school were forbidden by their school teachers from wearing the tamlḥaft in the classroom, but their mothers expected them to dress appropriately once home from school. The fabric changed over the years, from wool to polyester, and the decorated trim on the hem was no longer only white thread but instead contained sequins and plastic pearls, as dictated by fashion's whim. Regardless of its material composition, the tamlḥaft remained a crucial index of Ashelhi-ness. No Arabs wore it, preferring instead overwraps of heavy or gauzy cotton, unbelted and attached without safety pins. The Tashelhit woman's tamlḥaft was internally considered beautiful, albeit denigrated by outsiders to the community who saw it as exotic yet antiquated, as Maggi writes of the Kalashi women's distinctive dress and beads in Pakistan (2001). The temporary tattoos (*tanast*) Tashelhit women and girls painted on the forehead, nose and chin with wild pistachio ink (*igg*) for festive occasions were also banned from the classroom; young female students were already abandoning the facial decoration displayed by their older sisters and other villagers on religious and secular holidays, lest they receive a scolding or beating from the teacher if the ink had not faded when school resumed. Teachers considered such bodily adornment and dress to be anti-Islamic and antithetical to modernity.

As the young people began discussing where they would find three rabbits they wanted for a stew, the spry elderly cobbler who had been sitting with us dramatically pulled out a silky brown and white rabbit from under his beige wool jellaba. The young men and women laughed and cheered in delight as the cobbler offered it to the group as a gift. Saadia, Hassan and Ftuma then headed out in the February drizzle to knock on village doors, asking who would sell a rabbit. The three returned shortly to the house with a gold and white rabbit, saying they could not find a third. Hassan and the young women talked in a hushed voice about how much it cost, then rounded up the 70 dirhams (around $7) from the youths present and headed back out to pay the woman who had sold them the rabbit.

At 5:30 pm, a half hour before sunset, three of the young migrant men, a gaggle of young children and I headed towards the house of a modest shepherd, one of the few resident men. We planned to ask him to slaughter the rabbits, in the manner required by Islamic doctrine. I walked down the path with Hassan, an emigrant in his mid-twenties, who held the rabbits by the ears, asking him why he or one of the others would not perform the slaughter. Hassan responded that a good Muslim man who prays should slaughter. "To be honest," he said, "I don't follow religion enough to do it."

The young men were in a bind: they wanted to fulfill their role as village men, yet their history of urban residence meant they were religiously emasculated through their incapacity to slaughter, a privilege of Muslim masculinity. The young men substituted a temporarily masculine man – a resident shepherd – who ordinarily was himself emasculated because of his weak economic position. The shepherd appeared at the door when his daughter called for him. He wore a black jellaba raincoat and rubber boots, and ducked to emerge through his front door and onto the path. Laughingly he exclaimed, looking around at the mixed-sex crowd, "As though there's no one here to slaughter? Look at all of the men!" The half-dozen young emigrants present laughed, but handed him a borrowed large butcher knife anyway. The young men looked relieved to stand back during the slaughter. One girl of about five years old stood on a rock behind me and squealed as the knife neared the rabbit's throat. I turned around and whispered to her, "I'll cover your eyes until it's over." She nodded her head up and down and I placed my palms over her eyes, relieved myself to have an excuse to look away. When a young boy called out, "Oh look it's still alive!" and the animal thrashed against the stone ground, I turned around. The spectators pulled back as the rabbit thrashed about then surrendered. The second slaughter went more smoothly.

Aisha Ali, an especially animated grandmother who frequently encouraged young people to throw zerdas and enjoy themselves, going so far as donating rabbits herself, rose from her customary sitting place near the wide path and lent a hand. Taking the butcher knife in her hand, she energetically removed the rabbit's head and pulled the skin around its neck to insert the knife, exclaiming, "I'm not embarrassed, I'm not shy" (*ur ad ḥššamġ*). She worked on the two animals quickly, throwing the skin and unusable organs on the ground. When she opened the second rabbit's abdomen, she implored, "Look! It was going to give birth." Hassan held the skinned animals uncomfortably at a distance from his body. A young boy gathered up the entrails and took them out to a nearby field, where he called the dogs to catch what he threw out. With the gutting complete, the children scattered and the young adults headed back to the house. I remarked twice, once on the path and once back at the house within earshot of one of the young women, that with three young men you would think there would be a single man among them who could slaughter. Hassan, who had not seen himself religiously observant enough to slaughter, noted quietly, "You got me there, that's enough teasing" (*waxxa tḍuwwrt gigi, safi*).

In the kitchen, Hassan orchestrated the meat preparation, as he would soon orchestrate the stew preparation and then the entertainment. He told me to hold the carcass still as he pulled on parts then cut the animal into small sections for cooking and eventual distribution among the zerda participants at the meal's conclusion. Three of us cleaned the meat and gathered up the inedible parts, like the fat kidneys, for the cats waiting outside. In the old stone house across the path, the young women heated the open wood-burning fire to make the bowl-shaped bread (*tannurt*). Hassan cut the onions and coriander, put it all into a casserole dish with the meat, salt, pepper, and paprika, and took it over to their older house, where they no longer lived, to cook.

The other young emigrants sat by the side of the cooking preparations, chatting as the young women prepared coals and bread. The young people moved busily back and forth between the new and old houses, bringing cooking and dinner dishes, cassettes, and the braziers on which the *ṭajin*-s (clay stewpots) would cook. They laughed and joked as they worked. A few young men crouched in the old house as the women lit the fire, speaking quietly in the thick of the blinding wood smoke. At one point as I headed for the door I overheard Mokhtar from a neighboring village, who rarely returns, talking to Ftuma. He was saying, "I like tamazirt; the mood (*amarg*) here is down-to-earth (Ar. šaεbi) and people don't put on airs (*ššiki*)." Ftuma responded, "Even here outside you'll find ššiki. Some girls don't come out anymore. They don't hang around and laugh like the rest of us." The girls knew she was talking about the shepherd's daughter; this had been a matter of some concern in recent evening conversations. "Still," Mokhtar said, "it's not like the city. I keep coming back here because I like it."

Mokhtar and Ftuma had different frames of reference for ššiki or snobbishness. In Casablanca, ššiki took on proportions Ftuma could scarcely imagine, given the city's conspicuous consumption. Class distinctions were more marked in urban areas. In the village, as Ftuma had told me on other occasions, certain young women acted ššiki by refusing to converse with men in the evenings. Unmarried village women did not snub Mokhtar, for they considered him as a brother; the young men told me that in the city, the infrequent mixed-sex interactions were loaded with expectations. In the village, Mokhtar had prestige by virtue of being an emigrant with the perceived potential to bring in significant remittances. Young village women did not distinguish among emigrants by job description or salary – the important factor was simply that the men worked.

Later as we sat and ate, Mokhtar talked about Casablanca. His father was dead, and he had gone to Casablanca in 1974 as a small boy. He has been there ever since; one of his sisters married a man in Marrakesh and another stayed in Casablanca and married. Mokhtar lived in a basement room that his employer offered him rent-free while working for a distribution company delivering Nestlé products. He rode a scooter around the city to a major department store and several convenience stores, counting the inventory. He considered the job a step up from an earlier inventory job he held in a corner grocery store. He made about 1,400 dirhams a month ($140), enough for his basic expenses and meager savings. He cooked in his basement room on a small butane gas stove. As he spoke to me that evening, he punctuated his description of this meager existence with, "All is fine, thank God, I'm working and that is all that matters." He articulated his work philosophy, one that I imagine his fellow villager men would embrace: "If you don't have troubles/responsibilities (*lhmm*), you have nothing. The person who sleeps untroubled just needs some lousy work to remedy the situation."

As the stews simmered in the entranceway, I ducked to cross the threshold of the upstairs tamṣrit (guest room). Mohammed motioned to me to take the place next to him on the carpets spread on the floor, offering me a cushion. I moved it to protect both of our backs from the cold wall. We sat quietly with three other emigrants, listening attentively to a cassette of Aznag and Ben Wakrim's *tinḍḍamin* that I discuss in Chapter 5. Whenever someone entered the room and made noise, the boys ordered "*fss*!" ("be quiet!") and leaned in closer to the tape player. Omar sported a baseball cap turned with its bill to the back as city boys did, even though he had lived all of his 20 years in the village. He tried to make small talk with the others in Arabic, suggesting he was street smart. The emigrants chastised him for speaking Arabic. As Mohammed explained the tinḍḍamin lyrics to me, Omar translated over my shoulder into Moroccan Arabic. Mohammed ordered, "Explain them to her in Tashelhit," to which Omar responded, "It's hard to explain what they're saying in Tashelhit, it's easier in Arabic." I told Omar that Mohammed made the lyrics entirely understandable without translation into Arabic.

Discussing the tinḍḍamin, the young men and I engaged in commentary on their own emigrant predicament, using it to assess the truth value of the poets' moral claims. Hassan left the stews at several points to try to replace the tinḍḍamin cassette with one of his recordings of popular Eastern Arabic music. Each time, the other young men vetoed his unilateral will. The young women and adolescent girls were still baking bread in the open fires in the downstairs courtyard, not yet physically present to voice their musical preferences. Cassettes were one kind of *tifawt* (lit. light; metaphorically money, goods, or ideas) that emigrants contributed to the village's stock.[6] Bringing tifawt was an ideal promoted in informal discourse as well as in speeches by Hassan II. Those who brought tifawt to the countryside – literally by installing electricity, or metaphorically by sending remittances – were the least active in maintaining it. Young emigrants saw the tamazirt as the Janus face of their northern urban lives. As Mokhtar told me, "Casablanca, it's all about money (*lmal*). It's not about people or truth. Everyone who's there is there to make money, and that's all. But here [in the village], this is why we work hard to make the money. This is life. This is who we are."

When the meat was cooked we relocated to the second-floor storage room, a low-ceilinged room with bags of grain and extra dishes along one wall, but otherwise reserved for special occasions. I had last sat there with the young women a year and a half earlier while they sang the tizrrarin into my tape recorder that Saadia would then play back during her wedding preparations. Plastic mats and wool rugs still padded the cement floor and bright blue paint decorated the bottom half of cement-coated walls. The place was inviting. In the entrance area stood a half-dozen four-foot tall bags of barley grains. We placed braziers in this area and pulled out the two clay stewpots to prepare dinner. Hassan piled the meat into the two dishes for the final simmering, rearranging pieces to assure that they contained the same amount of rabbit meat; Mina moved a leg from one plate to the other. Hassan cut more onion into rings atop the meat, then tomato and sprigs of cilantro, in the same way that he had garnished ṭajins in the Casablanca restaurant where he worked. He replaced the lids and we moved into the main room. With the dinner ready, the young man called out "Six and six," indicating that there would be two ṭajins for twelve people, and they should seat themselves around the low tables accordingly.

One of the young men produced a camera from his jellaba pocket. A young woman jumped into action to arrange the image that henceforth would be the visual reminder of the post-Ramadan zerda of that year. Rural dwellers frequently composed photographs to include a boom box or clock among the group in the photo, even if this meant they had to bring in the clock from another room or even a neighboring house. The commodity's value was in its indexical properties of urbanity and modernity, and its presence in the image seemed intended to deflect attention from the juxtaposed rural indexes of the photo's subjects evident in their dress and their surroundings (although the contrast instead was striking, at least to this outside observer). When people later circulated these photos, even an urban Moroccan would identify with the electronics in the photo. As such, rural and urban dwellers shared the positive valuation of consumption and leisure activities.

Rural youths' self-presentations drew on an urban, material-laden standard by which Moroccans throughout the country measured prosperity and modernity. Yet rural people did it according to local aesthetics, as with the tamlḥaft design fashions. Each year, new embroidery designs appeared in the markets, several named after that year's Mexican soap-opera heroine (including Guadalupe in 1996 and Celeste in 1998). Colorful plastic jewelry came in and went out of style; plastic marked the rural dweller off from the urban dweller who preferred gold jewelry or wore nothing if she had no gold. Scarf styles varied from year to year, not only in color (bright yellow was popular one year) and design (white fringe was popular another year), but also the style of tying and/or pinning the scarf. Some years, fashion dictated wrapping the scarf under the chin and safety-pinning it on the back of the head in the ixwani (lit. brother; Islamist) style. A few years later, exposing the neck and ears was fashionable. Older women typically covered only their hair, exposing their necks and ears as well as face. Mountain fashion relied on the market, but it followed its own aesthetic sense. What made new market items preferable to other items was that they signaled the user's ongoing engagement with the market economy through the male networks that linked country to city. The newer, cleaner, or more unused an item was (like a market-bought blanket), the better, regardless of the quality of its materials. Anything from the market was better than the homemade, as the village women reminded me while weaving my rug, as I described in Chapter One. There was no nostalgia for the old, whether styles, ideas, words, or melodies. A person with old possessions was not cared for by men. New goods marked the owner as closely related to city dwellers, drawing symbolic capital from this association. Wearing an outdated tamlḥaft signaled that no man in the city was looking after the woman.

An ironic nostalgia on the part of young emigrants both divided and united them with the year-round village-dwelling young women. The unmarried young women, for their part, knew little besides village life. A few had visited relatives in Casablanca or Taroudant, but they were usually restricted to the house or carefully escorted around public places. This symbiosis between males and females held, on the whole. We ate close to midnight, sitting on the floor around two low tables. There was little talk while we ate quickly except for a few compliments to the chefs. As we ate, we moved through the cassettes, listening to part of one until someone exchanged it for another. When the communal dishes were empty, the young women pushed the tables aside and continued flipping through the cassettes.

The young men engaged in discursive analysis of the village life they were experiencing, listening to the singing poets debate the relative merits of city and country life. When the young women took their places in the tamṣrit, they were eager to hear the new urban trends on cassettes by rways (singer-songwriting poets). Each person who wanted to dance rose, alone or in pairs, some single-sex and some mixed, holding hands. Hand-holding between males and females was socially condemned, because it was indicative of physical and romantic affection, which according to local customs should never be displayed in public, even between spouses.[7] The young people gathered for the zerda, however, as fictive skin, which permitted this kind of close physical and verbal interaction. The tamṣrit was an intimate, safe zone, not accessible to outsiders. Friendly hand-holding and mixed-sex dancing could take place there in confidence and without impropriety.

As part of his ongoing attempts at attention throughout the evening, Hassan convinced Ftuma to take off her tamlḥaft (which was mine; she had borrowed it while doing laundry) and her orange fringe scarf so that he could dress as a woman.[8] He took on a falsetto voice and danced provocatively, shaking his hips. The young women laughed at Hassan's antics, but his male peers cast disgusted looks his way. The spectacle inspired amateur *anḍḍam* (orderer of words) Mohammed to compose a few verses on the spot.

But then came a crucial point in the evening, where the air of the event shifted. This often happened in group gatherings: the excitement built to a pitch which led to either intensified order or, instead, chaos. These youths fell into synch, shifting from a passive listening engagement with music to active production of music. The central focus shifted from males to females and from the city to the countryside. We had been listening to Tashelhit rways commercial cassettes and the young women rapidly shrugged their shoulders up and down as they had seen the professionals perform on their solar-power televisions, a dance with sexual overtones according to local standards. We had moved through a Kuwaiti cassette whose hit "Yallah" ("Let's Go") was popular in Casablanca nightclubs that year, and we had listened to the young men's anonymous club music in Spanish and Egyptian Arabic. The young women had passively consumed enough music. They got up to sing and dance.

One girl called out an agwal verse (see Table 2.1) and another called back. The rest of the youths, male and female, joined in the chorus. The lyrics of the first line of the agwal were from the last sung line of the rways cassette; the rest of the verses came from other sources. At first three of the young women overlapped in their turn-taking attempts, each unsure where the next would start in, but then they got organized. The older Kiltum, known for her skill in spinning enthralling adventure tales, whispered some lyrics to the outspoken Sultana, who listened attentively, holding the bottom part of the plastic basin she beat as a drum. While the first agwal wound down, Kiltum called out a verse about Moulay Brahim, a revered saint of the Moroccan South. Since her sister lived in Marrakesh, she visited periodically; this verse had symbolic capital, indexing her familiarity with a faraway and thrilling place. When the first agwal wound down a quarter of an hour later, people were in good spirits. There was a noticeable feeling of communion in the room.

At the pause Sultana organized the group by calling out, "Let Kiltum arrange this next one." The youths divided into rows and Sultana led. In her strong voice she called out the verses, most of which she repeated twice. The call and response segments of the sequence sometimes mirrored each other, but at other times contained two separate lines (A + A, B + B, or A + B, C + B). The young village women effectively shifted the "situational focus" (Irvine 1979) from passive listening orchestrated by urban young men to an active performance more typical of the countryside.

Hassan pulled me aside by the hand, away from the line of young women, and gestured towards the built-in microphone on his boom box;

he was going to press the record button, tapping his tape of pop Kuwaiti music against his palm. After the first recorded piece ended and there was a pause in the singing, Hassan played back the new recording to the delight of the young women, who had not suspected his move. They all listened attentively.

Hassan then took the empty five-liter orange oil jug out of Mohammed's hands and started to beat it to encourage another agwal to start up. Mohammed frowned and told him, "You don't know how, give it back." The youths stood facing each other in an oval formation in the long rectangular room. Sultana called out, "Okay guys, this is just for the girls. Take a seat!" The boys split up, some moving to sit against the wall and others picking up drums and relocating to the center of the circle of young women. Sultana announced to the group, "Ftuma and I are going to call this one." They called out the first verse and the others responded. The young emigrants were effectively silenced with the young women's insistence on a serious rehearsal. Hassan was among those who could not drum correctly. The young women tolerated the young men's participation in the music-making until it morphed into a more serious opportunity to experiment with new lyrics and turn-taking. When the right drum beats were needed, a village resident needed to perform them – not an emigrant, even a music aficionado. All fell into place; order was restored. The agwal got everyone involved in some form; the sweat flowing despite the freezing winter night air, and afterwards the dancers collapsed on the floor, laughing. The gender role-play, Western-style hand-holding, and (by local standards) provocative hip-shaking had faded. After trying out the urban practices, the young women steered the event back to indigenous leisure activities, to making rather than consuming entertainment.

An adolescent girl too young to have been invited to the zerda but old enough to be out at night came into the tamṣrit and called to one of her peers that her *amsqqr* (pl. *imsqqrn*), the adolescent boy she sat and talked with, waited outside for her. Male suitors from other villages offered young women the chance to flirt and show off their verbal agility, wit, and composure. After all, much of domestic life involved talking, and young women nurtured self-presentations as reasonable, smart, and well behaved, as well as fun. When small groups of young men visited from other villages, there was always the chance of meeting an amsqqr, "one who sticks," a chatmate with whom one has private conversations (within view of the other young people), which led either to a marriage proposal or to boredom that ended the tête-à-tête. Itinerant male visitors, on the other hand, were not welcome at village zerdas, where only intimates gathered.

Although he was a latecomer to village life, Hassan assigned himself a central role in the zerda as it unfolded. (Converts are often the most zealous advocates.) He was uniquely vain in his self-centeredness, asking others to photograph him throughout the evening with his camera. His friends obliged, documenting him cooking the stews, serving them, dressing in drag, and playing the wash basin as a drum. Together these images documented his identity as a tamazirt-dweller at the village zerda, consciously producing ideologically informed metaculture. His objectification of the event was total, and his peers appreciated his cooking more than his behavior. Since he had grown up in Casablanca, his annual visits to the village had started only a few years previously. As a teenager, he devoted himself to learning Tashelhit and acquainting himself with his laṣl. A few nights earlier, he explained to me that laṣl is a driving force that youths try to fight, but to which they eventually surrender. "Take for example your father's tamazirt," he said. "Even if you never spent time there, at some point you'll want to go there and make it your home, too." This, he told me, was what he had done. In Geertz's terms, Hassan expressed a primordial attachment encultured in his fundamental sense of identity and grounded in a congruity of blood, language, and custom (Geertz 1963), or as Fishman framed ethnicity, a "kinship phenomenon" or continuity within the self and within those who share an intergenerational link to common ancestors (Fishman 1980). Hassan had solidified his connection to Ida ou Zeddout by attending regional weekly markets and attempting to get involved in decision-making circles. He invested materially and had begun construction on a stone house nearby. During the summer following the zerda, he married a cousin from another Ait Musi village, and she immediately accompanied him on his return to Casablanca. They planned to spend their vacations in the tamazirt, but she was glad to leave it. She had longed for the city for years.

Hassan was the most removed of the young emigrant men from village life and the least constrained, but with an ideological and emotional link that he eventually solidified materially. At times his late self-insertion into village life became evident. He drummed poorly. He danced like a city man. He knew his way around the Casablanca dance clubs and could rattle off entrance fees and clientele. He was familiar with the illicit: he bragged about knowing how to roll a joint, dangling a rolled cigarette paper from his lower lip. He mockingly slurred his speech throughout the evening, claiming in a drunkard's voice, "I drink" (*ar ssaġ*). He appeared so confident about his masculinity that he spent the evening in drag, dancing alternatively as a Tashelhit village woman, a professional raysa, and a hip city man. His palms were soft: he was a stranger to manual labor.

The social organization of the activity reflected gender conventions: the young men paid for the meat, while the young women provided flour, vegetables, spices, and labor for fire-making and bread-baking. The conventions mirrored other gendered contributions to the community: men's money and meat, outsider commodities considered necessary and brought in; women's unremunerated labor and harvest of the earth, the most fundamental food, bread, of the humblest of grains, barley. Cooking on special occasions was prestigious and thus a man's domain, and as such it was distinct from the women's everyday cooking chores (tawwuri). These young people also experimented with alternative arrangements: young men and women held hands, one young man cross-dressed, and there was mocking reference to urban hashish-smoking and alcohol-drinking.

In youth culture in the Anti-Atlas, the material and the symbolic came together in generating an understanding of the tamazirt as a distinctive place. The young emigrant men brought news of the outside world to the unmarried village women, who in turn reminded the emigrants why they tolerated their difficult urban lives. Both urban and rural made the other possible; they were in a symbiotic relationship – but they also struggled over the means of representation and the necessity of emplacement in them. Women retained the main responsibility for language socialization, Tashelhit language maintenance, and upkeep of the homelands and its associated cultural practices. Yet men monitored them for their correct usage of these material and discursive resources: pure Tashelhit speech (awal), competent musical performances, frugal allocation of domestic resources, and agrarian knowledge.

Williams (1973) writes that nostalgia for the country is linked to nostalgia for childhood. Particularly for Ashelhi men like Mokhtar, who left the country at adolescence, innocence and the countryside disappeared simultaneously from their lives, leaving in their wake a nostalgia for both that surely informed young emigrants' sense of relief in leaving the city behind, at least for short holiday periods.

Consequences

Gendered language maintenance

Women have been crucial to the reproduction of the countryside, of Tashelhit language, and of Ashelhi identity. As repositories of both (past-oriented) nostalgia and (forward-oriented) aspirations, they bore the brunt of performing authenticity for the estranged men whose relationship to the land and language was more compromised. In order for older women to become repositories of tradition and conservators of knowledge, they had to be socialized into that role from an early age. By adolescence, as young women approached marriageable age, they were already marked as incontrovertibly rural, integral to the landscape, the rightful heirs of ancestral land and language. Ishelhin knew well that

Tashelhit language was not simply in their biological makeup; in this respect, their ideas about language acquisition differed from that of the Haitian diaspora in New York who presumed that children would speak Kreyòl regardless of the language environment (Schieffelin and Doucet 1994). Constant contact with emigrants, both kin and non-kin, amply demonstrated to mountain women that children learned Tashelhit only when adults spoke it with them. Beyond the matter of linguistic input and communicative competence, Tashelhit-speaking young women needed positive valuations of Tashelhit and the rural world it evoked in order to continue to speak it.

While in some respects most Tashelhit women had no choice as to which language to speak with their children, others did. Fḍila, for one, actively resisted the hard labor (tammara) expected of her in both domestic and agricultural spheres, refusing outright to plant or harvest. To the consternation of her mother-in-law, Fḍila simply refused to do many chores when asked, or performed them so incompetently that she was unlikely to be asked again. She cajoled her husband, a university-educated emigrant to Casablanca working in dry goods distribution, to work longer hours, accumulate more money, and bring her and their two young sons to Casablanca as quickly as possible. Her daughter was born there. Fḍila was from Mrait, another tribal section of Ida ou Zeddout, but despite her rural roots, she set her sights on the city from a young age, even more so when her parents retired to the city. When I last saw Fḍila in 1999, she stopped by my house in Taroudant en route to the mountains. She was dressed in an ornately decorated white caftan under her jellaba, ample gold jewelry, and a modest headscarf. She had put on significant weight, especially visible on her hips and chin, clear markers of a woman who does not labor. Whereas she used to be tanned year-round from outdoor work, Fḍila's skin had faded to a pale white. In Casablanca, she told me, her husband rented a two-room apartment and had it decorated with sofa cushions and gilded pillows for her arrival. She was living the life many young village women dreamed about, far from the physical labor and the woolen rugs used for bedding, about which the women at the loom had complained. She used to tell me, modifying a proverb, "It's not time that passes; it's people who pass the time" (*ur d izri luqt; mddn zrin luqt*). The other village women were not as scornful of their homeland as was this woman, as much as they all complained about it. Few sought to sabotage household finances to demonstrate their incompetence. Instead, many sought inspiration from the city through the young men who returned periodically. In turn, women provided authenticity and sanctuary for the young men as they forged lives that linked the disparate places. Most women, like Fḍila, knew at a gut level that a man's place was in the city. A woman's place, many reasoned, was in the homeland.

The burden of instruction

Tashelhit-speaking women in the mountains were primarily held accountable for teaching Tashelhit to their children. This was not a conscious effort, but rather the result of the child's monolingual Tashelhit environment prior to schooling. In families residing in the plains and towns, when the mother spoke Arabic and no Tashelhit, even if the father spoke Tashelhit, children simply did not learn to speak Tashelhit, although they may have had a passive understanding of some Tashelhit words. Moroccan mothers spent significantly more time with their infants and young children than did fathers, whose role was restricted to play and periodic discipline. This was particularly true of mountain families with absent fathers. Children raised in the Anti-Atlas inevitably spoke Tashelhit, as it was the only spoken language there, outside of institutional contexts such as schools and health clinics. There was more ambiguity in towns, where women often chose to become Arabic-dominant out of the belief that bilingual input would hamper their children's academic development.

This language ideology is captured in a song by Raysa Fatima Tabaamrant, a commercially successful Tashelhit singer-songwriter with roots in the Ait Baamran area of the Anti-Atlas. In her 1998 song *Ayuz nm a Tamaziġt* ("Bravo, oh Tamazight"), she pleads to Tashelhit speakers, especially mothers, not to abandon their language and beliefs (awal) and roots (laṣl), couched in metaphor, allusion, and praises to Hassan II to ensure that her message not be construed as critical of the monarchy. The lyrics constitute an appeal to Imazighen who have abandoned their language, culture, and home villages while simultaneously acknowledging the reasons many people have done so:

iwa a tawtmt tamaziġt a talli yusin	Oh woman, oh Tamazight, you who are holding
arraw iggi wạfud ns at asn tmmal	the baby on your lap, you who are teaching him
ad akk^{w} izwarn d tmaziġt ml tt i warraw nm	Start with Tamazight, teach it to your son
ad ur ijlu laṣl da iwalan afus nm	so that the one in your hands doesn't lose his roots
. . .	
// wa han ạfṛux ad mẓẓiyn aġ illa imal	// It's in this young boy that the future rests
a ṛṛuḥ inw a tamaziġt //	Oh my soul, oh Tamazight //

aḥ a laṣl aḥ a bab ns walli t ur ittun	Oh roots, oh those who don't forget you
mamnk ittzyan ṛbbi ġilli ġa ttilit	how beautiful God makes it wherever you are

It may be "in the small boy that there's hope," but he is the raw material for the mother to instruct. She is equally responsible for counteracting pressures from the Arabic-speaking schools, institutions, and media that disfavor the Berber vernaculars. Rife with tension and verging on desperation, Tabaamrant's lyrics render urgent the primary caretaker's actions and words, yet they express the anxiety of the emigrant man more than those of the monolingual Anti-Atlas woman who typically knows no other language. Indeed, the plea is directed towards women in the plains and towns who may speak MA to their children:

illa ma as innan ajj afṛux a nit iḥṛš	There are those who say, "Just leave that boy, he's smart
iġ as nmla tamaziġt ira ġar itlf	If we teach him Tamazight he'll just be lost
ass na ġ ṛuḥn lmdrst ur issin awal	The day he leaves for school, he won't know how to speak."
a ġikad iga tḍḍayt n wawal nnaġ	This kind of talk weakens our force
imma tiġri trxa dar wanna tnt iran	Yet studying is easy for those who want to learn
/// iġ iḥṛš warraw mẓẓiyn rxan a issan	/// If the small child is smart he will easily understand
a immi nw a tamaziġt ///	Oh my mother, oh Tamazight ///
. . .	

In these verses, Tabaamrant summarizes the most pervasive language ideology that leads parents to speak Tashelhit to their children: speaking Tashelhit to children impedes their acquisition of Arabic. Linguists and anthropologists may disagree, but this folk view has strongly influenced language shift in plains and towns and accellerated the decline of bilingualism among urban children. These lyrics play on the dual meanings of awal as both talk/language and power/force (Lortat-Jacob 1981:92). In the skeptic's voice, the young boy who starts school speaking Tamazight will not know al luġa ("the language") meaning Arabic, the language of the schools. But this is counter to "our awal," meaning both our way of thinking and the force behind our language which binds us together. The detractor to Tabaamrant's message risks weakening the group as well as the language.

In this song, Tabaamrant also intimately links language, land, and women, calling Tamazight "my mother" and "my soul." There is a glorification of women for their ability to perpetuate language and community, but while potentially empowering, this role may be imposing. Indeed, the focus remains on women's actions and words as the keys to reproducing the social group and its in-group communicative code. Free will is strikingly central to Tabaamrant's lyrics as what guides a woman's actions, and it is more powerful than the structural position in which a woman finds herself.

The Real Language Institutes: The Feminization of Berber Language

A review of high school records in Taroudant in 1998 indicated that the majority of students were born in the 1980s to parents who had emigrated from the adjacent Western High Atlas mountains and the Sous plains. The vast majority of those students were monolingual MA speakers in 1998 with little or no comprehension of their parents' Tashelhit language, and this was the most common language biography in Taroudant-residing families. Pegging aspirations for children's upward mobility on state schooling, these families largely excluded Tashelhit from their homes, excepting the occasional resident Tashelhit-speaking grandmother. If all immigrants from the Anti-Atlas and Western High Atlas followed this pattern, Tashelhit would most likely cease to be spoken altogether. A case-specific account of the shift would require emigration rates, origins and destinations of emigrants, and domains of language use for multi-generational families.

There were certainly Tashelhit-speaking women living in cities and towns, increasingly in secondary regional capitals such as Taroudant and Tiznit as well as the major industrial cities of Casablanca and Marrakesh. Yet many native Tashelhit speakers became Arabic-dominant speakers once they settled in these urban areas. If they married locally and sent their children to state schools, within one to two generations, linguistic Arabicization and cultural Arabization were generally complete. There were exceptions, certainly; the financially secure, such as wealthy merchants, tended to retain Tashelhit in the home, whereas the financially unstable, such as wage laborers, were more likely to shift towards the national lingua franca, Moroccan Arabic.

Why should it concern anyone whether Ishelhin continue to speak Tashelhit? Many Moroccan laypeople, including many Tashelhit speakers who have relocated to towns and shifted from Tashelhit to MA as their primary vernacular, argue that retaining an attachment to Berber and continuing to speak it constitutes an impediment to upward mobility and national citizenry. Certainly Berber monolingualism limits a person's participation in an Arab-centric nation that has long disregarded the diversity in its midst. Recent scholarship has emphasized the ecological consequences of language loss around the world; the argument is frequently forwarded that humanity as a whole loses resources and knowledge when indigenous languages cease to be used. Biolinguistic diversity tends to be represented in terms of an objective importance to humanity (Maffi 2001). Yet this universal human good sometimes comes at the expense of specific individuals who are disfavored in the process. When women are kept monolingual and unschooled for the perceived good of the community, in part because their illiteracy is understood to guarantee the maintenance of an ancestral language, their human rights are compromised. Gendered spatial practices have helped Ishelhin maintain their Tashelhit language. We might ask whether it is worth the price, and whose interests are furthered.

More than language is lost in language shift. Worldviews shift, and they shift in directions guided by forces outside the source community, reinforcing hegemonies that make themselves convincing through people's material and emotional needs and even their desires. The interests of the minority group are necessarily sacrificed to those of the dominant group, and herein lies the moral difficulty with embracing language shift as a natural historical process and a morally neutral side-effect of globalization or the expansion of the market economy. Whole communities (or even individuals) do not move from speaking one language to speaking another on a whim; they do so in times of crisis, resignation, or necessity.

As more and more Ishelhin "let the land go," as one Anti-Atlas grandmother phrased it, the land itself became more symbolic and less of a material resource. Someone needed to work the land, to maintain its symbolic value, but the actual work itself was beneath the dignity (and outside the abilities) of most men who modeled masculinity after financial success as merchants. Grown women in the Anti-Atlas mountains often remarked to me when they saw me reading or writing that they could not read or write; they were animals, several claimed. It is difficult to convey the horror and sadness I felt when first hearing this, especially given how socially inept and verbally inarticulate I considered myself during fieldwork, in sharp contrast to the women's eloquence and expressive panache. The women's bald self-denigration embarrassed and confused me, coming as it was from some of the most self-assured women I have ever known. In one August 1996 instance, teenaged village women were informally practicing their agwal in the early evening in a village clearing. Their guide, a woman in her late thirties, drummed a steady beat on an empty oil jug, calling out lyrics for the young women to repeat, and walked the length of the two semi-circles of singer-dancers. At one break in the rehearsal the song leader turned to me and said, "We're just donkeys, unlike you educated Europeans (*iṛumiyyn*, lit. Romans). We can't read; all we know how to do is plant and harvest and feed the chickens." The hideousness of the remark took me aback as it contrasted so sharply with the beautiful song and dance the young women had just completed. I objected: "But donkeys don't make amarg (music, moods) as you do; they can't bring about such beauty. I can't bring about such a mood, either, or sing such beautiful songs." She remained unconvinced, and although I spoke truthfully, this was further proof that country people were the antithesis of city people.

Indeed the Tashelhit women who moved to the cities let their music go when they left their land; some explained that this was the consequence of urban life where there was no open field to perform the collective aḥwaš song and dance. Even at urban weddings in large halls, professional bands were hired to entertain. Tashelhit was so integral to these women's sense of themselves, as rural people and as women, that many of them could not imagine Tashelhit in urban life. The absence of Tashelhit expressive culture in urban emigrant communities thus seemed integral to the process of urbanization – in the cities, professionals entertained, not laypeople. The idea that an emigrant woman might strive to perpetuate expressive culture, including speaking and singing practices, in an environment hostile to it was counterintuitive, even nonsensical, and it fell outside the pattern they had witnessed many times over as community members emigrated and raised children in the cities. Again, it seemed, the women reinforced the persistence of their constrained roles; they perpetuated the status quo that placed them squarely in the countryside. This was just their *lɛada n tamazirt*, they explained, just the customs of the countryside, and thus outside the scope of debate.

The feminization of Tashelhit language and Ashelhi identity has contributed to and accompanied not only the decline in its number of speakers in absolute numbers, but also a decline in the language's status. Tashelhit has come to be associated with rural, illiterate women who are about as far from national policy-making debates as possible. This has a number of repercussions for its speakers. First, it means that *monolingual speakers of Tashelhit language are almost exclusively female.* Most men are bilingual, at least; they learn Arabic in state or religious schools and by working in commerce in the northern cities to which they emigrate at adolescence. In this respect, it is expected that a man will learn Arabic, and that this will further his economic opportunities and broaden his life chances. Women who stay in the countryside have no similar opportunities for learning Arabic, and for those women and girls who do pick up some colloquial Arabic in primary school, or in extended visits to relatives in Marrakesh or Casablanca, back in the countryside Arabic is socially dispreferred. Thus there is little audience or incentive for Arabic. Men from the countryside who speak with Arabs and anthropologists tend to use a colloquial, working-class Arabic learned from interactions with clients or at the market with sellers.

Second, *Tashelhit language is feminized* in that it is generally understood by both men and women that the mother is responsible for ensuring that her children learn Tashelhit. Without maternal input, children do not learn Tashelhit even if their fathers speak it. Mixed families in towns – where fathers are Tashelhit speakers and mothers are Arabic speakers – do not learn Tashelhit. In this respect Tashelhit really must be the "mother tongue" (Davies and Bentahila 1989) in order for a child to learn it.

I turn now to consider expressive culture as shaped by political economies, first in the Anti-Atlas mountains, and then in the Sous plains.

Part III

Consonance: Homeland

ullah amkd usiġ aḍar a illiġ nssn
is ur inxlf ġid d lmakan inu
I swear I won't lift my foot until we know
that here is no different from my place
– Ida ou Zeddout tazrrat

ana jit, j'en ai marre
I've come, I'm fed up
– Najat Aatabou (1983)

Chapter 4

Building the Homeland: Labor, Roads, Emigration

Liver, just be patient	*I have one disappointment*
Liver, just be patient	*I went to the* timizar *(homelands) and the* tiqbilin *(tribes)*
Liver, just be patient	tammara *(hard labor) is what people endure, night and day*
Liver, just be patient	*Who is looking in on them? Who cares about them?*
Liver, just be patient	*Who knows the goodness of the ancestors?*
Liver, just be patient	*Those who forced out the colonists with their bodies and their words . . .*
After all	*This is what the times have brought us*
Liver, just be patient	*Today cities are all they care about*
Liver, just be patient	*As for the timizar of the mountains, they belittle them*
Liver, just be patient	*I never saw a paved road reach them . . .*[1]

– Mhand El Moussaoui and Mohamed Al Qadiri, sung tanḍḍamt (Voix Assabil, 1999)

As the zerda dinner party in the last chapter demonstrated, the significance of locality for the Anti-Atlas mountain people of Ida ou Zeddout took on a different meaning for those who were emigrants (in Casablanca, Marrakesh, or occasionally France) estranged from their lands than for those who were year-round residents, that is, married women, their unmarried daughters and pre-adolescent sons, and the occasional male shepherd or truck driver. Zerdas were rare; hard labor was daily. For emigrants – mostly men – the *tamazirt* (homeland, countryside or rural place; pl. *timizar*) was an almost fictive land, a place that in reality they visited once or twice a year. For rural women, on whom the labor of socially reproducing the tamazirt largely fell, the tamazirt was a place of decidedly unsentimental hard labor (tammara), contingency, and anxiety. Women carried this responsibility with an abiding ambivalence. The demographic distribution of Ishelhin between cities and villages followed this gendered pattern, although more families reportedly relocated to the cities in order to school their children and withdraw from the pressures of maintaining a rural home. Even for those who followed the prevalent pattern, men's and women's investments in the land may have shifted throughout the life cycle and according to individual fortune.

What, then, made a place a tamazirt, and how did Ishelhin perceive its distinctiveness? How were place distinctions involved in the ways Ishelhin of the Anti-Atlas mountains classified themselves and others into distinct social groups? What was it about tamazirt that made it such a potent "home" that was "conceived and lived in *relation* to practices of coming and going? How, in such instances, does (women's) 'dwelling' articulate, politically and culturally, with (men's) 'traveling'?" (Clifford 1997:6; emphasis in the original). The Moroccan Arabic correlate to tamazirt, bled, did not carry the same emotional charge, nor did it have the connotations of a coherent community. The ebb and flow of people, mostly men, between the mountains and the cities made women acutely aware of their dwelling in the tamazirt, that is, of their non-movement.

Most everything made or brought in by Anti-Atlas residents is a colorful antidote to the dry mountains: navy-blue tamlḥaft wraps with glittering gold and silver embroidery, red leather slippers (*idukan*), older women's red, green, and black headbands securing their gauzy black headcoverings that resemble American doo-rags, younger women's yellow or orange headscarves, rugs, toys, striped blankets, powder blue or white Nissan and Peugeot trucks. Even cartons of carrots, tomatoes, pomegranates, and green peppers and hanging goat carcasses render market days festive and give the illusion of abundance. Produce and meat are purchased at weekly markets or from itinerant vegetable sellers, whereas clothes, batteries, and candles are purchased either from a small village store (run by a middle man who makes regular trips to town and resells items for a small profit), or trips into Taroudant, which may be spaced months apart, according to local pickup truck drivers' schedules and the fees charged. Most villages have at least one man working in France, Spain, or Belgium, and most families include emigrants to Moroccan cities. Anti-Atlas mountain dwellers produce little for their own consumption aside from barley, some almonds, and some wool.

Unlike areas of the High Atlas and Rif mountains with abundant water sources, the Anti-Atlas mountains of southwestern Morocco do not sustain their inhabitants. They never sustained them well; one wonders if they ever sustained them at all. Men emigrate in search of work and schooling, a tendency that intensified under the French Protectorate and now comprises all but a few post-adolescent males in any given village. The area's emigrants, like Moroccan emigrants on the whole, return to their home villages an average of one or two times a year. Official statistics note that of Moroccan male emigrants, 36.6 percent return to their home village once a year, 15.2 percent return twice a year, 8 percent return eight times a year, and 28.3 percent do not return at all. Women emigrants who pay return visits do so at slightly lower rates, although 35.9 percent of women do not return at all (CERED 1995:179). Regional affiliation remains salient in important respects, not least of which involves the networks of employment that shape the earning potential of men who support their families back in the countryside. In regions in which a network in Casablanca, Marrakesh, or Tangier is in place, post-adolescent men typically leave their native villages for most of the year to earn money in petty commerce.[2] The Ida ou Zeddout have been migrating since the early days of French occupation, although they were not among the first Ishelhin to establish commercial interests in the northern cities. There are no reliable statistics available concerning the contemporary rural–urban migration specific to this region. Among the scarce sources on Soussi emigration, only one mentions the *commune* center of Igherm (in Ida ou Knsus) by name, although not Ida ou Zeddout or Indouzal. Benhlal (1981) contrasts the East Anti-Atlas tribes of the Igherm area (and specifically Ida ou Zekri, Ida ou Knsus, Ida ou Naḍif) with those of Tafraout and Ida ou Gnaḍif. The Igherm-area tribes were known for shoe craftsmanship, first in Marrakesh and then in Salé. Emigration from the Igherm area followed thirteen years of struggle against French colonization, when the Moroccan qayds (French Protectorate-approved regional rulers), who ruled rural lands as agents of the Makhzen, expropriated the scant natural and human resources of their areas of governance and drove large numbers of men to northern cities. These Igherm area natives had been sedentary agriculturalists. In the late 1970s, according to Benhlal (1981), there were thousands of Igherm-area natives in Marrakesh working as cobblers, living frugally and returning to their home villages during the harvest or planting period for a month or two. According to migration statistics in the first Protectorate era tribal report for the Ida ou Zeddout (Clement 1949), migration from Ait Musi was relatively light: sixty-two men and no women were temporary migrants in Casablanca, and five men were permanent emigrants – two temporarily migrated to Marrakesh, and twelve had settled there definitively. In contrast, the Ait Tafraout[3] fraction of the Ida ou Zeddout had 206 men and women in Marrakesh and only fifteen in Casablanca.

By the 1990s, most Ida ou Zeddout emigrants were based in Casablanca, and Ait Musi men were particularly present in the package liquor sector. Controversy surrounded this market sector, however, with some devout Muslims refusing to work in šrb (Ar. lit. drink; alcohol) despite its profitability. Many others considered the virtue of providing for one's family a more important criterion.

Most Ida ou Zeddout men returned once or twice a year for a few days or weeks, establishing a pattern of moving and dwelling that filled the stomachs and souls of Ishelhin, sometimes meagerly, sometimes copiously, by their modest standards. The mountain inhabitants managed with few resources and yet seemingly remained, as the French Protectorate authorities commonly phrased it, "very attached to their customs." Such claims – common in colonial documents, ethnography, and travel writing about Berbers – provoke more than describe, and beg the question of what it means for a group of people to be "attached" to customs, to place and to language, or to abandon customs, places, and languages. This matter is particularly pressing when the attachment indexes a marginalized subjectivity repeatedly erased from national history and the popular consciousness of the broader nation-state that frames individuals' lives. Furthermore, it invites us to consider how individuals and groups are differently situated to produce, consume, circulate, and assess the meaning of both "custom" and "attachment."

When people circulate, so do ideas, beliefs, practices, and material goods. Some external influences – languages, ritual practices, interactional norms, dress styles – become part of what people consider their own. From both inside and outside the Ashelhi linguistic community, some critique the villages about which I write for their lack of authenticity, remarking on the ways that rural Ishelhin have absorbed outsider (read: Moroccan Arab, never Western) ways of eating, speaking, singing, dressing, interacting and practicing avoidance, marrying, even burying their dead. Each element of daily life is potentially fraught with meaning to someone, indexing collective belonging, signaling a person's attitudes towards what he or she considers his or her community, its past, and (perhaps most importantly) its future. Authenticity is not merely a concern for anthropologists. It was part of the rhetoric of everyday life in southwestern Morocco, and it burst through to the surface of people's consciousness as they assessed each others' actions. It was not only emigrants returning to the village who were aware of cultural difference. Even villagers who had not left what they call the tamazirt made assessments about authenticity and change because these processes affected their daily affairs. Assessments of talk, clothing, or material goods were moral judgments about their speakers, wearers, or owners.

Anti-Atlas mountain residents welcomed periodic breaks from the daily tedium of their household and field chores in the form of visitors or special occasions. In the Ait Musi village where I worked, there were weekly visits from the vegetable seller, and from the bread and candy station wagon. Each week an elderly blind man rode his donkey through the region buying eggs from households and selling them to others who had no chickens. Itinerant merchants of silver, ready-made clothes, and herbs provided periodic diversions as well, and enriched local residents' familiarity with current affairs in other parts of the mountains and in the towns. Festivities such as the annual local saint's veneration or *maɛruf*, the Id Imqqorn (Ar. 'Id Lkbir) and the summer wedding season were discussed and rehashed for months on either side of the events. When there was seemingly nothing going on in these villages, residents were tireless in their efforts to invent something, even if it was retellings of stories they heard or movies they watched while visiting a relative in Marrakesh or Casablanca. While many local people complained that they would prefer to move permanently to the city, they resided fully in their villages in the meanwhile.

Emigrant men's remittances marked the countryside physically in the form of large, colorful cinder block houses they built around the stone village's periphery. Men brought back Arabic language, too, and sometimes a reverence for the social capital symbolized by colloquial Moroccan Arabic (MA, *darija*), that sat uncomfortably with the disdain with which they regarded its native speakers. Emigrants brought back, as well, an increasingly urban support for a form of Islamic orthodoxy that accommodated the more internationally oriented tendencies of urban Arab Islamists. Like emigrant men in many other societies, they were both part of the village community and apart from it, owners of ancestral lands with the right to farm it, but whose everyday lives bore little relation to that of year-round mountain residents (Baumann 1987; Ferguson 1999; Turino 1993). In return, the women who stayed in the tamazirt socially reproduced it through the Tashelhit language they used and taught their children, their practices of saint veneration and the annual rituals associated with it, and their material contributions to tending the ancestral lands and maintaining their symbolic as well as material value despite the typically meager harvests.

There is ample discourse in the Moroccan newspapers, as well as in the political rhetoric, about developing the countryside and increasing its capacity to sustain its inhabitants. Rural development efforts, particularly water, electrical, and sanitation infrastructure, increasingly bring elements of urban life into the homes and habits of a population sector long marginalized and following an alternative system of symbolic capital. For some, the infrastructural development better integrates rural populations into the homogenous national fold while it decreases regional variability and the richness of expressive culture for which Morocco is renowned. Fears about the effects of rural change stem from urbanites' fantasies about themselves and their own pasts. Native villagers seeking jobs in the cities cared little for the romanticized notions that many urban people had of the countryside, yet oftentimes emigrant men, too, objectified the homeland. Indeed, bundles of discursive oppositions circulated among town and rural dwellers: traditional-modern, authentic-corrupted, old-new, difficult-easy, country-city, Berber-Arab, ignorant-enlightened, illiterate-educated, female-male. Each of these characterizations is a signifier with no essential, enduring referent. Each is a shifter generating meaning only within the specific context and by the interlocutors using it (Silverstein 1976, 1987; Galaty 1982). Ethnic, regional, spatial, and moral evaluative labels were relative concepts disguised, yet not pragmatically operative, as empirical facts. Language and ethnicity mapped increasingly onto these dichotomies, generating meanings that were only beginning to be contested by some Ishelhin who were disfavored by them.

In this rural homeland, in contrast to Moroccan cities and provincial administrative centers, Tashelhit was the uncontested lingua franca. As such, the tamazirt had become an organizing symbol as well as a physical location for perpetuating the Tashelhit language as an index of ethnic identity. Migration did not erode the aspects of Ashelhi identity specific to locale or grounded in language. Rather, migration led to an Anti-Atlas understanding of community as comprised of present and absent members. In this way, men and women dialogically related absence and presence. The song text opening this chapter suggests as much; one could hardly mention the timizar without reference to the cities. Cities materially sustained village populations, while villages morally nourished the urban Ashelhi population, a mutual reliance documented elsewhere (Ferguson 1997; Williams 1973; Turino 1993). For people from the Anti-Atlas mountains, this set of evaluations was mapped onto material practices and discursive representations, the two domains on which I focus my discussion of homelands in this and the following chapter. The production of these practices and representations are historically situated, and thus the "cultural territorializations" (Gupta and Ferguson 1997:4) I describe here should likewise be understood as products of their particular political economy at the historical moment when I documented them, although some may remain true for years to come.

Contemporary villages and ancestral lands are more than mere dwelling places or repositories of imagined histories. They are integral to the ways people rationalize and experience the present, and they are crucial sites for negotiating the boundaries of a dispersed community membership and the roles of individuals within it. By considering migration and homeland *together,* as dialogically related but produced through distinct processes, anthropologists may more fruitfully explore how people endow places with meaning when community boundaries and memberships are contested. In such circumstances, gendered and ethnic subjectivities are constituted less in terms of place (or even places) than in terms of movement between places and means of engagement with them through social networks.

For other societies as well, we should consider the concomitant processes of migration, homeland-building, language maintenance, and gender construction in the making of individual and collective subjectivities. Gupta and Ferguson (1997) argue that "imaginings of place" shift under changing political circumstances. Similarly, I am suggesting that men's and women's differing engagements with political economies impact their "senses of place" (Feld and Basso 1996). Drawing on Ashelhi understandings of human activities as well as this scholarly literature, I extend the notion of performance beyond that of representation, in order to analyze manual labor practices alongside discursive practices. Negotiation and contestation pervade performances of both "speech and sweat" (Povinelli 1993:32), conditioning which individuals perform authoritatively, what they should perform, who can critique others' performances, and what role performances play in constructions of place and identity in the wider context of a diversely constituted nation-state. In instances where people differ over their senses of place, the tension may point to the "topographies of power" in play (Gupta and Ferguson 1997). For the overwhelmingly monolingual and non-literate women who populated the southwestern Moroccan countryside in the late 1990s, "home" and "homeland" connoted hard labor, not nostalgia. Nostalgia was rare even among the minority of women who had accompanied their fathers and husbands to the city, throwing into question whether the nostalgic impulse necessarily accompanies modernity (Ivy 1995).[4]

Material and Demographic Constitution of the Tamazirt

allahu akbar swa gis yan iššša wakal
ġwalli iġabn ġ iggi ns ur a tn zrrġ
I swear the one who bit the dust is the same as
Those who strayed far away whom I no longer see
– Ida ou Zeddout tazrrart

The Anti-Atlas mountain population is divided administratively between the provinces of Taroudant, Tata, Tafraout, Biougra, and Agadir. Within the Province of Taroudant, the Ida ou Zeddout live in the low rolling hills of the Anti-Atlas located about 70 km southeast of the provincial capital, Taroudant, and the Oued Sous. The Ida ou Zeddout area is administratively within the annex (Ar. da'ira; Fr. *cercle*) of Igherm. This annex registered 61,308 residents (divided into 12,051 families) out of the Province's total of over 551,000 residents in the 1994 census. The Igherm annex is divided into 428 communities or districts (*jmaɛ*-s). The fraction of Ait Musi, within the district of Walqadi, has 3,398 people divided into 698 households. The Ait Musi village in which I primarily worked had one hundred official residents divided among twenty identified households.[5]

Despite these statistics from the Ministry of the Interior, it was difficult to confirm numbers of mountain hamlet inhabitants for several reasons. Methodologically, we must question the documentation that verifies residence: a person's identity card may be registered in Ida ou Zeddout even though the person resides undocumented in Casablanca for all but two weeks each year.[6] Conceptually, too, we can ask what makes a person a resident: village of origin or participation in a community. The rural sector division of the Ministry of the Interior uses a formula whereby six months of residence in one place makes a person eligible for census in that place, but it is not clear how they confirm residence. I was not in a position to initiate a census of these lands myself, for I witnessed the extent to which suspicion surrounded attempts to count belongings, property, or household members, even when the census-taker was a trusted and familiar community member (Hoffman 2000b).

Unlike Ishelhin in the Sous Valley whose villages abutted Arab villages, the Ida ou Zeddout were what city and plains residents call mountain people (*ibudrarn*; sing. m. *abudrar*: ab (man) + udrar (mountain); fem. *tabudrart*), squarely situated in the tamazirt. In the late 1990s, a deteriorating one and a half lane paved road ran from Taroudant through Igherm south to Tata, with linked dirt roads leading to several Ida ou Zeddout villages. State services were few and far between; a few villages alongside the road had electricity, but solar-powered batteries and panels were more common energy sources. Each cluster of hamlets shared a primary school; boys tended to leave for the northern cities after completing their fifth or sixth year, and almost all girls left school by their fifth year. Women and their children coordinated domestic and agricultural tasks according to their household needs and parents' aspirations for their children. The nearest middle school in Igherm was far enough away to require boarding, but it lacked boarding facilities for girls. A modest health clinic opened in 1999 in Walqadi, the market center that also housed a pharmacy, foodstuff supply store, elementary school, and administrative offices.

Ida ou Zeddout land is owned by the Ida ou Zeddout, not by outside commercial agricultural interests that operate in much of the Sous Valley. The land yields little, however, and so their migration and wage-labor activities have brought about changing relations between these mountain horticulturalists, their land, and state institutions. Dwellings in the Anti-Atlas mountains are typically made of stone and mud, in contrast to the mud-and-straw brick (pisé) dwellings of the Sous plains and the slightly elevated Ida ou Finis villages. This reflects the increasingly rocky quality of the soil as one moves higher into the mountains, but even once into the hills the proportion of rock to soil varies not only between villages but also within the landholdings of each. For this reason and because of the variability of soil's performance on different sides of a given village, an individual's landholdings tended to be dispersed. One parcel, for example,

Figure 4.1 Market day in Walqadi

may be in direct sunlight during the bulk of the day, and another parcel shaded by a hill at all times. French tribal reports for the Ida ou Zeddout, Indouzal, and other neighboring Anti-Atlas tribes summed up their assessments of the land and its resources as part of *le Maroc inutile:* "not of interest for colonization".

The Ida ou Zeddout ascribed to the perspective that roots, or laṣl, provided insight into an individual's behavior, morality, and ideas, a concept widely noted for Arab society (cf. Abu Lughod 1986:41–6; Geertz et al. 1979; Rosen 1984:21–5). On the other hand, as in many other societies, Ishelhin held that the places where people dwell weigh heavily on the ways they live their lives. In such a view, places themselves have moral characters that reflect the histories of their occupants, and town and village dwellers frequently evaluated the moral characters of various places they either visited or heard about from others, an approach documented elsewhere (Ferguson 1997). For example, village mothers told me, and I saw in instances like the zerda dinner party, young emigrant men behaved respectfully with young women during nighttime socializing hours outside in common spaces on Ida ou Zeddout land. But the mothers surmised that these same young men probably harassed young women on the streets in Casablanca where they were outside the "grip of patriarchy" (Sadiqi 2003:167) whose benefit was to protect rural women and girls from unwelcome male advances. Many Ida ou Zeddout claimed that people's behavior was conditioned by the places in which they dwelled, albeit somewhat according to their laṣl.

The tamazirt was a place of laṣl, a wholesome and moral place, in contrast to the city. Its moral character stemmed not so much from the behavior of its inhabitants – for they ranged in actions and conviction as do people anywhere – but due to the understanding that people in the tamazirt were the opposite of *xalḍn* (ethnically mixed). Although mountain dwellers occupied a range of socioeconomic positions, the crucial point in this assessment was that they, collectively, were not Arabs (*aεrabn*), a category that encompassed urban bureaucrats, Western Sahara desert residents, and Arabs of the Levant and Arab East alike. People in the tamazirt were Ishelhin with some shared understanding that, unlike in much of Moroccan society, there was no disadvantage to their identification within that space. In the tamazirt, most residents placed a high value on Ashelhi-ness. In a very tangible way, the tamazirt was the one space free of the cultural, linguistic, and moral hegemony of Arab urbanity that pervaded public and private spaces throughout Morocco. It is clear, then, why such a place attracted its migrants back year after year to celebrate the religious feasts, weddings, and harvests that socially reproduced the community.

Next to this appealing moral and social universe, however, were the grim realities of the tamazirt. These realities explained the repulsion towards the tamazirt felt by many of those who lived or visited there, as well as those who refused to visit. When an urban Arab called someone a šlḥ (Ar. fem. šlḥa, pl. šluḥ), it signaled that the person referred to was a native Tashelhit speaker who lived in the tamazirt, or who used to, or whose parents did. That residence history meant that Ishelhin, while perhaps retaining a more solid sense of roots than those who had abandoned their place of origin, inherently lacked the quality of urbanity that made a person a Moroccan citizen. A set of lifestyle characterizations was indexed in the label Ashelhi. Ashelhi meant an agricultural existence compromised by consistently disappointing yields from rain-fed barley fields and dependent on outside goods for survival. It meant uncertain income, with men working in faraway places that women were rarely allowed to visit. It meant a dearth of modern conveniences such as electricity and running water. It meant limited access to fresh produce and meat from markets and restrictions on women's public movements that forced women to rely on the few available men and boys to procure the market goods required by their households. For men, it meant temperance in financial matters and oversight in domestic affairs despite long absences from the village. For women and girls, most of all, living in the tamazirt entailed an expectation of tammara (hard labor): gathering wood, hauling water, baking bread in open ovens, weaving blankets for brutal winters. It meant gashed legs, sore backs, burned hands, and scratched, leathered faces.

Laboring: Tammara Makes a Tamazirt

> Too long a sacrifice
> Can make a stone of the heart.
> O when may it suffice?
> – W.B. Yeats, "Easter 1916" (1924)

Within the space of the tamazirt, a series of repeated acts of labor constituted the routine activity of rural dwellers. This labor, as Eric Wolf stresses, is always social, and is deployed by an "organized social plurality" whose individuals expend energy ("work"). The laborer, then, always stands in relation to other people. The controllers of social labor are "assigned to their positions by the system of deploying social labor" (Wolf 1982:74). For Anti-Atlas female laborers, crucial subsistence chores included tending the land, collecting fodder for donkeys and cows, and preparing four daily meals. The lighter, tedious chores were known as tawwuri, a word whose root suggests repetition, a circular movement, but also forward movement (from the Arabic root ṭ-w-r, to develop). While female labor assured the maintenance of rudimentary material living conditions, its importance extended to the normative moral order of Ashelhi society. Respect for the fields (*igran*)[7] and willingness to exert oneself physically to ensure their upkeep comprised a normative work ethic. Women and girls told me they desired to flee the constant contact with the land; city-dwelling male emigrants told me they were nostalgic for it. For both men and women, however, women's labor was understood as central to the social reproduction of the tamazirt. Bodies were constantly in motion between inside and outside spaces, with little absolute protection from the elements given the animals who needed tending, the wood that needed collecting to heat water and bake bread, and the constant visits by interdependent neighbor women in need of an aspirin, a handful of tea, a length of rope, a box of matches, or a piece of advice.

While the cooking and cleaning of tawwuri was women's work anywhere in Morocco, tammara was limited to rural women. The hard labor – especially agricultural labor – was once assumed by men and boys. As men's normative space became the cities, however, increasing numbers of young male Ishelhin in the late 1990s balked at agricultural work in favor of urban wage labor. Men's disdain for agricultural labor – and its influence even on marriage and divorce patterns – was documented as early as 1939 by Igherm's Native Affairs bureau chief, Marcel Turnier:

> [M]en scorned this thankless work [farming] and we noted many marriages in the sowing season; at harvest time, on the contrary, the number of

> divorces increased, the men hoping always, despite customary laws, to profit alone from the fruits of the earth. (Méraud 1990:340)

Women who remained tied materially to the land six decades later shared men's pessimistic assessment of the land's productive capability. There was a symbolic dimension, however, in that many Ishelhin saw these weakened (and for some men, weekend) ties to the land as indicative of a break with the place and their ancestors. In an increasingly market-oriented economy, the barley grown by the Ida ou Zeddout had become the poor family's substitute for the more sought-after bread wheat (farina).

The moral overtones of this economic shift permeated narratives like the one I collected from a grandmother living just outside the market town of Igherm in a village of Ida ou Knsus. Her critique was targeted at young people as well as her peers who embraced the market-orientation of the younger generation:

> When I was young we planted for over a month, not like the week we plant these days. Back then, if you didn't plant, you didn't eat. There was no cooking gas, no electricity, no oven. You hauled wood on your back to make bread. In the morning we ate meal and made couscous. There was no wheat flour – everything was barley, barley, barley. The [Igherm] market was held on Friday then, until the French exiled the king [Mohamed V] to Madame Gascar [Madagascar]; then they changed the market day to Wednesday. People wanted to pray on Friday – they didn't want to go to market. The market wasn't so big then; there weren't all the trucks there are now. Now every Wednesday is like a festival!
>
> Now few people care about planting and harvesting. They work a week or two, that's all. They don't care at all. Like these girls, even the men and the guys who have gone to school, they don't want to work the land. If you go and look at it, you'll see a lot of land left fallow. They say, "Look, there's bread in the market, there's barley and ground wheat, what more do you want." They want to let it go.

The "they" in the grandmother's critique were young women and older women, as well as men, who valued state education over farming, the mass-produced over the homemade. She used her description of horticultural activities in her youth to comment on the present ("They don't want to work the land") and to project into the future ("They want to let it go.") (cf. Basso 1996; Stewart 1996). Such assessments bridge temporalities (Goodwin and Goodwin 1992), constructing a moral order in which physical laboring is not only endured but positively valued.

Whether women and girls "let go" of their fields, or instead planted and harvested for a week or a month each year, tammara extended beyond the fields. Most mornings, girls and women headed out of the village into the "forest" (*tagant*) of sparse uninhabited land to gather fodder for their donkeys and cows. Several times a week girls pushed out further beyond the mountain for firewood. Wood collection for their open clay ovens was left to adolescent and teenaged young women whenever possible, who set out in pairs, singing as they walked up the hillsides towards the fields and out of view. From the village below, their laughs were audible. They spaced their destinations so as to favor their success in finding weeds and small trees; one pair would head in the direction of the tomb of the local patron saint and the other pair, with their scythes and ropes, would go beyond the dry riverbed (*asif*). Their yelled greetings reverberated back to the village as they called out to other young women collecting atop other hillsides. The occasional man spotted on a trail became a target for their heckling. Collecting wood was the worst of their tammara. The heavy loads on their backs ripped through their first layers of clothing; the weight exhausted them.

The women and girls took turns handling household chores. Shortly after sunrise, the one with breakfast duty fired up the wood stove, over which she heated water in a meter-high copper jug for face washing, prepared the barley and olive oil porridge (*azkkif*) and the sweet coffee, and then baked the tannurt for the late-morning breakfast. Smoke rose from the smokestacks across the village. Young women returned for the late morning breakfast with swollen tamlḥaft wraps over their backs, filled with fodder or wood. Returning from the path by the river, they stopped to rest their laden backs momentarily on the dirt ledge that they dryly called "our [mountain] airport." They headed back into the village, where they dispersed to their homes, some to contiguous stone homes in the village

Figure 4.2 Mother and daughter planting barley, Ida ou Zeddout

core, others to palatial pink-painted cinder-block structures on the village margins. Whether they walked through wooden or metal doors, these girls and women dropped their loads of grass and wood in the same way, baked bread on the insides of open ovens in the same way, and laid out their blankets on the floor to sleep in the same way. Discrepancies in wealth visible in domestic architecture disguised similarities in work activities inside and outside domestic walls.

Tammara was considered by both the women and men I knew to be a female activity. When fathers, brothers, and sons were home from their urban jobs, they were only marginally involved in lightening the laboring load. Men scoffed at the idea that they might assist in wood and fodder collection. The task of cutting and carrying wood was one activity that men considered characteristic of Tashelhit female identity. This point was illustrated for me a few weeks after a storm. The village women had chopped down some of the trees that a strong wind had shredded. The approximately 50-year-old Lalla Rqia and I headed out with a handsaw the size of a bow and a few yards of rope to chop some of the trees that the wind had downed. The wood we cut was on her fields, but since we had worked together, custom dictated that we split the wood. Half of it we hauled on our backs to the house of Hajja, her cousin, where I was considered part of the household. We dropped our load on the back path in front of Hajja's courtyard. Lalla Rqia called out to her adult son, home from Tangier, to bring the donkey from Hajja's house and secure its metal saddle designed for hauling heavy loads. The son looked embarrassed when he brought out the donkey and geared her up, snickering that he was doing women's work. We led the donkey back to the riverbed and hauled branches out of the fields as we walked. It was not so much the weight of the wood that was hard to bear, but that the branches bit into our backs and shoulders, finding our every soft spot. The man's role in the task was holding the donkey still; he did not saw branches or haul wood. All the while he wore a lightweight jacket that looked as if it would have torn had he lifted the slightest branch. Even then, Lalla Rqia and I decided how to load the donkey with each six-foot-tall stack of wood.

When I loaded up the first of three stacks of wood on my back, Lalla Rqia apologized as women conventionally do when a guest or high-status person labors: "I'm sorry I'm making you work." I answered conventionally as well, saying it was no problem, and as I expected she made no further comment on my participation in the task at hand. Her migrant son, on the other hand, offered a running commentary on my participation in the chore, with such remarks as "You're going to carry wood?" then "Oh look you're carrying wood!" and finally "Was it hard to carry wood?" Uncomfortable with his suggestion that my laboring was unusual because I was an educated foreigner, I tried to downplay the novelty of the situation with such non-sequiturs as "Work is work" and "The world is full of work." Lalla Rqia said to me, "I'm used to work and you're not yet." Her use of "yet" seemed to imply that I would eventually get used to the work or maybe that I was able-bodied but not yet knowledgeable. Lalla Rqia's son headed back to the village steering the loaded donkey. Lalla Rqia handed me a few sprigs of a bitter grass to nibble as we strolled through the fields. She led, pointing to the plants on the right and left saying, "There are so many names for the greenery."

Lalla Rqia approached the task at hand as a chore to accomplish, and I was available to help. Her migrant son, in contrast, indicated through actions and words that only certain categories of people were appropriate participants in the task. As an outsider who broke through those conventions, then, I was behaving in a way that elicited assessment – my actions framed labor as an aspect of dwelling that characterized a Tashelhit woman.

While the activities of gathering and cooking were ongoing in the countryside, agricultural activities were part of an annual cycle. The phrase *iśwa usgg^{w}as*, literally "The year was/is good," characterized a bountiful harvest. Ida ou Zeddout villagers no longer plowed and harvested collectively as villagers told me they used to. Each household (*takat*) worked its own land with family members or hired workers, especially darker-skinned workers from Taggmout near the pre-Saharan outpost of Tata, as the French military officer Clement remarked a half-century earlier (Clement 1949). As one young woman explained to me, the reason for this shift from collective to household-centered labor was that families with little land no longer wanted to work the land of the larger landowners. Every household thus determined for itself how much labor its fields required. Some villagers told me that working collectively without the assistance of hired workers simply took too long. Under the household-based system, most groups finished in two to four weeks; when they used the tiwizi collective harvesting system, a longer period was required. Moreover, as one young woman explained, collective harvesting was messy: it conflated the spheres of work and play (cf. Caton 1990). The Ida ou Zeddout strove to keep each activity in its place, whereas for those who practiced tiwizi, as the young woman explained, "You look at them and you can't tell whether it's their harvesting season, or their wedding season, or what it is, it's all messed up (*mxrbaq*). People are coming in from the fields dirty and then going to weddings." In an orderly community, villagers finished harvesting and then celebrated, as in Peruvian Andean villages in which the silence of monotony is broken by the monthly festivals, "the reverse side of life's cloth" that nevertheless carves into the monotony of everyday labors on either side of the event (Turino 1993:1). The "liability to personal labor" may have integrated into the existing Berber tradition of collective labor, as Bidwell argues, making it "accepted by the people" when imposed by French Protectorate authorities (Bidwell 1973:187). There were practical reasons for completing the harvest in early summer as well, while there was still enough wind to separate the hay from the chaff, and before the intensive, still August heat. If the barley sat in the fields in the summer sun, the grain became brittle so that the shaft fell apart and dispersed the seed. Moreover, it became more difficult to work long days as the temperature rose. For all of these reasons, villagers told me, each family worked alone or with its hired workers to harvest as quickly as possible. The seasonal workers lived in their employer's house, and they fed them and paid them according to the year's price. In 1997 the rate was around 100 dirhams ($10) a day because there was so much work after the heavy rains. In contrast, the 1996 rate was 40 or 50 dirhams a day, closer to average daily wages for manual laborers in the Sous, the least experienced of whom earned 30 dirhams a day, about half of that earned by the supervisor or master (maɛllm). In 1998 there was insufficient rainfall for a decent harvest and thus outside workers were not employed. I suspect that an increased disparity between families' landholdings is partly responsible for the decline in the practice of tiwizi. The system was best suited for situations of parity, it seems. Outside of personal landholdings, as Bidwell notes, "the tribe agreed to work in common for some specific purpose such as the plowing of lands of a widow or those of a marabout, or building a mosque" (1973:187). Such a willingness to work was not lost on French Native Affairs (*affaires indigènes*) authorities in the countryside whose archival traces suggest that (forced) labor projects improved their subjects' living conditions.

In the Anti-Atlas, the cyclical anticipation for the arrival of men and boys for the Id Mqqorn (the Great Sacrifice) and the August wedding season, and their inevitable departure, involved ritualized interactions surrounding comings and goings. Families tended to keep to themselves, and visitors timed their arrivals and departures so as to encounter the fewest villagers possible. When visitors left the village, friends and family accompanied them to the foot of the village to say their goodbyes. Ideally they left quietly, and there was little insistence to stay. The silent resignation of the village women at these departures differed notably from the insistence of women in the towns and plains that the visitor should not be in such a hurry, that a longer stay would be more reasonable. Mountain women made no such plaints, respecting a visitor's timing and presuming the visitor knew his or her constraints better than they did. Most of those who left in this way were emigrant men visiting what they called their homes; they were the ones who procured and paid for the consumable and material goods that came into the household. Among the many Ishelhin who called the tamazirt home, however, only a fraction were year-round village residents. Women joked that they were themselves better fit than men to take the harsh conditions of the village.

Central to my concern, then, is the question of who comprised the village community and the distinction between tamazirt residents and those individuals who considered the tamazirt their laṣl. How was the gendered experience of moving and dwelling constitutive of residence and origins? How had migration and ideas about urbanity transformed what it meant to be rural, and vice-versa; that is, how were ideas about the tamazirt implicated in what it meant to be urban? Indeed, would there have been a tamazirt in the Anti-Atlas without out-migration? Before addressing the question of how the mountains emotionally and morally sustained emigrants, I turn first to the concept of occupying space and then to the marital patterns and the material ways in which towns facilitated mountain life.

"Full" Places: Dwelling Makes a Tamazirt

Although a person could be Ashelhi outside the tamazirt, a tamazirt ceased to be a homeland when it was no longer "full" (*ɛmmrn*). For a homeland to retain its value, it had to retain its population. Places that were good were verbally assessed as full, implicitly filled with people. For instance, women either studiously avoided or intentionally moved through spaces in the countryside or village that were ɛmmrn. In many instances, women's talk about a place being full euphemized the presence of men. The expression was used in other contexts. To say that a saint's festival would take place a certain day, for example, one said that "it will fill up on [Tuesday]." Taroudant had become a desirable place to live, one woman from Touraght told me, because it was full, meaning that people were building new cinder block homes there, and the markets were so crowded that moving about in the late afternoon shopping and strolling hours was challenging. Taroudant was worth visiting during Throne Day festivities, yet another young woman told me, because it "fills up." One plains villager with whom I was out walking one afternoon looked at me in confusion when I pulled out my camera to take a picture of the landscape, scolding, "You're turned the wrong way. Take a picture the other way, of the village, over there where it's full."

Humanity was dependent on sociability in Ashelhi understandings. Likewise, a person who was solitary was less human, less civilized, in the original usage of the term, where civil relates not only to things urban but by implication also things social. Groups of people were included or excluded in part dependent on their sociability. Individuals spent their lives surrounded by people. Solitude for women invoked fear and boredom, while for men – if not voluntary – it signaled a lack of integration into the social milieu. People lived, ate, and worked in groups, sleeping several to a room. Indeed, for young women in particular, sleeping alone invited the spirits (jjnun), and through my years living in Morocco women and girls often expressed concern for my safety when I slept alone at night. Claustrophobia, if rural women ever experienced it, certainly was not acted upon. A common praise used for both men and women in MA and borrowed into Tashelhit was allah yaεmarr ha ad-dar, literally "God fills up his/her home." The expression was used to praise and solicit God's blessings: "May God fill up her/his home." To say that a woman will "fill up your house" is to say she will be a good wife and mother, bringing children, other people, honor, and a joyful mood to a home. A full house was inhabited by blessed people.[8] The opposite is a curse, allah ixxli ha slεa, literally "God clears out his/her supplies," meaning "May God destroy his/her home, family, and fortune." The divergent ideas behind the running disagreement I had with rural women about the appeal of Taroudant and Casablanca was their frequently expressed admiration for cities because of the throngs of people milling about in them, precisely the kinds of crowds for which I had little tolerance. It also explained, in part, the good-natured mood with which town residents withstood hours in lines waiting to pay utility bills in crowded, unventilated rooms, which at times took on a festive atmosphere, each person jockeying for recognition by the bureaucrats tasked with collecting the paper slips and cash due, not a one queuing up.

By extension, people were understood to live in occupied places, and the more full a land was of people, the more human its residents were believed to be. People who lived in the hinterlands were called jackals (*uššn*), dogs (*iyḍan*), worthy of contempt, uncouth, sub-human. One Indouzal man explained to me from the top of a pickup truck as we passed a hilly land with stone houses perched high above and nothing but argan nut fields all around, "They grow everything for themselves here, carrots and almonds and barley, they don't even buy or sell at market. Jackals are what they are." Subsistence was not positively valued. On the contrary, the absence of the most basic of human encounters – the market transaction – signaled an absence of humanity. This comment echoed through the mountains, ringing the same theme as that uttered by city folks against non-urban folks. Civilization is a relative concept, but rural people used and highly valued it as denoting urban manners, in its original sense.

A term borrowed from Arabic into Tashelhit indicates the opposite of tamazirt, the wilderness or outback (lxla). The term evoked for Swasa images of the Sahara, desert(ed) places, sparsely inhabited, perceived as dangerous. People in such places were believed simply not to ascribe to the same rules of social behavior. An insult aimed by an Ashelhi at a person who was uncouth or antisocial is "desert Arab" (*aɛrab n lxla*), linking the concept of wilderness to that of Arab – a bedouin, or a Saharan – a lawless, rootless person.

Homelands Inhabited by Strangers

a immi d baba qnḍat i ṛṛḥmt inu
nfuġ awn ifassn nga tarwa n mddn
Oh mother and father, prepare my burial
We've left your hands now we're strangers' children[9]
– Ida ou Zeddout tazrrart

Judging by discursive constructions of the tamazirt as a place into which one's roots burrow, the tamazirt would seem to be a place to which residents could trace their ancestral origins. In a broad sense, this was true; in the mountains Ishelhin seldom married Arabs as did Ishelhin living in the plains and towns. The Ida ou Zeddout were largely endogamous; in Ait Musi, the Ida ou Zeddout farqa (Fr. *fraction* or tribal section) with which I am most familiar, there was only one native Arabic-speaking woman living in the tamazirt, married to a shepherd whose roots were allegedly in "the Sahara." Others called the couple "Arabs"; they had been accused on more than one occasion of employing magic to ruin weddings. Whether this couple had malicious intentions towards the Ishelhin is less important for our purposes than the fact that their being "Arabs" made their Ashelhi neighbors distrust them. Beyond the primary social distinction of native language, however, what were the boundaries of "there" in the countryside?

Many of the people who occupied a given tamazirt – women – arrived there through the typically once-in-a-lifetime movement that accompanied marriage. Since few men resided full-time in their native villages, their wives and young children largely populated the hillsides. These women were only rarely raised in the same village as their husbands, but they were usually from the same or a neighboring taqbilt. In the late 1990s, a young woman in her twenties or thirties was likely to marry a man connected to her through kinship or shared infrastructure – someone who lived along the same path or road, a construction worker originating in another region of Morocco, or a relative of a family member's husband, to cite a few of the pairings I witnessed during fieldwork. The women in any village lived there because their husbands had laṣl (and land) in that village. Each woman perpetuated her husband's fortune, small or large, and raised his children. The women who worked and socialized alongside one another, borrowed buttermilk from each other, and cooked annual meals in honor of the local saint, were not related, and usually they did not know each other before they became neighbors. Their husbands, in contrast, grew up together, each going his own way to provide for his family. The men were estranged by choice or necessity. The women were brought together by circumstance, fate (*larzaq*), God's will, which they said governs where each person will spend her days. As one young woman sang in a wedding verse that was neither clearly mournful nor hopeful:

ignwan d ikaln ad ur ittmittiyn	Movement stems not from skies and earth
imma larzaq ar yadlli ttmittiyn	it stems instead from fate

Given this residency pattern, it was striking that adolescent girls and young women who talked about marriage, as they did frequently, did not talk about the women amongst whom they would live. Instead they talked about the wealthy migrants who would whisk them away to Casablanca and remove them definitively from their dreaded annual planting and harvesting labor. They talked, joked, teased each other, and sang about good men, attractive men, men who were straight and honest (*maεqul*). Shortly after each young woman married, however, her husband returned to the city. The new bride then had to adjust to a village full of unfamiliar women, a household with a mother-in-law, sisters-in-law, and older wives of brothers-in-law whose wishes and habits took precedence over hers. For young brides, then, the moral character of her groom's tamazirt was conditioned by networks of women residents.

Older women who had experienced their own dislocation and that of their daughters and other female relatives were more aware of the importance of female village networks. The transcript below captures the rude awakening that awaited the bride and the importance of garnering allies in the groom's village where she would assume a subservient role to female in-laws according to their number and ages. The conversation was nestled between long sessions of singing in the first day of 20-year-old Saadia's two-day wedding in Ida ou Zeddout in August 1997, the young bride who played my cassette of tizrrarin sung verses rather than having her friends sing during her secluded days. Saadia sat on the floor, shrouded by a white sheet and red face veil that marked her liminal status between virgin and wife. Women came to her to wish her well, relieve her worries, and offer advice on marital life. Two elderly women (Lalla Aisha and Lalla Awish) offered Saadia assurance that the groom's village, Issdrim, was full of good women who would look after her. They reminded Saadia, however, of her impending low status in the groom's household and suggested how she might modify her behavior to ensure good relations with her in-laws.

Figure 4.3 A shrouded bride accompanied by female mentor and friend, Ida ou Zeddout

Transcript 4.1: Advice to the Bride

Lalla Aisha:	((bending down at the waist to address the bride)) You're not on your own any more.
Saadia:	I hear what you say (safi).[10]
Lalla Aisha:	There's only your mother-in-law in the [husband's] house, right?
Saadia:	Two of them [=older female relatives]!
Lalla Aisha:	Two of them!
Saadia:	Yeah.
Lalla Aisha:	Don't get mad at [your mother-in-law] until she dies. Because it will be difficult.
Saadia:	Oh no.
Lalla Aisha:	Well, may God protect you. ((Standing up; to Lalla Awish)) She's just getting a taste of it now; their bad side hasn't come out yet. When it does she'll remember me.
Saadia:	Yeah.
Lalla Aisha:	((leaning down, to Saadia)) So he said to you,[11] to [your father] Hussein u Belqas, and I said to him, I said to your mother, I said, "Aisha" she said "yes." I said to her, "For God's sake, give your daughter to [a suitor in] [the nearby village of] Issdrim. You'll be near her. If you die she'll be by your side. She'll even drop water in your mouth. If you're sick, she'll run to your side. All your daughters will be together there." She said to me, "Oh my sister, may

	God help you." You'll do what's good. Well, may God forgive us.[12] ((Stands up))
Saadia:	May God help you. May God help you.
Lalla Aisha:	((Leaning down again)) So my daughter, our Rqia is there [in Issdrim], there's Haj Hmu's daughter, there's our Houria. So God help you. ((Standing up))
Saadia:	Amen, dear one, Lalla Awish, may God accept your gifts.
Lalla Awish:	((bending down, to Saadia)) Pull your head together. Pull your head together.
Saadia:	Okay. Thanks.
Lalla Awish:	Pull your head together. Don't go around, "ha ta ta ta ta" [chatting]." If you come in, like to here?
Saadia:	Yeah?
Lalla Awish:	Be quiet, that's all. Shut your mouth. Watch. Check things out. Notice what they do. Look out. Whatever you're going to do, announce it first to your mother-in-law, ask her if you can do it. My daughter-in-law always waits on me. She has prepared so many meals for me! ((Stands up))
Saadia:	As for me, if she'll be patient with me, I'll leave her alone.
Lalla Aisha:	Yeah, all the time. Until you've borne a lot of children. Well, may God make things good for you. ((Both elderly women turn to leave))
Saadia:	Amen, Lalla Awish.
Lalla Aisha:	((Turning back)) May God help you. You haven't seen anything yet. That's enough. May God pardon us.
Saadia:	Amen.
Lalla Aisha:	If you enter a place, don't be overly enthusiastic. Keep this shut ((pointing to lips)). Just keep your mouth shut. Pull your head together. The chicken said – this is what they say happened [signaling a proverb] – it pecked at a shell; it thought it was corn. The shell got caught in its beak. They say this really happened. May God help you.
Saadia:	Amen.
Lalla Aisha:	Hey, times are hard! Don't act as though they are easy.
Saadia:	((emphatically)) It's not easy! It's not easy!
Lalla Aisha:	May God forgive us.
Saadia:	Amen, dear Lalla Aisha. May God accept what you offered. ((Lalla Aisha and Lalla Awish leave.))

Saadia: ((with worried expression, to unmarried friend Kiltum who overheard conversation)) Am I really going to have to ask before I do everything?
Kiltum: Well, there you are.

The elderly Lalla Aisha rose to leave numerous times, each time asking for God's blessings on the bride, then thought of something else she felt compelled to add. Saadia accepted the advice without hesitation, at least until the elderly women were out of earshot. At that point, she confided her surprise to her peer at the suggestion that she might have less freedom than she was accustomed to: "Am I really going to have to ask before I do everything?" Her friend offered a neutral response in empathy. The strangers in Saadia's husband's village, like those of each new bride, would socialize her into the ways of maintaining her husband's tamazirt. In Issdrim as in other Anti-Atlas villages, women comprised the demographic core. The responsibility for perpetuating a tamazirt, an inhabited place made meaningful through labor, rested on these women's shoulders.

From Emigration to Remittances: The Circulation of Goods and Symbols

Just let us be, we can't explain it all
These times are hard, they're like a Frenchman
Men have disappeared, they're [rare as] remedies
The wind takes away those to whom women give birth[13]
– commercially recorded tanḍḍamt by Ihya and Othman (1999)

Lefebvre states, "*Social spaces interpenetrate one another and/or superimpose themselves upon one another.* They are not *things*, which have mutually limiting boundaries and which collide because of their contours or as a result of inertia" (1991:86–7; italics in the original). While some Ishelhin conceived of the tamazirt as a "thing," a particular kind of rural space, historically the boundaries of specific timizar have expanded and contracted as state authorities shuffled administrative borders (Hoffman 2000b). It is not so much that these rural social spaces "interpenetrated" or "superimposed themselves upon another," but rather that they co-existed, collided, and regrouped in popular imaginations. Today, roads are central to the coherence of a geographical space as a region, promoting certain interconnections and patterns of movement over others. But roads resulted from a history of conquest, land seizures, and ultimately reliance on market and urban centers. What Ishelhin told me about the history of road building in their lands, as the Hawsaphone Mawri of Southern Niger told Masquelier (2002:829), primarily concerned French colonial-era conscription of labor for road building. Marriage patterns for Anti-Atlas people from past generations suggest more interconnections across hilltops as people walked mule paths through the terraced lands. Increasingly, however, mountain residents came to rely on *lḥdid* (Ar. ḥdid, lit. iron; vehicles) for transportation – and thus asphalted roads – and many footpaths were abandoned, no longer cleared, flattened and widened by foot and animal traffic. The new pistes (rocky dirt roads) redefined the interconnections between tribes, tribal fractions, and market centers. Yet the boundaries of a given homeland were never as fixed as French Protectorate administrators pretended.

If the Anti-Atlas mountains ever sustained the local population, no one I knew remembered those times. Reliance on home-grown grain, however, diminished only over the course of the last generation. Oral remembrances indicate that residents used to keep small vegetable plots of carrots, turnips, and lentils in addition to the staple crop of barley. Yet documented rainfall averages over the past century do not support this recollection; during the drought of 1936–7, emigration towards urban areas reached historic numbers (Swearingen 1987; Hoisington 1984:85). Dependence on other market goods and on migrant work remittances goes further back. The first documentation on the Ida ou Zeddout, a tribal report (*fiche de tribu*) circulated by Native Affairs officer Clement in 1949, notes that as early as the 1920s local men engaged in long-distance trading and commerce to ensure their families' survival. Roads and transportation facilitated both male emigration to the cities and their easy return to the homelands. Road building went hand in hand with military and political conquest from 1912 through 1934 as France brought the final dissenting tribes into its sphere of administration and control. Roads spurred the out-migration of Anti-Atlas men, a process that radically reshaped the region's political economic system which, in turn, shaped a shift in language practices and language ideologies.

By the 1990s, the procurement, delivery, and payment for household staples were organized and relatively reliable. The system's smooth functioning depended at every step of the way on men, although its primary beneficiaries were women and children. Mail, food staples, and fresh produce from the cities were delivered to rural market centers. Each cluster of villages had one or two men who crucially linked villagers to goods and information. Drivers of small trucks served as intermediaries between the inhabitants of Ida ou Zeddout and its surrounding tribes and the emigrants living in Casablanca and Marrakesh. Migrant men in Casablanca periodically boxed supplies of canned fish, soap, and flour for delivery to their village households; some sent four-foot tall woven baskets of vegetables. The truck drivers turned a good profit, according to women, who occasionally expressed their bitter resignation at the drivers' exigencies and erratic schedules. Each driver serviced a set of villages and occasionally kin in other locations, and he delivered goods directly to the villages or dropped them off in the Ida ou Zeddout market hub of Walqadi for distribution. Migrants in France assigned a family member in a Moroccan city to procure household goods. The foreign emigrant sent a money order to an urban-dwelling relative, or deposited the funds into a Moroccan bank account. Emigrants who visited the village assessed whether goods indeed arrived and what might still be needed, then they reported back to the Casablanca relatives to order further shipments. Emigrants also brought goods with them when they visited their homeland.

This system secured the basic household necessities for most mountain dwellers. Little has been written about the influx of consumer goods into Anti-Atlas households, with the few sources describing material and architectural changes that migrant revenues have facilitated. Alahyane (1990), for example, argues that migrant remittances have altered what he calls "traditionally tribal" communities. As the migrants periodically return to their villages with gifts, both domestic aesthetics and architectural styles change. In addition, these gifts bring about further mutations in rural dwellers' economic interactions with the cities, although Alahyane does not consider means other than gifts through which goods enter the villages. For example, rural women are more likely to save the few almonds from their own trees to sell at market when they can serve their guests market-bought peanuts and hard cookies. This introduction of material goods, Alahyane contends, has fueled rural girls' dreams of marrying into an easier urban life. Men I spoke with, however, found that young village women were increasingly less appealing marriage partners because their austere living conditions and rural laboring had not prepared them for the high standards of household cleanliness expected from urban Moroccan wives. The seduction of television, powered in many places by solar-charged batteries, exacerbated young women's frustrations according to Alahyane (1990), for it neither responded to rural needs nor reflected the non-Arab half of the Moroccan population. As a result, young women failed to situate themselves in the Moroccan national public, yet they longed to experience the world beyond the village they inhabited.

Financially successful migrant workers have tended to announce their prosperity by building ostentatious, colorful cement-block homes in their native villages. Yet the visibility of such signs of rural gentrification obfuscate the more mundane contours of the countryside's dependence on urban centers. While Alahyane usefully identifies material goods introduced into Anti-Atlas communities as their populations have shifted from subsistence horticulture and pastoralism to migrant revenue-dependence, he overlooks the persistent socioeconomic diversity of mountain communities, perhaps even exacerbated by the wealth of some among them. In the Ida ou

Zeddout section where I worked, for instance, there were two stone homes for every cinder block house under construction. Cinder block rarely replaced stone altogether, but rather seemed to creep up around the village edges. Some of the massive villas built over the past two decades comfortably housed three generations and seated 500 wedding guests. Yet the literal stone core of each village remained inhabited, each wall melding into the next, with roofs of varying ages, their wood-burning stove holes topped with the chipped lids of clay ṭajin cookware, fastened to rock and mud, punctuating the village's sky line. Indeed, the newer villas are further distinguishable from the stone core by their non-contiguous placement relative to other village homes and from shared spaces such as the mosque, storage units, and animal pens.

Several Ishelhin explained to me that if only villages were equipped with urban conveniences such as electricity and running water, fewer men would flock to the cities. Others directed my attention to the countryside's advantages: exhaust-free air, neighborly familiarity, and distance from the urban plagues of drugs, alcohol, prostitution, and juvenile delinquency. From the perspective of the men moving between the tamazirt and the city, life was improving in the countryside in numerous ways. Older men recalled the days of dissidence (*siba*), inter-tribal warring, brutal qayds, famine, illness, nakedness, and widespread ignorance about religion.[14] Older women – those who remained in the tamazirt – recalled those times as well, yet they did not contrast them optimistically with the present as did men. Carrying out their tammara day in and day out was still oppressive to women; they told me they were becoming less patient for its rewards.

Conclusion

The Ishelhin among whom I worked were aware that their relationship to their ancestral land was loaded (symbolically and morally) and contingent (materially and demographically). Appadurai calls the making of locality "an inherently fragile social achievement" (1996:179). Yet the persistence of locality-making in the Anti-Atlas mountains, through moving and dwelling, suggests that the arrangement might not have been so fragile. It was, however, highly contested – and highly orchestrated, as the mixed-sex zerdas demonstrate.

A question I often heard mountain residents, both women and men, ask visitors to their villages, whether foreign anthropologists or urban relatives, was "*is tšwa tmazirt*?" ("Is the tamazirt good/nice?" or "Do you like it here?"). Although rather abstract, the query suggested to me that tamazirt was different from other places, and as such, deserved assessment. If the visitor responded in the affirmative, the resident sometimes laughed, maybe pointing to a burn on her wrist or a rip in her clothing or uttering a list of all that the countryside lacked: faucets, electricity, rest, schooling. Posed by tamazirt dwellers, then, the question appeared rhetorical – the resident expected a negative response. Yet it may also have been a phatic plea for assurance that the countryside, its women, and their language would not be forgotten by those who tested their fates elsewhere, those they sustained morally and on whom they depended materially.

Chapter 5

Voicing the Homeland: Objectification, Order, Displacement

Allah ukbar a ddunit tkufrmt
ar ukan taṭṭat bnadm waxxa suln
Oh world, I swear, you heathen
You separate people while they're still alive
– Ida ou Zeddout tazrrart

Mother: *manis idda baba?*
Where has Father gone?
Toddler: *baba bayḍa*
Father [went to] Casablanca

With male emigration common since the 1920s, mountain communities have long accommodated practices of moving into their sense of self and community, as well as into their discursive strategies for managing persons, places, and the relationship between them. This was not only an impersonal empirical fact: it was reinforced as an understanding through practices that naturalized it. Adult women in the Anti-Atlas socialized children from a young age to know that their fathers were away in the city. I often saw mothers play question and answer games that drew on the child's early ability to pronounce the sounds *b* and *d*, the two consonants of *dar bayḍa* (Casablanca), with or without the *idda baba* (and without the conjunction *s-* or "to" she will learn to prefix to placenames). While children raised in the mountains rarely saw their fathers, the father's presence and authority were repeatedly invoked by wives, daughters, and daughters-in-law.

For emigrant men, it was the distance from urbanity, as well as the requisite *tammara* (hard labor), that made a place a tamazirt. Among those emigrants who objectified a singular tamazirt, there were gradations between timizar. An assessment offered by one young emigrant illustrates this point. Returning from the village of Tikiwin where he had attended all-night wedding festivities, the young man exclaimed, "Tikiwin: now that's a tamazirt! It has a great view (Arabic mandar), a two-and-a-half hour walk by foot from the road, no truck access, perched on a steep hill." The village of Tikiwin fit his perception of what a tamazirt should be – difficult to access, with a beautiful view. (It was in the mountains, after all.) It was a hard land where, nonetheless, people still gathered socially and sanctioned the collective representation of their homeland as such.

By locating timizar on an implicit continuum between city and country, the young man used a discursive distancing mechanism unfamiliar to most rural-dwelling women. There was a gendered difference in what men and women considered the qualities of a tamazirt, and gendered discourses for expressing them, marked more because of the different ways men and women engaged with the countryside than with anything inherent in the sex/gender system (Rubin 1975). In this sense, then, gendered discursive practices were indexical of placements in space more than biological constitution. For the young emigrant, "traditional" practices and accessibility were characteristics that made Tikiwin a tamazirt. For women, a tamazirt was instead characterized by those people who filled it up, their relations (blood or affective) to other families, the quality and quantity of hard labor that life there entailed, villagers' styles of dress, speech, and food – how the place felt up close. For women, there was no relative scale of tamazirtness; any occupied, named place in the mountains was a tamazirt. The term itself had a neutral valuation in women's usage. Male emigrants and female agriculturalists were differently linked to the material realities of the land. Not surprisingly, they had different conceptual frameworks for understanding both what constituted the tamazirt and ways of talking about it. In this chapter, I examine gendered song and talk to explore discourse about the tamazirt in two related senses: discourse as a cultural domain of knowledge (Foucault 1990 [1978]), and discourse as a way of talking (Sherzer 1987). What follows explores male and female senses of place as mediated through the modalities of talk and song.

In Raymond Williams' classic *The Country and the City* (1973), the distinction of the country(side) as an entity apart from the city is a byproduct of capitalism. His case study is England, and he traces the history of the country–city dichotomy through depictions of both country and city as they emerge in literature from the fifteenth century. The kind of nostalgia for a lost bucolic past that typifies turn-of-the-century writings on the countryside accompanied dramatic shifts in European agricultural economies.[1] Williams suggests that further studies of country and city should be done for places outside of England, but that the commonalities between English rural history and the contexts that postcolonial novelists describe suggest a common, universal place-making history of capitalist expansion. The case of the post-Protectorate Anti-Atlas mountains supports this facet of Williams' argument while necessitating a gender dimension that Williams overlooks. Williams rightly compares nostalgia for a lost rural past with the mourning of the passing of childhood. In this sense, it is fitting that men who left the tamazirt at adolescence sensed the most nostalgia for it. Those who did not undergo such physical distancing – women, most notably – did not yearn for earlier times, because for them there was no break in the developmental time that they could map onto distinct rural and urban places.

The exploitation of one social group by another – here, of land-dwelling women by landowning men – allowed for the construction of a social order where tamazirt could figure centrally. The self-conscious observer, Williams argues, has an enduring history, incarnate in the young emigrant who returned from the "real" tamazirt on a steep hill (presumably contrasted with his own village's gentle slopes) to tout its authenticity. A quick glance at the multiple timizar suggests some of the economic variability that Williams writes characterizes the countryside at any given moment. How can we understand the concept of a singular, unified tamazirt when its inhabitants participate in strikingly different political economies, with different land tenure systems, and consequently experience the countryside so differently? Moreover, how does an individual's gender further delimit the range of practices that alternately challenge and reproduce exploitation in the countryside? Williams poses the question of land tenure in terms of modes of production that pertain between landowners and tenant farmers, yet his analysis presumes that the rural resident or laborer was male. He mentions women in passing without considering how gender affects participation in the construction and reproduction of the countryside. For Ishelhin at the end of the twentieth century, gender was the primary identity marker that conditioned a person's engagement with country and city.

Understandings of place may rise to the level of discursive consciousness in metaculture (culture about culture) (Urban 2001) when triggered by an apparent contrast. This is clear in the following exchange taken from my fieldnotes of September 1997. A high school-educated father who worked in the northern city of Khouribga took a break from videotaping the *aḥwaš* collective song and dance performance in the cleared space behind the village by the dry river. The occasion was the marriage of a young Ida ou Zeddout woman to a young man from a village alongside the paved road.[2] The father, in his thirties, asked me what I thought of the aḥwaš and the tamazirt in general. Usually I would have responded with a phatic remark about liking it, a remark intended to build solidarity more than to offer an assessment. Instead, I told him that I thought the tamazirt was complicated (*taɛqd*). He responded, "Well, you're only interested in tradition (*taqalid*), in customs (*adat*), not in what's modern (εsri), right?" I said that no, I don't see customs as something stored in a freezer; he followed this allusion. I continued, "With so much movement between the city and country, the villages don't seem so isolated." He said, "But people in the tamazirt are very interested in *l'autenticité*," using the French term. He clasped his hands together and smiled, saying "Tight, they hold onto their customs tight." We looked out at the dancing young women as he took up his video camera again and I wondered silently, are these young women holding tight to their customs, considering this is all they know? Perhaps it is more as Sadiqi notes, that men are the ones who "cling to their indigenous traditions, but assign the responsibility to guard those traditions to women" (Sadiqi 2003:229). From this perspective, the father was not just recording his daughter's participation in the collective song and dance, but was also creating a document that attested to the women and girls' fulfillment of this responsibility.

Participants in this event were disparately placed relative to metaculture, but they were all engaged in producing it. The resident village girls and women performed for the group, and the videotaping father, one of several at the event, captured the performance on videotape to play and replay for family and friends in Khouribga. The videotaping allowed the father to make a cultural artifact about a cultural practice that he experienced already as an artifact. The father assessed that participation in the women's collective agwal was limited to those who held tight to their customs, rather than considering the residency requirement that more commonly delimited inclusion and exclusion (Hoffman 2002a). Absent from his interpretation were the intricacies of the social negotiations over not only who performed, but also how, what, and according to whom – all dynamics that, from a local resident's perspective, may have taken precedence over an embodied desire to perpetuate ancestral ways.

As people grounded their fortunes less exclusively in one place, the *concept* of place, and more specifically of a homeland, became more discursively developed and symbolically loaded. The homeland as symbol was increasingly objectified or "thingified" (Taussig 1992) by rural–urban emigrants, who were primarily but not exclusively men, turning the homeland into a discursive construction as much as a geographical location. Amazigh activists in Morocco and abroad, as well as Radio Agadir programming in Tashelhit, presented and represented the Tashelhit-speaking community to itself and to Arab Moroccans, drawing heavily on images and sounds from the countryside to do so. In rural areas, residents were more discerning of differences between villages and tribal subsections. Only more recently have Ishelhin begun developing solidarity with other Imazighen whose first language is not Arabic (Crawford and Hoffman 2000; Silverstein and Crawford

2004; Ouakrime 2001). Discursive representations of an objectified homeland in the media, school texts and everyday discourse influenced how rural dwellers outside of direct urban and state influence understood the constitution of their local identity and the boundaries of their community. That is, the objectification of the homeland entailed a concurrent process of subjectification (Heidegger 1977), meaning that Ishelhin became part of the tamazirt at the same time that the tamazirt became part of what it meant to be Ashelhi. In this nexus between the self and the world, the tamazirt became meaningful, through the care with which Ishelhin linked here and there, and joined the present with both the past and the future. With this perspective in mind – that people in out-of-the-way places apply their own logics to puzzle through broader social and political economic processes – we can explore how cultural and linguistic assimilation of Ishelhin into an urban, Arabic-speaking citizenry was far from inevitable, at least for those who maintained ties to the tamazirt. It was not only material and personal ties to a tamazirt that fueled men's nostalgia. The discursive construction of tamazirt – as a concept even more than a place – was likewise responsible.

Emigrant men were more prone to objectify a singular and unitary homeland, whereas year-round mountain residents (primarily women) used the term tamazirt to reference an inhabited land or a place which could be as small as a hamlet or as large as a foreign nation-state (such as *lmaġrb*, Morocco; *marikan*, America or *fransa*, France). What emigrant men talked about as *the* tamazirt was for year-round residents a highly diversified conglomeration of multiple timizar, multiple inhabited places. One village girl made this clear to me when she called out names of villages visible from the hillside where we walked; even the next village over was "another tamazirt," provided people considered it substantively distinct in its social relations, material practices, or topography.

Women and men used sung and spoken registers to express contradictory attitudes towards the tamazirt in general and specific timizar in particular. Normative conventions governed the stances towards rural lands that were integral to each verbal genre and condoned by members of each gender. The dissonant discourses among Ishelhin operated much as did the twin discourses noted by Abu-Lughod for the Awlad Ali people of the Egyptian Western Desert, whose spoken discourse stressed modesty and strength and whose poetic discourse permitted talk about vulnerability and love (Abu-Lughod 1986). Like the Egyptian Bedouins, among the Ida ou Zeddout one discourse was not truer than another. Rather, Zeddouti discourses comprised a communicative and conceptual repertoire from which individuals drew to express ambivalent language ideologies about their dwelling places, their language, and the cultural and material practices associated with both.

Figure 5.1 Singing tizrrarin at a wedding, Ida ou Zeddout

Tamazirt in Song

Just as Ishelhin distinguished between conversational speech (*tjmmaεt*) and meaningful speech (*lmεana*) (El Mountassir 1992), they also construed singing (*lhawa, lεb*) as something apart from and more valuable than conversational speech. The contrast in part shaped the ways people distinguished everyday life (*tudrt*) from extra-ordinary festive events (*timġriwin*, sing. *tamġra*, or *lfṛḥ*). Broadly speaking, life for year-round residents of the Sous Valley and Anti-Atlas mountains was a balancing act between two extremes of human existence: hard labor (tammara) and the play (*lhawa*) that often involved music. In moments of transition, most notably weddings, "having something to say" (*illa dars ma ittini*) took on elevated importance. Collective identity was publicly displayed in these contexts, in contrast to the practices of concealing knowledge prevalent in other discursive domains.

Women singing the tamazirt

Ida ou Zeddout women talked informally, at least with outsiders like myself and by their own reckoning with each other, about how much they wanted to flee their hard labor for the conveniences of Casablanca. But their public, sung voicings on the tamazirt implied no urban counterpoint. That is, in song, tamazirt simply meant "place" or "land" and had to be qualified further. An example from my fieldnotes of August 1996 is suggestive.

On the day before an Ait Musi wedding, around eighty women and girls gathered at the groom's parents' home for dinner after their evening walks. The courtyard was lined on three sides with long plastic mats, and the women sat with girls and infants scattered in front. Zayna, a fair-haired 12-year-old girl in a faded navy tamlḥaft approached me with a playmate. I addressed them in Tashelhit, and Zayna smiled and looked away, uttering her name. The bolder friend was the only female at the wedding dressed in a multicolored urban-style caftan with a gilded belt rather than the tamlḥaft. She declared to me in Moroccan Arabic, with her hands on her hips, "I don't understand Tashelhit." I wasn't sure if she was posturing in front of the foreign guest, acting *šširki* (Fr. *chic* or putting on airs) by stressing her ignorance, or whether she was an outsider to the festivities perhaps invited by her fair-haired friend, and so I asked her who she came with. She said her aunt brought her down from Casablanca, pointing to a woman dressed in a black tamlḥaft, black net scull cap, cloth head covering and red tie wrapped high around her forehead in the custom of the year-round residents. "Tashelhit is so heavy," she continued. "It's hard. But Arabic is easy, it flows. You can say what you want in it, the words come easily. Not like Tashelhit. You can't talk so easily in Tashelhit. Tashelhit is ugly (xayba)." Her aunt jumped in, leaning forward towards the girl, "*You're* xayba, you don't even know your language." She switched to Tashelhit and turned towards us, "She's just like the other kids in Casablanca. They don't even know where they're from. Look at her," pointing to her niece, by then seated with her legs tucked to the side and her calves exposed, "She doesn't even wear pants under her dress. She runs around naked like they do in the city." I turned to Zayna and asked her, "Is Tashelhit xayba?" She smiled and looked down again, shaking her head from side to side to indicate disagreement. After dinner a short while later, Zayna pulled me aside as we waited outside the house for the aḥwaš group singing and dancing to start. "Tashelhit isn't ugly," she said, "I like it. My friend just says that because she doesn't understand it." Both girls lived and attended school in Casablanca, but the fair one insisted that the tamazirt was better: "In the city all my friends talk about is school. In the village we talk about everything; it doesn't have to be important. And in the village, my friends don't lie. Sometimes it's hard because I want to write letters to them when I'm in Casa, and I can't because they can't read." She shrugged her shoulders: "So I just see them in the summer." Meanwhile, two dozen white tamlḥaft-clad teenagers and a few younger girls came out the front door and lined up in two semi-circles as the men warmed frame drums over the nearby fire. The girls started to sing a cappella, and Zayna repeated that she would not join the singing because she did not know the words. She joined the dancers anyway, but after a few tentative moments swaying with the others to the music, she retreated to the center blanket with the male drummers, and sat with her legs tucked beside her, pants under her dress concealing her calves, gazing at the resident girls as they sang.

Such interactions were common to the large summertime gatherings I attended over the years in which full-time mountain dwellers and urban residents, often of the same family, came together for vacation (*ɛuṭla*) and celebrations. In these gatherings, when the community performed itself back to itself, not everyone was equally authorized to voice the homeland through singing. They reconciled the comings and goings of community members, the interaction of schooled and unschooled, the confrontation of city and country.

Associations people make between places and languages engage moral economies and strings of associations – such as, in the view of the Arabic-speaking girl's aunt, an abiding disrespect that manifested not only in the girl's inability or unwillingness to speak Tashelhit, but also her alleged refusal to acknowledge "where she's from," and her immodesty in going barelegged rather than wearing the modest calf-length leggings (*ssrwal*) under her skirts. Zayna could not fully participate in the agwal, not because she refuted her Tashelhit roots, and not because she couldn't speak Tashelhit. (She could.) Despite her Tashelhit fluency and appropriately modest behavior and dress, she lacked the requisite communicative competence (Hymes 1972) that comes with full-time residence in the mountains. Knowing "where she's from" – having a sense of place – is an activity that is lived collectively, not just felt individually. Basso states, "Relationships to place are lived most often in the company of other people, and it is on these communal occasions – when places are sensed *together* – that native views of the physical world become accessible to strangers" (1996:109). His view echoes Boas' conviction that places are social constructions *par excellence* (Boas 1934 in Basso 1996:74).

Here I want to turn briefly to consider representations of these social constructions as found in women's community song I recorded among the Ida ou Zeddout between 1996 and 1999. The verses here were improvised to suit the context, combining fixed forms and creative inspiration, and

Figure 5.2 Wedding guests arrive from the bride's village at dusk, Ida ou Zeddout

performed by women who lived in the tamazirt year-round (Hoffman 2002b). The Ida ou Zeddout sung verses engaged contexts – histories of people, places, and gathering occasions – as much as they indexed earlier performances from similar occasions. Community song provided women an opportunity for socially condoned commentary on community identity, place, and morality. Such genres of folk music, Lomax observes, "produce a feeling of security for the listener by voicing the particular quality of a land and the life of its people" (Lomax 1960:xv in Bohlman 1988:52) – or at least, here, the female people of the lands.

Not surprisingly, "tamazirt" appeared frequently in the women's community song I recorded – indeed, this was in large part how I became interested in it as a key cultural theme. Verses signal *a* tamazirt and not *the* tamazirt, where the indefinite article *a* indexes a neutral use of the term, in contrast to the definite article *the* that points to an affect-loaded concept. Definite and indefinite articles are not necessarily marked directly in Tashelhit, but must be inferred from surrounding words and context. For example, the first verse below warns that one should pause before entering a tamazirt "until the people of that tamazirt welcome you there." Here the term *ayt tamazirt* refers to the inhabitants of a village or place, the owners of the land on which one should not trespass. In that sense, the verse refers to an individuated tamazirt and not to the countryside in general. Clearer yet was a verse in which the vocalist took the voice of the new bride, plaintively observing that she was given to a land where she knew no one and had no one to show her around. We can presume that this bride moved from one rural village to another, and not from the city to an undifferentiated countryside. Such contextual cues hint at female vocalists' reference to different timizar as distinct from one another, and at the particularities that evoke homesickness in a new bride.

I recorded the following *tizrrarin* (sung verses; sing. *tazrrart*)[3] at sunset during wedding festivities in August and September 1997 while women sat in a domestic courtyard waiting for coffee and, later, for dinner. The first verse was sung just after the arrival of women from the bride's village; they indicated publicly yet subtly that they had not been welcomed with coffee. The verse drew on an Anti-Atlas aphorism on normative guest behavior:

iġ ilkm yan imi n tmazirt irard aḍaṛ	If you arrive at the edge of a land pull back your foot
ard as nnan ayt tmazirt mrḥba srk	until the people of that land welcome you

In the following verses as well, each sung separately, tamazirt referred to particular hamlets or clusters of villages:

fṛḥan lɛtubat n tmazirt	The paths to the tamazirt are happy
han angbi ikšm d imawn nnsnt	Guests have passed through their gateways
haya g^{w}ma tamazirt lli saġ nnan	Oh brother, here is the tamazirt they told us about
iga gis ujddig n flayu taffiwin	There are bundles of peppermint flowers [virgins]
bismillah iga win iġ ira yan	Bismillah is for when one is going
akk^{w} nt iffġ a tamazirt ikšm i ṭayaḍ	to leave you, oh tamazirt, [and] enter another

In the following verse, a grandmother in her mid-fifties took the voice of the bride:

ha iyyi fkiġ i tmizar ur xaliḍġ	Here I am, given to an unfamiliar tamazirt
ur iyyi gis baba ula immi qnḍġ	My father isn't here, my mother isn't here, I'm lonely
ur iyyi gis id dadda maġ immaln	There's no older brother to guide me

The most significant move most women undertook was from their parents' home to their groom's home. Marriage in rural Morocco was more about this change of residence than about romance. The common Tashelhit way of saying "She is going to marry a boy from Tililit [village]" was *tra*

Tililit, literally "She wants Tililit" and meaning "She is going to Tililit."[4] The theme of movement was reflected in wedding verses, reinforced by their being sung while moving and in liminal moments such as during the bridal procession.

a ṛbbi bqqa ɛlaxir iga win iġ ira yan	"Be well" is for when one is going
akk^{w} nt iffġ a tamazirt ikšem i ṭayaḍ	to leave you, oh tamazirt, and enter another

In the following verse, another woman from the groom's village addressed the bride, urging her to relax now that the day she had anticipated had arrived:

a ġilli s bdda tddit lġrḍ inu	The place that has always been your destiny
a hati tlkmt t id a taft ṛṛaḥt	is where you've arrived; be at peace

The following verses do not mention lands *per se*, but rather refer to the movement involved in marrying and the accompanying mix of thrill and apprehension. Sung by mothers and grandmothers, the verses offer consolation to the young bride:

zayd a awddi zayd ukk^{w}an	Go on, my dear, go on
imma larzaq ad llan dar mulay ṛbbi	Still fate is in the Lord's hands
ar ttawin yan s illin ur itam	It takes you where you never imagined
ullah amkd usiġ aḍar a illiġ nssn	I swear I won't lift my foot until we know
is ur inxlf ġid d lmakan inu	that here is no different from my place[5]

In the first verse above, movement is divinely ordained – a common theme in Anti-Atlas sung and spoken discourse about geographical displacement. The second verse, sung by an older woman from the bride's village, assures the bride that women are looking out for her best interests, even if she will no longer be in their company. The last verse above was sung by a woman in the groom's village, addressing the bride, acknowledging what was commonly understood to be the bride's desire to marry a man from a distant village in order to experience a new land, something that seemed unattainable. The verse's implication is bittersweet, however. One local young woman explained its meaning: once you've drunk from a stream, do you remember that you were parched before you drank? Or rather, as this metaphor alludes, once you've moved far away from your people, will you remember how you ached to travel? The question is rhetorical, but there is reassurance nonetheless in the acknowledgment. Elsewhere I have distinguished between the social functions performed through the verbal genres of talking and singing (Hoffman 2000a). Here I examine a subsection of sung voicings that are part of a larger normative moral order in which men and women have differential license to publicly express attitudes towards a/the tamazirt as a point of allegiance and place in which to dwell.

The tizrrarin verses singled out here from an ever-changing repertoire were among scores strung together over the course of a single wedding night. The verses shared not only the theme of relocation, or mention of tamazirt, but an articulation of community boundaries. They exemplify common verses sung during the summer wedding season. Such stylized verbal expression engages themes of movement and dwelling found in more mundane conversation, evoking competing normative moral universes. This is not to reify the false distinction between too-loosely identified "formal" and "informal" genres. Ethnographic descriptions of public oratory suggest that the difference lies more in the extent to which events or interactions are rule-governed. A woman in the groom's village may sing to the new bride, "Find your rest." But as Lalla Aisha demonstrated in her advice to the bride Saadia in Transcript 4.1, the young bride was expected to behave otherwise, to follow other commands: "Shut your mouth. Watch. Pay attention."

Men's song: "arranging" countryside and city in song

The gendered discursive constitution of place distinguished men's song from the women's songs I have just discussed. In men's aḥwaš collective song and dance and the accompanying sung verses (*tinḍḍamin*, sing. *tanḍḍamt*), men were granted license to sing about tamazirt as an object of discursive analysis. One example strikingly illustrates this license. During an August 1997 aḥwaš wedding performance in Ida ou Zeddout by a group of men from neighboring Ida ou Knsus, the sung refrain was "*tama tamazirt/amarg amarg ay*," linking homeland (tamazirt) and music/mood/longing (*amarg*). Stringing these two concepts together was telling, because the tamazirt was precisely a place of amarg, of music and nostalgia. Each person brings his/her own amarg to an encounter or a space. The phrase "The amarg of my homeland pains me" (*yaġ iyi amarg n tmazirt*) means that I long for my homeland. Ishelhin also say "your amarg pains me" (*yaġ iyi amarg nm/nk*) implying that your absence hurts or more simply put, "I miss you." Galand-Pernet brings the word amarg back to its root, w-r-g, "to dream," from which the word amarg would mean "that which brings together dreams" or "the realm of visions, the play of imagination, of illusions" (Galand-Pernet 1987 in Rovsing Olsen 1997:30). In the wedding refrain, amarg was a mood, a music, a dream, not simply a conglomeration of clapping hands, legs and shoulders pressed together and swaying in unison, heads alternatively held high to call out verses then chins down to the ground as to wait through the call's response. Together, the words baldly celebrated the intertwined tamazirt and amarg that brought the men to the gathering in the first place, linking two identificatory symbols absent in their emigrant lives in northern Arab cities.

While it may seem that the residency requirement for voicing the tamazirt was waived for men, where emigrants featured prominently, the best male *inḍḍamn* (sing. *anḍḍam*, lit. "orderer" [of words] or dueling poet) were considered to be resident men, as I will explain shortly. While young women sang about the displacement marriage brings, young emigrant men's music took the form of easily transportable cassette-recordings. In form and content, this commercial music mediated between city and countryside. In this section of the chapter, I examine one genre, the tanḍḍamt, and the ways in which it resembled and departed from the live performances of tinḍḍamin that punctuated the collective song and dance of the men's drum-accompanied aḥwaš in the Anti-Atlas. I focus on discourses of displacement and social identity in one recorded tanḍḍamt, where the moral quandaries the lyrics suggest are endemic to migration and city living for the Ashelhi young men.

Physically moving between the city and countryside, and within a sex-gender system in which a man's absence was part of his presence in the homeland, men's voices mediated the experience of economic and social displacement. Young Ashelhi men dominated the market for tinḍḍamin cassettes. For young men aspiring to take the floor as inḍḍamn at weddings, moussems, and other large public gatherings in the countryside, commercial recordings as well as live performances served as models for their own compositions. What mattered to listeners was neither the source of the sung poetry, nor the extent to which it mirrored a live performance. The truth value, cleverness, and aesthetic qualities of the sung verse were more important, combined in the person who "has something to say" (*illa dars ma ittinin*).

Sung poetry was particularly valued by young emigrants, as the poetic exchanges were directly related to their own preoccupations: spatial displacement, masculinity, and morality. Social identity informed by the migration experience was a central theme that young emigrant men found meaningful in tinḍḍamin sung poetry. While in Casablanca, young men listened to what these inḍḍamn, originally from the Sous or still residing there, pronounced about life there or about collectively held values or even national or social politics. Traffic, gendarme corruption, administrative bribery, and sexual crimes committed by a high-ranked police commissioner in Casablanca were among the events on which inḍḍamn commented in the late 1990s. When they returned to their villages, young men listened to these recordings when they gathered, and many memorized the lyrics. Some composed their own. Unlike young women, young men rarely sang out on public occasions, although they might join the aḥwaš chorus backing up the more established and older inḍḍamn. As with the Khawlani balah performers Caton (1990) describes from Yemen, the Anti-Atlas inḍḍamn authorized to participate in poetry duels were typically married men from the community who positioned themselves as central to rural affairs, even if they lived most of the year in the city.

Marginal to the economy in Casablanca, young emigrant men developed new social networks with their co-workers and sometimes, with time and inclination, their fellow villagers. As often as not, however, cassettes and their annual or bi-annual return to the village were their most solid links with what most of them continued to consider their laṣl, their roots and ultimately, the allegiances that shaped their economic conditions. Many of the young men who felt pride in this musical genre slept on makeshift mattresses in the back closets of the stores in which they worked. During their first years, they often worked as unpaid apprentices for their employers in the hopes that eventually the owner would compensate them with a daily, weekly, or monthly salary rather than an annual "bonus" they could take home to their mothers (usually a 200 dirham, or $20, bill, which prompted laughter from a mother over its insignificance). Some commercial and non-commercial inḍḍamn poet-singers lived in towns for much of the year. Few "real men" lived in the villages year-round, for one who "is a man" (*igan argaz*) is honest, provides materially for his family, stands up for his interests, and makes decisions rather than letting a mother or wife make them. There was a widely accepted link between maleness, economic success, and toughness that put wealthy merchant emigrants on top of a social hierarchy.

When it came to male singer-poets, then, these links created a tension. Men who lived in the cities commanded authority in their homelands, but living in the tamazirt helped an amateur anḍḍam to develop his skills. As one young rural-dwelling anḍḍam in his late twenties from Ida ou Naḍif, Mhand El Moussaoui (an excerpt from whose first cassette opens Chapter 4), explained to me:

> If they [inḍḍamn] live in the city, they don't know *awal* (talk, words) any longer. They get Tashelhit mixed up with Arabic. It's better for them to stay back in the village. If they live in the city they won't know how to talk, for example, about plowing (*tayrza*), about harvesting (*tamgra*); they won't know the condition of the tamazirt (*lḥal n tmazirt*).

In his view, the poet needs to know more than the language with its grammatical and lexical elements. He needs communicative competence, and he needs to know the concerns of rural people and their "condition" – that is, he should be the kind of journalist expected of bards in many societies with their specialized knowledge and vocabulary. How can he comment on the affairs of the day without an intimate familiarity with life there? But knowledge was not sufficient. The anḍḍam's talent lay in his gift of quick-witted, spontaneous eloquence which he demonstrated in the course of verbal duels during live performances. What distinguished an anḍḍam was his originality, familiarity with the conditions of the tamazirt and ability to incorporate the community's shared agricultural and moral values into his verses. He also, however, needed to deliver a commentary on national or international events in the song's closing, called the *tamssust* (wrap-up, lit. shaking down, sweeping up). The audience also judged him by his ability to draw on metaphor, allusion, and word play in conveying the group's preoccupations without explicitly referring to them.

The tension, then, was that the linguistic skills and familiarity with the agricultural terminology required for a singer-poet's success could best be developed through rural residence. Rural male residents, however, commanded little social authority in their communities, regardless of the extent to which villagers relied on them for slaughtering or marketing. If men who were less financially fortunate set the standard for communicative or musical competence, there would be a shift in the symbolic value accorded to migration for men. The privilege of singing out tinḍḍamin verses in public aḥwaš performances was reserved for older men who were more established in the community, and among them, those who were more poetically adept than the average man. The practice required that its utterer have social capital, acquired either through economic capital (which in this community earned him symbolic capital) (Bourdieu 1977) or through a talent with words, symbolic capital acquired outside of the institutional setting of schools with which Bourdieu is most concerned (Bourdieu and Passeron 1970). It was not the words alone that commanded authority; the authority of the one who voiced them made them authoritative (Bourdieu 1991). A man who lacked symbolic capital and ventured a duel anyway was greeted with chuckles from the audience and soon retreated to the chorus, ceding his place to another more qualified contender.

When a well-known anḍḍam took the lead in arranging the verses in a live performance, other pretenders "picked up" (*ad ittasin*) verses in response, vying for the position of the suite's arranger. Young men did not call out unless specifically encouraged to do so by more senior men. The crowd listened attentively as smaller-time inḍḍamn attempted to usurp the leader's role. Tashelhit sung poetry was composed for specific occasions and on given themes. Anti-Atlas inḍḍamn varied in the level of their recognizability and their talent, but they were indeed specialists. Any man could participate in the collective song and dance of the aḥwaš chorus, but only the talented few dared take on the experienced poets in this spontaneous verbal dueling. There remained a significant difference with the Yemeni tribal *balah* song genre Caton describes, for he writes that "[Khawlani Yemeni] Poets are not specialists. They only do especially well what everyone else in the population ought to do as a matter of course" (1990:50). One of the effects that migration has on tribal Yemeni society, Caton argues (1990:267), is that

> young men forget the speech acts of tribal social intercourse, such as greetings and the challenge-and-retort routine, which we have seen to be the mainstay of performance poetry. Children do not have access to formal instruction in this art but must acquire it through direct experience of rhythm, rhyme, alliteration, and speech acts to be found in ordinary conversation. If young men are deprived of this early experience, they lack the training to compose very competently.

Younger Yemeni composers are more likely to stress the topic of the poem, and pay less attention to stylistic concerns.

The same seemed to have happened among younger Anti-Atlas men for whom cassette tinḍḍamin served as poetic models, who stressed the topic of the song more than its poetic structure or the spontaneity of a live performance. These verses punctuated the aḥwaš collective refrain. Rovsing Olsen captures the texture of the back and forth between the "poetic jousting" of the inḍḍamn and the chorus. She remarks that the chorus has the unusual responsibility to predict, "– in unison! – the end of a poet's effort" before collectively repeating the verse and giving the anḍḍam a rest (Rovsing Olsen 1997:38). The unison "spontaneous" chorus is only one source for collective musical productions to fall apart, and the singers keep it together, sometimes looking at each other for cues and other times looking impassively ahead. Men who participated in an aḥwaš may have been year-long village residents, but many were urban merchants who savored the opportunity to travel to other tribes and villages with the men from their village during a summer vacation (Schuyler 1979). The dance brought together subsistence farmers with wealthy merchants, local administrators, and unemployed educated young men. Male performers in aḥwaš groups ranged in age from their twenties to seventies, with the leader typically a man in his fifties who had been performing all of his life. The performance alternated between group singing and movement and pauses in the dancing in which male soloists, selected by the group leader, sang out verses.

The content of live tinḍḍamin verses was typically political commentary (on local elections, or state or police corruption), praises of the bride's or groom's family or village, mentioned by name, descriptions of the land from which the singers hailed, or news about geographic regions otherwise cut off from centers of information. Verses that were particularly catchy or clever got taken up in the young women's agwal that followed the aḥwaš. Young women no longer composed their own lyrics, they told me.

The *asays* performance circle among the Ida ou Zeddout was not meritocratic and indeed was more accepting of poets with social capital. Yet audiences were not so callous as to dismiss a clever anḍḍam who lacked status if he could think quickly and lyrically on his feet. The elderly blind itinerant egg vender who bought and sold from his donkey, for example, joined the asays at an Ida ou Zeddout wedding once. He offered what my companions considered well-composed and meaningful verses on how the heart guides when the eye does not see, responding to another anḍḍam's string of verses that used sight as a metaphor for knowledge. The audience and other inḍḍamn poets affirmed the roaming salesman's words as wise, encouraging his performance with verbal affirmations such as "it's true" (*lmaεqul*), "that's the way it is" (*ġikan ad igan*), and "he has something to say" (*illa dars ma ittini*). As a result, this man of normally low status occupied the proverbial and physical floor in the performance circle for several verses, until he exited of his own accord. Dueling poets more typically outwitted one another in an attempt to have the final say about the truth of human nature. Eventually in these duels one of the men called a truce. Each poet then offered his own tamssust, a longer set of uninterrupted verses closing the segment.

There were important differences between live performances by inḍḍamn and those of the cassette recording studio. Abdelmajid Araaman, a cassette seller in Taroudant who began recording inḍḍamn such as El Moussaoui and Al Qadiri on his label Voix Assabil in Agadir in the 1990s, explained to me that in live contexts poets find themselves facing other poets who try to outwit, shame, or speak more truthfully than them. A performer must think fast on his feet. He must also respond to the desires of the audience (*tasukt*; Ar. suq, lit. market). For this reason, the anḍḍam rarely repeats verses previously sung, unless they are considered part of a classical repertoire as proverbs are in many societies. When an anḍḍam did perform appropriated verses, he changed the melody so that he was not quoting musically as well as literally.

In contrast, the inḍḍamn who recorded in a studio planned and rehearsed their points and counter-points in advance, as well as the turn-taking with the aḥwaš chorus. The spontaneity and unpredictability of the live event were absent. According to Abdelmajid, "Just about anyone with the right connections can fill up a cassette. But in a live performance, the older, more established poets carefully screen those they allow into the asays." El Moussaoui described that when he debuted in the asays circles of the Igherm region, the older men only reluctantly accepted his interventions. With time, though, the older poets encouraged him to join their duels. Regardless of which men voiced tinḍḍamin verses, my point here is that they were granted a license to express uncertainty over their social lot and their timizar that is outside of women's permissible expression.

Displacement and Conflict in Men's Mass-mediated Tinḍḍamin

In mass-mediated tinḍḍamin, abstraction and objectification about placement and displacement in social identity paralleled that of the young migrant men I knew who bought and listened to the cassettes so avidly. Transcript 5.1 below is an excerpt from the commercially recorded tanḍḍamt the young emigrant men listened to in its entirety at the zerda in Chapter 3. The cassette was released sometime between 1996 and 1998 by two Soussi singer-poets, Omar Aznag and Hassan Ben Wakrim. The singers verbally assumed the roles of childhood friends, one of whom moved to the capital city of Rabat and the other who remained in the countryside. Through these roles, the men debated the relative virtues of rural and urban dwelling. Listeners accept the biographies of the two singers for the rhetorical purposes of the song only, but this does not diminish the song's truth value. The scenario evoked by the two poets is a familiar one: a migrant man leaves his homeland for the city and seems to forget his village-dwelling friend who used to keep him company. But this migrant is no simple greedy caricature, for he presents an argument as to why occupying the city is a way for Ishelhin to stand up to the Arabs who have historically predominated in the centers of power.

Hajja's 16-year-old son Mohamed worked through a preliminary Arabic-script transcription with me of the text below during one of his infrequent visits to Ida ou Zeddout in 1998. Mohamed emphasized that the words reflected the resignation men feel about finding that their tamazirt holds no future for them, but yet feeling its pull. This pull makes them keep their home, wives and young children in their native villages. The uncertainty the singers express towards the values of the Sous and the city merits exploration here. The two singer-poets represent different life paths Soussi men can take: working in commerce in a city or remaining in the countryside as a shepherd or wage laborer. Each of the singer-poets alternatively idealizes the other's position and yet justifies his personal choices. Here, the tanḍḍamt text is paused for clarification. Line phrasing here follows breath patterns; it thus appears uneven from one turn to the next.

Transcript 5.1: Tanḍḍamt: Omar Aznag and Hassan Ben Wakrim

Ben Wakrim, "migrant merchant":	
bismillah *ḍlbġ ṛbbi ad xiyyrn ass nnaġ*	Bismillah I ask God to make our day good
ad ur gis ddunub ad gin lḥasanat	So there won't be sins, there will be goodness
ad gim nttsllak a ddunit ar k^{w}nt nffġ	We'll get along with you, oh world, until we depart
Aznag, "mountain shepherd":	
ad gim nttsllak a ddunit ar k^{w}nt nffġ	We'll get along with you, oh world, until we depart

ya bismillah ra ddaġ nbiks ad kšmġ i ssuq	Bismillah we're getting ready [lit. tying our belts], I'm entering the circle
a bn wakrim a ttajir sslamuεlikum	Ah Ben Wakrim, oh merchant, hello to you
is mqqar k nsqsa a daġ tnnit lḥaq	Is it all right with you if we just ask for the truth
isahl d flak ṛbbi tammara tukik	God made your labors easy, you have no more troubles
mami trit imurig ad k^{w}n sul issiḥil	What do you want with amarg, why are you still concerned with it?

The song format is conventionally framed in both its opening and its closing. Ben Wakrim opens the song with a standard supplication to God for goodness and peace. He closes with a plea to his fellow anḍḍam to cease the debate. In between, starting with Aznag's response, each verse responds to the previous verse in theme and sometimes in word play with lyrics introduced by the other, the subtlety of which are lost somewhat in my colloquial translation. Aznag, then, also inserts himself in the market, or public song circle, and provokes his dueling partner Ben Wakrim by addressing him ("oh merchant") and questioning Ben Wakrim's participation in the verbal duel in the first place because of what he says is Ben Wakrim's easy city life: ". . . you have no more troubles / what do you want with this music, why are you still concerned with it?" That is, Aznag implies that the music and the mood that they are creating are particular to people in hard times, and inappropriate for those with a leisured life.

While the city dweller may express nostalgia about the amarg (music or mood-making) of the countryside, Aznag puts the nostalgia in the perspective of its quality as marker of Ashelhi identity. The listener understands that in this instance, to be Ashelhi entails certain disadvantages, especially poverty. Ben Wakrim responds not by questioning whether city dwellers should participate in amarg, but by confirming his modest situation:

Ben Wakrim, "migrant merchant":

εmar ajji daġ ljir ur iyi xṣṣan	Oh Omar give us a break, I don't need to be whitewashed
ur nra a iġ ittsbaġ ils nk ula afus nk	We don't want you to build us up
a mani ġ giġ ttajir ma aġ srs issn	Where am I a merchant? Who can attest that I am?
a han ur dar nġ lbank ula luṭlilat	Here we have no bank [account] or hotels

"Where am I a merchant?" Ben Wakrim asks. That is, he has not accumulated the wealth that would first be spent on a villa or other conspicuous consumables. Still, Ben Wakrim saves Aznag's face by suggesting that Aznag called him a "merchant" to "build him up," implicitly in the eyes of the others present. Aznag replies with a bone to pick:

Aznag, "mountain shepherd":

nkki ġayda nẓṛa ẓṛant akk^w *lxalayiq*	What we see is just what everyone has seen
as ak nniġ ur igi lḥal ak^w*n ṛšševmġ*	It's as I told you, the situation isn't fabricated
ġass lli gik ẓẓlḍ nstara kullu sus	When you were penniless we wandered the whole Sous
ġass ad iġ k^w*n riġ nbrrmawn tilifun*	Today if I want you (pl.), I have to phone

Ben Wakrim has become inaccessible, Aznag accuses, barring a phone appointment, even though he used to be so modest that they wandered the Sous together. Ben Wakrim responds with a slight, justifying his decision to leave the Sous as a search for something better, and he situates Aznag's decision to stay in the Sous as a futile effort in the age of modern technological pursuits:

Ben Wakrim, "migrant merchant":

awal iġ gan ṭṭnẓ ad tn ur ittini yat	If words are lies, it's better not to say anything
ṛẓmn irgazn ġ iggi n wayyur i ṣṣarux	Men send satellites to the moon
a sul a ukan tsiggilt aġaras n sus	You're still looking for the path to the Sous

Aznag then reiterates what Ben Wakrim understood from Aznag's opening verses: that Aznag is trying to flatter Ben Wakrim while Ben Wakrim is trying to put himself down.

Aznag, "mountain shepherd":

ar k nttal ar tsiggilt a xuya ad k nluḥ	We are building you up, brother but you're putting yourself down
awal ur gin ṭṭnẓ lsas a ftn usiġ	Words aren't lies, a [solid] foundation they're built on
wa yak lɛaṣima a ġn tlla takat nk	Right? the capital [Rabat] is where your home is

By employing the idea that awal (talk or words, implying truthful words) is at the root of communication – a frequently recurring language ideology in Tashelhit song – Aznag attempts to bolster his own credibility, and returns to the idea that Ben Wakrim lives in Rabat. Ben Wakrim confirms that Rabat is indeed where he lives, and justifies his decision to be there rather than in the Sous. His words are scornful:

Ben Wakrim, "migrant merchant":

nlla ġ lɛaṣima giġ gisnt alaxir	The capital is where we live, I am well there
a flġ ak Sus ili gisn ar k nit issus	I left you the Sous; stay in it until it shakes you out
iskr nit gik jjuɛ askiwn ḥrranin	It even made you hungry, [made you grow] bitter horns

This is a terribly unnostalgic depiction of the implications of difficult living conditions on the Soussi's fundamental well-being (hunger) and sociability (difficult personality). The phrase "*fld ġ ak Sus ili gisn ar k nit issus*" is a play on words: the Sous (*Sus*) shakes you out in the way you shake out (*issus*) insects and crumbs from a blanket before lying down on it to sleep. The "you" is singular, addressed to Aznag, attempting to account for Aznag's bitterness towards his dueling partner. Aznag responds with equal venom, letting Ben Wakrim know that the people in tamazirt also do not want him there, for when he was there, times were bad: perhaps he was responsible.

Aznag, "mountain shepherd":

wa dduɛa nga tin s ṛbbi ukan a tt ikmml	We're pleading to God to fulfill our wish
a k^{w}*n yasi ġ tmazirt a k ur nttannay*	to take you away from tamazirt altogether so we won't have to see you
ġass lli ġ gis tḥaḍarm ad kkiġ afus	The day you (pl.) were around, I was in hard times
ibbi n unẓar ssrbis illa f lxnšat	The rain stopped, [there were] lines for [ration] sacks

Go away, Aznag effectively urges: you carry misfortune. Having risked insulting his own ancestors, Ben Wakrim suggests that "those who bore us" bear no blame for the way things turned out; there was nothing they could have done to prevent the situation. Instead, "Arabs grabbed all the best cities," leaving Ishelhin to the mountains where they lived among animals:

Ben Wakrim, "migrant merchant":	
aw ukan irḥm ṛbbi willi aġ urunin	May God be merciful on those who bore us
iġwi waɛrab lmudun kullu xiyrnin	Arabs grabbed all the best cities
iggi n udrar aġ iga ušlḥiy arraw ns	Ishelhin put their children up in the mountains
a aruš d uẓɛḍuḍ a mi nkks akal ns	We had to steal land from porcupines and monkeys

That is, Omar sings, it is too bad that our parents were not so clever, but they did not know any better. Mountains should only be inhabited by animals, but since Arabs took the cities Ishelhin resorted to the mountains.

Aznag, "mountain shepherd":	
ašlḥi gan lbaz ikṣuḍ s warraw ns	The Ashelhi is a falcon, he protects his children
wa yuf lxla d tyuga ns ar ssan attay	The wilderness and its harvest are better for drinking tea
inna ran mun n d lɛql ula ššaraf ns	Wherever he goes, his reason and honor follow
wa han aɛrab ur igi ma ittwala a yan	The Arab is not the one you want by your side[6]
mqar lsan ddahab išš tiram nqqinin	Even if he wears gold and eats clean food
ass nna iswa ššrab a ak ur tli asafar	The day he drinks liquor, there's no remedy

Aznag retorts to the suggestion that Ishelhin live among animals by saying the Ashelhi is one of them, but a protective falcon, and an honorable one. Tending the harvest and drinking tea, he says, are better than living among untrustworthy Arabs. Despite difficulties and migration, Ishelhin retain their reason and their honor. Arabs lack both, he implies, as they are more concerned with material wealth (gold) and good living conditions (clean food). Moral decay marks the Arab's lot, however, issuing a warning to be wary of the Arab's intention. All the more reason to live in the cities, Ben Wakrim suggests in response; why should the person from Fes (the Fassi) get it all?

Ben Wakrim, "migrant merchant":	
wa han abujadi lɛql ixaṣṣa ak	Oh naïve one you need your reason
nga laṣl amzdaġ a aġ iksn akal nġ	We have roots [but] the settler took our lands
ġilli ġ illa ddahab iks awn nt ufasi	The places with gold were taken by the Fassi
fln ak nḥas skr gis tasila qn tnt	They left you copper; make horseshoes and wear them

Ben Wakrim uses the term *(t)abuji(t)* for a naïve adult who should know better, usually referencing mountain residents (*ibudrarn*). Those Arabs who usurped Ashelhi lands ("the dweller" and the Fassi) left only modest copper (*nḥas*), and those who live among it can only be donkeys. One of the traditional occupations of pockets of Anti-Atlas Ishelhin is coppersmithing, especially in Indouzal and other Ida-ou tribes who are believed to be descendants of the Tamdoult area south of Tata in the thirteenth century, historically noted for its copper production (Rosenberger 1970). Copper is considered a humble material, strong and reliable but lacking refinement. Since nḥas is also a colloquial term for bullets (Hart 1984:176), there may be wordplay here: Ben Wakrim suggests that Aznag make innocuous and useful horseshoes, not warring bullets, from what Ishelhin have. Importantly, Ben Wakrim thus perhaps suggests that Aznag not try to fight the way things are. The alternative reading that Latifa, my transcription assistant, suggested is that Omar is backward – why does he want to stay in the tamazirt? He is just like a mule, so he should just act like one and wear horseshoes.

Aznag, "mountain shepherd":	
a walayni tusi d ilmma tikrkas nk	Well now your mockery is clear to me
ddahab d lfḍḍa d iḥkam n tmġarin	Gold and silver and women's rule are inseparable
ur jji bḍin $\dot{g}^{w}$*id aḥlas a ra tilit*	The saddle is what you wear

That is, Aznag is saying, you're a mule ("the saddle is what you wear") if women rule over you. Aznag defends his position by attacking Ben Wakrim's masculinity, since Ben Wakrim is more concerned with wealth ("gold") than men should be. Preoccupation with gold and silver indicate lack of control; this plagues a man manipulated by women. Note that Aznag and Ben Wakrim share the same moral universe, ultimately, and are pointing out each other's consistencies. For both it is important to be a man, but the question is how to perform masculinity: by guarding one's children and peacefully drinking tea, or by reclaiming somehow those "good cities" full of Fassis.

Ben Wakrim, "migrant merchant":	
wa han ar k ntmnad ar k ittawi rriḥ	Here we're watching the *wind* sweep you away
lɛzz a iga yan iddan s lqasariyyat	Proud is the one who goes to the shops
ig lmal ġ ufus ig asmun i wanna ran	Money in hand affords good company

Ben Wakrim justifies the importance of money, for it allows one to keep the company one wants. Aznag reiterates his position that a man concerned with money allows women to control finances and decision-making:

Aznag, "mountain shepherd":	
wa iwwi k lġalaṭ ur awn t inni yan	No one dares tell you that you are wildly mistaken
wa niġ ak lɛaṛaḍ ns a mi yalla yan	I tell you, a person's honor is worth defending
ġikad ixšn yan iġ ttsuqnt tmġarin	It's very bad if women go to market

"To indicate that the world is topsy turvy," Bourdieu writes in his ethnographic treatment of the Algerian Kabyle house, "it is said that 'the women are going to the market'" (Bourdieu 1966:240 as cited in Kapchan 1996:50). In Omar's verse and perhaps the Kabyle use as well, women who "go to market" make decisions, thereby "ruling" over men.[7]

Ben Wakrim, "migrant merchant":	
šuwr awddi f lhawa nun d imurigi	Slow down, dear friend, with the tone of your song
šuwr awddi f lhawa a bab n umargi	Slow down, dear friend, with the song oh music-maker
šuwrat ukan a ššifur i iġarasn	Just slow down, oh chauffeur

At this point Ben Wakrim calls a truce, begging Aznag to be patient and not ratchet up the hyperbole: "hold on, wait a minute," and not to continue with *lhawa* (song or wind; that which sweeps one away) and the *imurgi* (amarg). He cedes the reins to Aznag by calling him the "music-maker" (*bab n umarg*). Following this penultimate section of the song, Aznag changes the subject for a brief *tammsust*, a "sweep" or "shaking out" in which he offers comments on global politics and especially American military domination as a close to the song.

Throughout this tanḍḍamt, there is extensive negotiation over what it means to be Ashelhi in different timizar. The singing poets move towards resolution and agreement by the song's end, sparring throughout and trying to outwit each other. As such, the verbal duel comments upon the maintenance of social identity despite geographical and economic displacements, migration, and urban challenges to a man's moral code. The "I" requires identifying the "Other." Duelers share a speech ideology: one who speaks should speak the truth. They share a gender ideology: men should not cede decision-making, especially in economic matters, to women. They even share an ideological orientation to wealth (although one ostensibly has it and the other does not): wealth can distract a man from his values. Within this shared vision of morality and gender roles, however, there are different paths that men can follow, each with its own logic, and each with its pitfalls. For the city dweller, a sense of injustice vis-à-vis "Arabs" plays into his calculation, for he wants his proverbial piece of the pie, and is tired of the advantages granted Arabs generally in Moroccan society. The sung genre in which conflict and one-upmanship are rhetorical conventions permits a liberty of expression. The rules of the game and the structure of the genre also require, however, that the content ultimately affirm the collective; the chorus repeats the last line of selected verses, signaling a collective voicing that confirms a particular voice. Although the poets' words must contain social critique and political commentary, this particular tanḍḍamt is not a call to any type of revolution. Even though it ultimately voices ambiguity about the lot of Ishelhin as men, it confirms the solidity of the moral universe that underpins Ashelhi society in both its country and city locations.

In song in the late 1990s, then, Ashelhi men engaged the concept of the tamazirt as an entity for contemplation and public commentary. Women's public sung voicings referred to tamazirt in its longer-standing meaning of a place or a village. Lacking the voice to turn tamazirt into an object of discursive analysis, women were effectively precluded from commenting publicly on rural places, on rurality as a state of being, and thus, on women's roles in these places. Such public commentary was relegated to men. For women, critique of the tamazirt was restricted to informal, everyday same-sex discourse.

Tamazirt in Everyday Talk

Conversationally, women referred to the tamazirt as place or village, as illustrated in the tizrrarin sung poetry above. But they also used the term in informal conversation much as men did in song, to refer to rurality more generally, and to the vast rural expanse marked by agricultural labor. This spoken discourse on the tamazirt mirrored the objectified sense in which men used the term in the aḥwaš refrain above. For men, the concept connoted nostalgia and homecoming – which they actively sought in their annual return from the city. For women, in contrast, it suggested hard labor and difficult times – from which they longed to flee.

Women's talk

Mountain women associated the hardships of the countryside with particular household items that simultaneously iconized and indexed rurality. Specifically, they valued many market-bought goods over homemade ones. White market bread was particularly valued, not only because it was made with bleached bread wheat (soft wheat) flour, rather than barley and hard wheat flour, but because it could be purchased ready-made. The countryside (Ar. bled), after all, is what gives its name to the adjective *abldi*, "country," as opposed to *aṛṛumi*, "European." An abldi cow is sturdy but small, whereas a high-maintenance aṛṛumi cow is a large Holstein variety that eats incessantly and requires shade, but in exchange for inconvenience and expense, produces large quantities of milk. Some town dwellers valued, for example, abldi eggs as being more flavorful than larger aṛṛumi eggs. Mountain dwellers, especially teenage girls, in contrast, seemed more unequivocally endorsing of just about anything that came from the market rather than the home.

I learned this through activities like weaving. When the women weaved the green and red rug I described in Chapter One, talk turned several times to commenting on our motivations for making the rug. The women and girls associated the activity of weaving with a lifestyle they preferred to avoid. The foreign anthropologist enamored of village handicrafts mystified them. Apparently, I was for them the ultimate symbol of material things, new, foreign, reliant on the market and therefore good, a contrast with things old and local. It seemed to puzzle them that the urban educated outsider found some redeeming quality in their tamazirt goods: home weavings, barley couscous, tizrrarin songs. It was unclear to them why someone would prefer to sleep atop stacked wool rugs on the floor (as most of them did), rather than on a hot foam mattress (*punj*, from Fr. *éponge*) under a blanket (as many urban Moroccans did). In this practice of weaving, the women literally were engaged in the production of an ideological sign: the rug was not just a material good, but by virtue of its being a sign, "reflect[ed] and refract[ed] another reality" that emerged as meaningful through social and situated human interaction (Messick 1987; Vološinov 1973 [1929]:10). Unmarried 20-year-old Ftuma opened this discussion during the weaving with a rhetorical question. Her 55-year-old mother Hajja piped in, as did Lalla Zohra, a decade Hajja's junior.

Transcript 5.2 (recorded February 1997): At the Loom

Ftuma: ((to me)) What do you want with an *aɛban* [handmade wool blanket]. A kašša [manufactured acrylic blanket] will keep you warm if you sleep. Why do you want to smell the stench of an aɛban you know Katrin?

Sleeping with a wool rug to keep warm was a marker of rurality. Ftuma considered blankets cleaner and preferable.

KEH: What?
Ftuma: I said to Lalla Zohra, we don't want your aɛban. Because we aren't up for it.
We just want a kašša and a mattress.
Hajja: Ah! To each her own.
Ftuma: We'll sleep on it, but tamazirt, no ((laughing))
KEH: Tamazirt how's that.
Ftuma: We don't want the tamazirt.
KEH: Why?
Hajja: Well look here, even {unclear} a blanket {unclear} we want to go to Dar Bayḍa or Taroudant.
KEH: What would you do there.
Hajja: My daughter and her reasoning (*lɛql*) there's nowhere she won't go.

Here Hajja used the term lɛql (Ar. 'aql) ironically to comment on their collective wistfulness. The word has multiple meanings in the Muslim world, from reason or social sense to intelligence and, especially in the Moroccan Sous, responsibility (Abu-Lughod 1986:90; Anderson 1991; Dwyer 1978; Eickelman 1976:138–141; Rosen 1984).

. . .
Ftuma: We want to go to Dar Bayḍa and we can't find a way there.
KEH: Yeah.
Ftuma: We don't know when we're going to go there.
Hajja: Being in Dar Bayḍa is hard, there are so many people there.
Ftuma: I'm always asking for God's mercy to get us there, just like [we ask for mercy to go on] the haj.

Getting to Casablanca seemed as unlikely to Ftuma as going on the haj, the holy pilgrimage to Mecca, and both were worth asking God for.

Zohra: Like a beehive of people all of them are doing like this ((gesturing with hands, fingers moving around in close bunch like swarming bees)). It's like this all the people are doing like this.

KEH: What's that?

Zohra: There are a lot of people there's a ((stammering)) crowd [C.A. jumhur] of people.

KEH: Yeah, there are a lot of people, a lot of people from the village.

Zohra: A lot, yeah a lot.

Zohra stammered while she searched for another word meaning crowd or gathering since I indicated I did not know *talilt* (beehive), even though I proceeded to nod my head signaling that I understood her hand gestures. The word she recuperated, jumhur, is a Standard Arabic word prevalent in Moroccan news and television programming to describe crowds of people, rather than the common MA term zham that would have better fit the context.

Ftuma: There it's nice. Dar Bayḍa. Dar Bayḍa is where people want to go, we're fed up with the tamazirt.

Hajja: Watch it; is here like there?

Literally, Ftuma said, "it's gone up to my head" (*tġli iyi ġ ixf*). Hajja asked rhetorically in response, is there even a basis for comparison between city and country? Similarly, Frye found that his Mexican informants used this rhetorical question to make an argument about the incommensurability of the two categories of "Indian" and "white," rejecting the question of why "Indians" looked so much older than "gringos" (Frye 1996:188–9). Ftuma continued:

Ftuma: Dar Bayḍa is where we want to go. Tamazirt, we don't want it.

Zohra: dadadadad

Ftuma: ((to Zohra)) Don't be so annoying. ((to me)) I was saying to you, we don't want the tamazirt, ((to Hajja)) she said "when you marry you'll go to the city (*lmdint*)".

Hajja She's right, maybe *lmdint n taššixt* (the saint's graveyard) ((laughs))

"Don't be so annoying (*ad ur tsdεat*)," Ftuma commands, played with the d-b-d consonants of Dar Bayḍa, and the verb sḍεa, meaning literally to trouble, to make noise, or to be annoying. She repeated the sounds "d-b;" "Don't be a pain in the neck" was what she meant. Zohra repeated the sounds from a word Ftuma had just uttered, in an attempt to keep the floor. I heard sḍεa (noise) used to refer to children who made noise, the Polisario that clambered for Western Sahara's independence from Moroccan rule, women who asked too much of their husbands, and guests who visited too frequently. The pun Hajja made here was cleverly suited to the discussion: lmdint is both the Tashelhit assimilated borrowing of the Arabic "city" (madina) and the Tashelhit word for grave. Here, the mention of the local female saint, or *taššixt* (from Arabic ššixa), referred to the graveyard adjoining her tomb where women frequently strolled and talked in the late afternoon hours. The idea was that it was likely that Ftuma would visit the "graveyard" ("the [lmdint] that is forever") before she makes it to the "city" (lmdint).

Ftuma: Maybe so {unclear} Just thorn bushes. Maybe so Katrin.
KEH: How's that.
Hajja: *dar taššixt* [at the saint's tomb]
Ftuma: I always say I want to go to the city, I want to go to the city, I want to go to lmdint, until I go to the real one. Until I go to the one that is forever.

. . .

Zohra: Tamazirt tamazirt is tamazirt hey you ((stuttering, to me)) Katrin.
Ftuma: Oof! Oof to tamazirt oof! May God bring it some disaster.
KEH: How's that, "oof"?
Zohra: It's [tamazirt is] not good.
Ftuma: We're fed up with it is oof.
((2.0))
Oof ah Katrin it's not good like this.

Young women increasingly set their sights on Casablanca, hoping to join the wives of financially successful merchants. These young women saw two ways for Tashelhit women to dwell in the world: they either worked the fields, or they stayed at home. They did not consider urban employment options; they rarely pursued adult literacy programs. One young woman summed up what several others told me repeatedly: "Tashelhit women don't work [for wages]. It's shameful. That's just how it is." Given the choice between a life of physical hardship in the mountains and less strenuous domestic servitude in the cities, their choice was clear. Barring that option, however, they did not seek to emulate urban ways within the village, but rather to appropriate the status of selected urban elements as their own.

One young mother of three, Muna, originally from Ait Mahmoud in the Western High Atlas, spoke with me about the differences between her homeland and town. We sat on low stools in her kitchen in Taroudant, peeling carrots for the midday stew. Which was better, I asked, Taroudant or tamazirt? Muna responded:

> Here [Taroudant] is good, but in tamazirt there's a lot of tammara. You have to chop and carry wood, you have to cut and carry fodder, you have to fetch water, you know what I'm saying? In the country, their situation isn't like the way of, the ways outside (*brra*) aren't the ways of the city. There is a lot of tammara as far as [rural] women are concerned.

But, I queried, did she not also "work" in the city? I reminded her that between her cleaning job at the neighboring high school, caring for her children and resident grandmother, and frequent visitors from the mountains, she usually had little time left for herself. Muna replied:

> The city, no. In the city what do you do: you sweep, you wash your clothes, you go to your job, that's all. Tamazirt you have tawwuri (household chores), plus you go out and bring in wood, you have to go to the forest, bring wood, cut grass from the river, carry water on your back. You have to carry your children on your back. You even carry them when you collect fodder from the river. Tammara. That is, the city is better, as far as I'm concerned.

Among younger and older women who dwelled in the tamazirt, as with Muna the emigrant to Taroudant, there was no nostalgia or praise for the amarg of the tamazirt as in the men's song. There were certainly aspects of rural life that women preferred to what they heard or saw about city life. What they wanted was to take the good and be rid of the bad. Women conducted their everyday lives according to a hierarchy of women residing in the village – but within parameters established by the absent males. I asked my host Hajja once whether she missed her husband who visited from France once a year for ten days. She responded by gesturing with a wide sweep of her arms around the courtyard in her cinder block house: "He makes all of this possible. Without him we wouldn't have so much as sugar or tea." Without the emigrant worker, her response suggested, there would be no tamazirt. Likewise, for married men, keeping their wives in the village allowed them to substantiate claims to a homeland where their honor was upheld despite Ishelhin's marginal status in the national Moroccan citizenry.

Men's talk

Movements of people in and out of the mountains and markets were part of what made times good; places were "filling up," and full places were good places. In collective taxis and pickup trucks between mountain villages and towns, passengers were often attentive to villages and fields by the roadside, and they exchanged assessments of places as well as news about their residents. Ishelhin guardedly monitored the dissemination of information about themselves and their communities, as much as they esteemed those who brought them news about other places. Thus conversations like the one below tended to be limited to men with shared histories, to the exclusion of women passengers (including myself; I listened but didn't participate). I traveled frequently around the Moroccan Southwest, so I was privy to a number of these discussions. The following conversation took place between a truck driver, in his mid-forties, and one of his male passengers, a dignified yet garrulous man in his sixties. I noted it down immediately after, for it struck me as exemplary of many other conversations I had witnessed. When times were bad, men attended market less frequently since they had little purchasing power and thus little clout. Buying and selling was only one part of what men did at the weekly markets in Morocco, where socializing, exchanging information, completing administrative matters, and soliciting opinions were equally important tasks. As Hart describes, market day is above all "a day of peace" (2000:13). Times may have been so good in Ida ou Zeddout that local men de-emphasized this sociality; men may have exchanged information quickly while they made purchases and sales. The older man made small talk as we headed down the mountains toward the Sous plains, all of us peering around the road's curves to the villages below whose growth these men had watched for decades. The two men alternated their comments, each agreeing with the other. The driver addressed his comments to his male passenger.

> Times are good, God has sent us goodness. Look at how many people are coming and going. Did you see the market in Igherm yesterday? Full! You couldn't fit another person. Look at all the busses full, the taxis. There are a lot of people in these times. It's not like it used to be. Now whatever you want, it's there in the market. Used to be there was no money, but now there's money.

The older man replied:

> Yes, look at all the houses in the tamazirt that are just locked. Their owners built them then come to spend two or three days there and then return to Casablanca. Things are good; people don't want for anything any more. Thank God there is money now; all you have to do is work and there's money. Look at the saint's festival [*lmusm*] they're going to have in the village. We're going to slaughter a cow. Times are good.

This older man asked the driver how his own village's moussem went. He answered, "So much goodness! So much meat! So many people!" (*ifk ṛbbi lxir, ifk ṛbbi tifyya, ifk ṛbbi bnadam*; lit. "God gave [a lot of] bounty/goodness, God gave [a lot of] meat, God gave [a lot of] people"). There is a tension here, however, in that locked houses can indicate that "things are good," but they can also indicate that the timizar are "clearing out", visually confirming that former inhabitants were unwilling or unable to adapt to the countryside's challenges.

An assessment of material conditions and an overview of general trends throughout the land beyond the confines of an individual's home – these were men's affairs. In tangible terms, paving the road did not lighten women's daily labors much; they tended the same fields, fed the same animals, hand-washed the same clothes, and cooked the same number of meals. Yet roads meant an increased quantity of goods entered their homes. Trucks brought vegetables, clothes, furniture, bleached white bread, and the candy bars whose wrappers littered the dry riverbed. Venders who lived in nearby villages continued to arrive on donkey back: the silver jewelry merchant, the herbalist, the blind egg vendor. Moreover, paved roads had an impact on village residency patterns, since with increased transportation, men arrived and departed more easily. Women did not outright fault the country's infrastructure for their men's absences. Indeed, some women told me that they were indifferent as to whether the men came or went, so long as they sent back goods and money. Pride and stoicism may have informed this discourse on men's absence, but so may a lack of a post-nineteenth century Western-style romantic ideal of marriage.

According to some women who were candid with me, however, the men sent little home. The younger generation, in particular, rarely returned to the village, sometimes because they had accumulated too little money to contribute to their households or fund their transportation. A few women told me that they had no idea how much money the men actually made. As one mother in her early thirties said, remarking on gifts her older brother brought on his previous visit, "All we see is what they want to give us. But I hear them talking, I know some of the men are making big money, living well in Casablanca, and then they don't let us come to see all that they've built. All we know is what they want to show us." Many women complained that "times are hard" (*išqa luqt*). Men occasionally did too, but they used the phrase rhetorically rather than literally, as a sign of empathy with someone experiencing tough times, and not as an assessment. Women's hard labor continued, along with a hefty dose of anxiety about managing a household while remaining uncertain about where their men were and unsure when supplies were forthcoming.

Conclusion

The philosopher Edward Casey writes that "A place is more an *event* than a *thing* to be assimilated to known categories . . . places not only *are*, they *happen*" (Casey 1996:27; italics in the original). In this pair of chapters, I have explored the specificity of one kind of place, the tamazirt or country homeland, as Ida ou Zeddout Ishelhin of the Eastern Anti-Atlas mountains in southwestern Morocco constructed it in the late 1990s. I have stressed that Ishelhin made their lands into dwelling places through the purposeful, interested, and participatory engagement that Heidegger (1977) contends constitutes the "care" of human existence. Individual instances of engagement with the tamazirt, explored in this chapter, contextualized the speaking present within memories from the past as well as anxieties and desires projected into the future. The ways that the Ida ou Zeddout sensed place evoked temporalities and bridged spaces.

In its multiple meanings – homeland, countryside, place of moods – tamazirt is a focal point for Moroccan Ishelhin. While recent scholarly discussions about homelands have focused on source societies and diaspora populations, I am proposing an analytical approach that situates identity not only *in* specific places but in individuals' *relations* to those places. Looking at the links between Ishelhin and land in a specific historical moment – whether focusing on estrangement or quotidian engagement – it becomes clear that urban emigrant men and rural-dwelling women, ostensibly from the same places, endowed land differently with meaning. Yet we see, too, that these practices were second order indexes (Silverstein 2003) that indexed gender (Ochs 1992) and language via emplacement. Thus while most of the Ishelhin I knew who objectified the tamazirt were men, some were female and did so out of a perspective borne of emigration or urban living, as with the immodest Arabic-speaking girl at the wedding I introduced early in this chapter. Similarly, men who remained in the tamazirt were emasculated by their lack of economic capital, yet potentially rich in terms of the kinds of cultural capital valued in sung poetry duels, where knowledge of the countryside was requite to a good performance.

In the song verse opening Chapter 4, the male singer-poet addresses his liver, the Berber repository of affect, begging for patience as he abides the derision he senses for the homelands and their inhabitants.[8] Such ancestral places are morally laudable, he suggests, for they were the last holdouts against the French military incursions, and home to those who "pushed out the colonists with their words and with their bodies." Western scholars are keen to distinguish between, on the one hand, the French colonial occupation of Algeria and West Africa and, on the other hand, the Protectorate status of Morocco and Tunisia. Yet this legal distinction did not resonate with Moroccans I knew who referred to the Protectorate period and, by extension, domination of any outside group over them, as colonialism (*listiεmar*). If indeed "today cities are all [people] care about," city and countryside may not be as mutually exclusive as the lyrics at first suggest. Instead, as I have argued here, the Ashelhi tamazirt is generated demographically, materially, and symbolically in relation to the city, as people move between and dwell in both spaces.

Part IV

Antiphony: Periphery

Let us cease to think of languages as if they should reflect some primitively given demarcation of the world, and learn to think about them instead as instruments of human action.
– Hymes (1984:25)

amarg a issalan yan urd lmut
imma lmut iġ immu yan igz akl
Yearning not death makes you cry
The dead find their rest in the earth
– Anti-Atlas tazrrart

Chapter 6

Transformation in the Sous Valley

The basic feature of Moroccan life is therefore the division of the population into plains-dwelling Arabic-speakers and mountain-dwelling Berbers . . . There is in reality a Berber core-area, situated in the very high mountains; an Arabic-speaking core area, situated in the plains and desert; and a very wide intermediate zone, where the two groups interpenetrate in varying proportions.
– B. Hoffman (1967:11, 40)

*Back in the early days (*zikk*), people didn't stay put! . . . Back when there was hunger . . . Whatever the people spoke in the land where they landed, they spoke it too.*
– Fatima Mhammd, 20-year resident of Taroudant, native of Arazan

The preeminent rural sociologist Paul Pascon wrote of Morocco that "All too often concepts of social structure are patterned after agrarian structures" (1986:197). Although Pascon published primarily on the Haouz plains of the Marrakesh area, the generalization holds true for the Sous Valley as well; populations in both areas are comprised of descendants of the twelfth-century Beni Hilal invasions, Arabized Ishelhin, and a smaller Tashelhit-speaking population. Those in the Sous plains are primarily agriculturalists, only some of whom own the fertile irrigated land they work, and wage laborers at local citrus and milk processing factories. Most land bordering the Sous River was converted from subsistence and pastoral use to commercial agriculture in the 1920s and late 1940s, primarily through private colonization. Europeans purchased land from Moroccans directly, usually for obscenely low prices, rather than through the official colonization through which the French converted much of Algeria's land from subsistence to commercial use, primarily vineyards and wheat fields (cf. Issawi 1982:126; Stora 2001:157–8).

One result of this political economic change is that many of the Tashelhit-speaking communities in the Sous plains display verbal expressive repertoires in which Arabic figures centrally, unlike their co-ethnics in the mountains. The present chapter describes the region's transformation from an early twentieth-century sleepy pastoral grazing land dotted with olive and argan trees to one of the richest commercial agricultural lands in the Mediterranean. The transformation brought about the emergence of a plains-wide, bilingual speech community that accounts, in large part, for the distinct development of language practices and language ideologies among this subgroup of Ishelhin Berbers. That is, land tenure systems have largely shaped the role of Arabo-Islamic culture and language among an otherwise Tashelhit-speaking population. By the late 1990s, the plains were tended by a rural proletariat identifying in some respects with the national Arab dominant narrative, but with a Berber history of displacement, famine, and transformation. Political economic factors were more important in shaping expressive practices than were governmental language policies, administrative practices, or innate differences within the Tashelhit language community.

Plains Arabs and Berbers share many aspects of agricultural and economic practices, architectural styles, customs, institutions, values, and diet. Despite these commonalities, plains dwellers at large festive gatherings such as weddings, circumcisions and saints' festivals reveled in the pleasures of deictic "microdifferentiation" (Tsing 1993:61), peppering their assessments with such observations as "There [in *x* village] men plow," "Here women stay at home," etc. They presented these conventions simply as the way things were, not one of several options, and certainly not as the outcome of historical struggles and collective experience, or reflective of land ownership patterns and institutions. Although plains dwellers themselves recognized the heterogeneity of the region, the plains-wide bilingual speech community – like other bilingual plains of Morocco – has gone unrecognized by scholars, administrators, and even cultural and human rights activists. The tyranny of the a priori ethnolinguistic group – as potentially homogenizing as the nation – has largely precluded political economic analysis.

Plains Ishelhin are arguably the periphery of the periphery, those who challenge the coherence of the Berber ethnic category to which they ascribe. By examining their ethnolinguistic praxis along with political economic histories, we can begin to account for variation among Tashelhit speakers in several related respects: in their relationships with those they call Arabs, in their bilingual practices, in the language shift of some groups from Tashelhit to MA, and in their participation in or (more often) absence from the Amazigh rights movement. The Sous Valley is geographically and metaphorically an in-between space where the subtlety of discourses about the tamazirt, so prevalent in the Anti-Atlas mountains, gives way to a preoccupation with things Arab and by association urban. Complicating matters somewhat are those people and places that defy the distinction between plains and mountains – as with the tribe of Arghen. Their lands were documented by Protectorate Native Affairs officials as comprised of both mountains and plains – an ancestry that eluded the consciousness of all but a few elderly and historically minded residents. Tribal consciousness was virtually absent in the plains in the 1990s, where solidarity instead was built more along lines of social class.

Marrying Up, Marrying Down

Although Khadduj did not think of herself as part of the Arghen tribe – as most people from Arazan (*ayt Irazan*) did not, despite a pre-Protectorate history of political organization that placed Arazan as the plains section of the Arghen tribe – she considered the neighboring mountains, now called Arghen, as the ideal place to "marry into." Khadduj's view was reinforced by the arrival several months earlier of her brother's wife, Aisha, from Arghen. Aisha and her mother-in-law sat on woven straw mats and sorted grain in the shaded hallway off the central courtyard of their pisé (mud-brick) village home, a good spot to catch the breeze. I chatted with Aisha as Khadduj got me the light blue cotton overwrap (Ar. lizar, lit. sheet) that her father insisted we both wear while gathering fodder for the livestock from the fields. Aisha told me about the narrow rocky road leading up the mountain to Arghen, visible from Arazan but accessible only by Peugeot truck. Then she offered an unsolicited assessment of Arazan, an implicit comparison with her native lands: "The customs here are nasty; it's hard for women" (*xšnt lɛadat n ġid išqa f tmġarin*). Her comment reiterated observations she had made earlier while the four of us sat cleaning pebbles and mouse excrement from a sack of barley. I asked her whether she had "gotten used to it yet" (*is tmyard?*) as women ask one another when they have changed places, either for a short visit or a relocation. She said that she had, *alhamdullah*, thank God. But, she added, her parents' mountain tamazirt was different from Arazan: among the Arghen, the girls and women socialized out of doors, did not cover their faces, and talked to men freely. In Arazan, in contrast, married women had to keep themselves covered and stay at home. Aisha remarked that before her wedding, "I'd never seen my husband and he'd never seen me!" which sent Khadduj and her mother Hadda into peals of laughter. Aisha asked me, "It's hard like that, isn't it?" Without waiting for my response, she continued: "My father and my husband's father are friends, and they proposed we marry, and so I said okay." She had returned to her natal village for the close of Ramadan, the month of fasting. Her mother and sister also had visited her in Arazan. The marriage alliance further strengthened relations between the families in Arazan and Arghen, and increased the frequency of their visits to both places, since Hadda also came from another Arghen mountain village.

Hadda's middle daughter Khadduj, in her late teens, had her heart set on marrying a cousin named Laεrabi, son of her maternal uncle who lived in Arghen. Before lunch, Khadduj produced a small torn piece of paper with the name Laεrabi written in French that she kept close to her breast, asking me rhetorically "What does this say?" After lunch she showed me a letter he had written her in Arabic, asking me to read it aloud to her and translate into Tashelhit. We progressed slowly since we were frequently interrupted; each time, Khadduj hid the paper under her skirts, saying she did not want her father to see it. She did not care about her older unmarried sister Nejmia knowing, however. The letter opened with the formal invocation bismillah ar-rahman ar-rahim (In the name of God the merciful, the beneficent). It continued in a decidedly more secular vein: Laεrabi wrote that he thought of Khadduj day and night, all the time, and with all his heart. He wanted to see her again. At the bottom he drew a heart and wrote "Laεrabi" in one corner of it, "Khadduj" in another, and below it qalb (heart) and hub (love). She asked me to write a response in French, noting that Aisha's brother would transmit the letter to Laεrabi once finished.

Khadduj and I, in our full wraps and she in her face veil (nageb), left the other women at home and set off for the fields adjoining the village, tidily tended, lush plots divided by raised irrigation canals that doubled as walkways. The calf-high barley did not yet bear buds under the olive trees; some plots belonging to the rays and the moqaddem – local political leaders – were fallow. We walked towards the Sous River, stopping under a shade tree. Khadduj looked around to ensure that the men and boys working the fields were scattered at a safe distance, then removed her overwrap, urging me to do the same. Khadduj and Nejmia discussed the identities of the people in the visible horizon, and little Rachida, Khadduj's 10-year-old sister, kept her eye on their grazing donkey, sickle in hand. We pulled weeds and tiny, yellow, calf-high flowers, and Nejmia directed me to pick only from those places without insecticide (ddwa, chemicals or medicine). At one point Khadduj's arms were loaded with fodder and a young man working in an adjacent field within earshot yelled out, "Drop that fodder, it has chemicals on it." Khadduj did so, not stopping to shield her face from the man, more concerned with keeping the pesticides away from her skin. I asked Nejmia how she knew which fields were safe. She pointed to the wilted hot pink wildflowers nearby, explaining "See those red flowers? If there weren't chemicals, they'd be opening towards the sun."

Khadduj told me to accompany her to the dry riverbed where the fodder was more ample. We picked along the way, despite her complaints about the paucity of fodder. I kept my eyes peeled in vain for *lxbbiza*, a delicious wild green that Khadduj said grew poorly around their fields. Elsewhere in the plains, this green was the kind of country food that men scorned and women savored, especially finely chopped and cooked with olive oil, plenty of garlic, and preserved lemon. When we had picked for a while by the dry riverbed, Khadduj sat down to rest in the shade of an olive tree. She urged, "Please Katrin, write me the letter." She pulled out a piece of paper and a pen from inside her dress. Unsuspecting, I laughed, remarking that she had left the house prepared. I took the pen and folded white lined paper torn from a notebook and asked her what she wanted me to write. She smiled broadly, asking me what Americans write in letters to their boyfriends. I told her that there was no rule, and that I was just her pen; she would have to tell me what to write. After several minutes of deliberation, I announced that I would start the letter with a greeting. Should I tell him you were happy to see him in Taroudant? I asked. She said yes, but that she did not understand why he did not show up at their appointed place at Bourar studio at Place Tamoklate on Throne Day, as he had promised. Was he telling the truth (*lmaɛqul*) or was he just lying to her? She did not want to hear any more from him unless he first told his mother and father that he "wanted" her, meaning wanted to marry her. She signed it. I told her not to tell anyone that I had written it, because I did not want to get in trouble with her father or the village men. She promised.

If I had not been around to help, she told me, she would have written back to him in Arabic. She knew enough from her two years in primary school, and read the letter to me and understood most of the words. She clearly had increased her reading level in the decade since she left school, something I had never witnessed among young women in the mountains. Once I started feeding her sentences in Tashelhit, she quickly departed from her first instinct which was to stick to the formalities of the Arabic letter. It was as though she suddenly realized she could express herself, since I would translate her spoken Tashelhit into written French, rather than repeating the stock Arabic greetings required of the standard Arabic letter-writing genre, suffocating to those who lack agility in the elaborate classical language (Djebar 1993; Kapchan 1996; Kaye and Zoubir 1990; Wagner 1993; Haeri 2003). We closed her letter with an ultimatum that Laɛrabi visit her before the Id lmqqurn. When I expressed surprise that her parents would allow a visit from their daughter's suitor, she explained that Laɛrabi was her maternal cousin. He came to the house periodically to talk, even when her father was home; she was convinced that her father knew nothing of their sentiments for each other. Even though they were cousins, she had only met Laɛrabi in the mountains at her brother's recent wedding to Aisha, and then they saw each other in Taroudant on Throne Day. "We haven't seen each other much, but now he can come to the house because he's family." I asked her whether she wanted to marry him and she said she did, if he asked; she smiled and asked rhetorically, "Is that bad?" She said she thought that it was better to marry a relative than a stranger who might beat her and leave her no recourse for complaint. Besides, she explained, his tamazirt was *fjjijn*: cool, relaxed, fun. Women went about outdoors, she told me; they did not have to cover up all of the time as they did in Arazan. The lhawa or air – both literally and figuratively – was good, Khadduj said, re-voicing much of what Aisha had claimed earlier in the breezy hallway.

I responded, "You picked the tamazirt where you wanted to live first and then you looked for a boy who lives there. Now I understand." She laughed, "That's right, what's wrong with that? You have to like the place you go to, and I want to know the boy before I marry him, to know his ideas." Later the following summer, Khadduj married Laεrabi and moved up the mountainside to Arghen, the fjjijn place where she could put away her face veil and walk about freely wearing only a headscarf. But important life-cycle rituals crucial to the social reproduction of the Arghen community remained foreign to her, especially the Tashelhit lyrics in collective song and dances that, as I explain in the following chapter, the people of Arazan no longer know.

The choice Khadduj made was not typical. She preferred to marry up, literally, into the mountains, rather than stay in the plains or marry into town. This was no social climb. Khadduj valued the clean air, relative freedom of movement, and the comfort of her mother's relatives nearby, but this was not a match that ensured economic mobility. The customs that kept her cloistered in Arazan were those of the Arabs, as she understood them. Indeed, plains Ishelhin took on many aspects of Arab plains cultural practices, including gender avoidance and physical concealment ("veiling"). Political economies increasingly merged and their fates became more intertwined. Combined with the mass migration down from the mountains to the plains during the 1920s and 1930s, under pressures of drought and famine, the populations of the Sous mountains and plains were increasingly linked, but their land tenure systems and economic means increasingly diverged. The plains communities in which Tashelhit speakers lived increasingly resembled Arab communities, even indexically as with dress, as in Figure 6.1 of the late Fatima Hamid in her blue lizar. Their Ashelhi mountain neighbors considered Ashelhi plains dwellers less "pure" because of their Arab-influenced expressive and cultural practices. In this respect, the plains discursively constituted a periphery of the mountain homeland, peripheral also to towns and cities, and their residents were conscious that plains villages afforded the advantages of neither the mountains nor the city.

Figure 6.1 The late Fatima Hamid in the blue lizar of the Sous plains

A Pitiable Promised Land

23 December 1917 – What is most striking, when you descend into the Sous valley, is the wide band of alluvion that this river deposits the length of its run. We cannot, for the moment, say anything precise about the dimensions of this double band of fertile terrain: there is no precise map of this region; there has not been a single detailed study of the *contrée*; we have sent no specialist there; we know nothing about the meteorology, nor the temperature, nor the diverse altitudes of this plain; we have not mapped the locations of springs, nor traced the ancient abandoned waterways (foggaras or seguias); we thus can have only impressions and not precise positions concerning the value of these districts. Accordingly, noting the abundant vegetation, the beautiful gardens, the numerous fields, one senses that this is one of the richest districts of Morocco where agriculture constitutes the central activity and the primary wealth . . .

The big difficulty to resolve, when one talks about the Sous, is that while some have only seen the river valley, which is very fertile, others know only

> the road from Agadir to Tiznit and its surroundings which are much less rich. Thus some speak of the Sous as an Eldorado and a promised land while others berate it. (Thomas 1918:111)

When Thomas wrote about geological contrasts in the Sous, the French Protectorate had recently secured its alliance with the Pasha of Taroudant, and would soon establish a series of agreements with rural qayds. Once Protectorate officials assessed the potential of the Sous Valley for colonization, they developed strategies for usurping or buying collectively held lands from the tribes who allocated water and land use rights. Colonization and agricultural development of the formerly pastoralist plains further distanced the plains' populations from the adjoining mountain communities that, in some cases, previously constituted a single tribe – as with the Arghen (see Fig. 1.2).

Arazan, 30 km and 45 minutes by collective taxi east of Taroudant along the Sous River, is at the heart of my discussion of the plains in this book, iconic of plains villages more generally. Arazan's population of 3,072 was divided into 425 households (takatin, sing. takat) (Ministère de la Prevision Economique et du Plan 1994). The village stretches alongside the paved road leading through Ouled Berhil toward both the mountainous Tizi n Test passage to Marrakesh and the flat paved road to Ouarzazate. In comparison to Eastern Anti-Atlas villages, Arazan and other plains villages had larger populations and were better serviced. Parts of Arazan had electricity installed in 1988; the part in which I worked received it in 2003. Running water was established a few years after I completed fieldwork, and by 2005 households had closed off the courtyard wells that used to provide their water. The village had a gas station, a regular long-distance taxi service, an agricultural delegation extension, a primary school, and a large market inside the village walls. Taroudant was the supply station for butane gas, food staples, batteries for the solar panels that powered televisions and lightbulbs, clothes, and home furnishings. Arazan's Thursday market, Suq El Khemis, has been an important regional institution since at least the Protectorate period, selling principally vegetables and meat but also housewares. Arazan is now the commune's administrative center. Like many other plains villages in the late 1990s, Arazan was simultaneously town and village. Land use was mixed in Arazan: some was owned and worked for household consumption, some was rented for small-scale commercial agriculture, and some was owned by large commercial farms. Farmed fields surrounded and divided the village's neighborhoods. The cinder-block mosque had a painted minaret, and a few mud-brick saints' tombs remained intact. The village was home to a community of Tashelhit-speaking Jews until their wholesale departure around 1968. A local guardian, Si Hmed Harim, guided visiting Jewish Americans and Europeans through what remained of the synagogue and the mellah, or Jewish neighborhood (cf. Deshen 1989).

The weekly market and administrative area comprised the village core, with new cinder block walls where older pisé walls had crumbled. In the residential areas, in the late twentieth century, pisé was the primary building material for the connected domestic complexes whose exterior walls framed the walkways connecting houses, fields, and public spaces like the mosque and school. Inside, residential complexes were comprised of sets of open courtyards lined with smaller rooms, adjoined by eucalyptus ceiling-beamed corridors with carefully placed skylights off the flat roofs. Rooms opened onto the courtyard through a single door and occasionally a window; ceilings were lined with cane and, budget permitting, the dirt floors were coated with cement on which plastic or straw mats and rugs or blankets heated or cooled the room, as needed. In the late 1990s, it was common for several grown brothers to live in one compound with their children and parents; only in the last generation have some couples sought the separate nuclear households more common among Arab than Ashelhi families. In the traditional patrilocal arrangement, homes contained separate sleeping and cooking quarters for each brother and his wife and children, with at least one shared courtyard, outdoor cooking quarters, and a common entrance to the village. Architecturally, the spacious dwellings, with roofs and storage rooms upstairs and wide open internal courtyards, operate similarly to Moroccan urban medina dwellings. That is, the rooftops of Arazan households adjoined one another and allowed easy access and ample visibility. Yet unlike urban medinas, in the plains residents did not allow themselves to walk between residences from the rooftops, nor to peer into neighboring courtyards; they jealously guarded their privacy. Arazan is in a strikingly flat region of the Sous where space is organized horizontally, in stark contrast to the High and Anti-Atlas mountains where vertical movements up and down mountainsides are more central to spatial perception.

Plains Ishelhin and Arabs: Parallel Histories, Shared Economies

Arazan's history of land usurpation parallels that of neighboring Arabic-speaking villages like Ait Dahman, a village less than an hour's walk across the Sous River. More commonly than marrying up into the mountains, as Khadduj did, Tashelhit-speaking plains women have tended to marry in the plains, even across ethnic groups, given the density of their social networks (Milroy 1987). Dahmani and Razani people, for instance, have forged friendships through family but also through agricultural and factory work. Monolingual Arabic-speaking Jamila of Ait Dahman explained land tenure this way, as I noted down shortly after we spoke:

> Before the French came, the land there belonged to people themselves. Under the French, El Tiouti took the land from the people and made them work it. After Independence, the lands stayed in El Tiouti's family. They've sold some of it, little by little. Much of it remains in their hands, so people have to rent the land from them or from the Habous. The rent is 100,000 rials [5,000 dirhams, around US$550–600] a year for a parcel (mlk; pl. malayk).

I noticed the thorn enclosure around the parcel and the aluminum door that was secured with a chain and a hook, but not padlocked. Looking out at her slim father in the fields in his oversized royal blue overalls and knee-high olive green boots, Jamila continued:

> This section of the land was bought by my father's father, and so all the land and the olive trees and banana tree on it were all theirs. They grew barley, potatoes, and mint that they sold at market. My father has just bought some more fields from Tiouti. On other lands, people rent only the malayk. If you rent the land to grow crops, you don't have the right to the fruit of the olive trees.

The daily domestic and work practices of Arabic-speaking residents of Ait Dahman, and even the physical environment, resembled Tashelhit-speaking Arazan: both had pisé residential complexes for extended families. Complexes linked to one another alongside narrow pathways that led to fields and the market area. Arazan and Ait Dahman had similar land tenure practices, a combination of privately owned and rented land. In contrast to the neighboring mountains, plains men worked the land, while women handled livestock and domestic chores. Women were more spatially restricted in Arab Ait Dahman than in Ashelhi Arazan, although women's and girls' movements were monitored in both. Dahmani women did not gather fodder from the fields as Khadduj and her sister did. Few residents emigrated into Ait Dahman, but a few Ida ou Zeddout men had moved to Arazan to work in the fields. There was little female presence in the public spaces; women visited with neighbors and performed chores together. Ait Dahman and Arazan shared musical practices at public festivities, and they hired the same *ššixat* (professional female musicians) from a nearby village, themselves a mix of native Arabic and Tashelhit speakers. Since Arabs did not tend to learn Tashelhit despite their proximity, Ishelhin accommodated the plains Arabs linguistically. Ait Dahman is in the Mnebha qbila (tribe) that, along with the Houara qbila stretching between Taroudant and Agadir, trace their ancestry to the Beni Hilal invasions, with all of the bravery (ššajaεa) and honor (ššaraf) associated with the "opening" (fatḥ; Islamization) of North Africa's hinterlands many centuries ago. Ishelhin in the plains, in contrast, had no illustrious history to flaunt. This is particularly evident in the village of Tiout itself, with its large proportion of dark-skinned residents with ancestry among the landless forgers of Indouzal and Taggmout who worked for Qayd El Tiouti under the French, some of whom resettled in plains villages like Arazan and Tazzemourt. Economic and symbolic capital was oriented outside their communities: on the one hand, towards the Ashelhi mountain homelands, and on the other hand, towards towns and cities.

Agriculturalists in the post-Protectorate period, collectively labeled fllaḥin (sing. fllaḥ) on their national identity cards, comprised primarily the country's rural proletariat. Yet the occupational category fellah conflated individuals' relations to the means of production and their primary remunerative activities, since it included owners of large commercial farms, day laborers, farmers with a few hectares of vegetables on a state-created farming project (mašruɛ), and mountain dwellers who plowed with a donkey and wooden t-plow. A few in Arazan owned some private land. The rest rented fields, or purchased the rights to harvest olive trees auctioned annually by the state's Islamic Affairs Ministry (ḥabus or Habous). Still others were sharecroppers in the xams (one-fifth) system, typically working for one-fifth of the harvest. The large farms were owned and operated by foreign companies, by the Moroccan royal family's company, or by wealthy Moroccans who, in the Sous, tended to be descendants of those favored by the makhzen or the former French administrators such as the qayds. Boukous reports that in the Ait Melloul/Ouled Teima area alone, 45,000 hectares of land were "opened" to colonists (Boukous 1977:74). Local people knew who owned which lands. Many aspects of village life revolved around these farms and factories: men worked the fields, and some women and girls picked the fruit for a daily wage of about 50 dirhams (a little over $5) for a twelve-hour day. Those who were fortunate found employment in the local packaging factories, which despite their seasonal nature paid 13 dirhams an hour in addition to benefits such as a bonus of 150 dirhams per month per child enrolled in school, health visits, and paid medications. As another bonus, occasionally workers brought home oranges. Family income cycles fluctuated with the citrus-growing season. Farm and factory employees made friends through work, and occasionally a friendship between workers led to marriage, as between a young woman I knew from Tashelhit-speaking Tazzemourt and a young Arabic-speaking man from nearby Ouled Aissa. Whether certain women could sustain the difficult manual labor, scratching, and bruising of fruit-picking was a subject of after-hours socializing among women connected to the industry. The fertile plains provided much of the agricultural produce that nutritionally supplemented the bread-based diet. Access to this bounty was limited by the relationship between agricultural worker and landowner. According to statistics compiled between 1994 and 1997, in Taroudant Province, 65 percent of the economically active population was officially engaged in this kind of seasonal employment (Taroudant Province Public Administration n.d.).

The Independence government since 1956 has furthered Protectorate-era land "reforms," even carrying out agricultural and land management projects designed then abandoned by the French (Swearingen 1987). The resulting rearrangement of rural space, created by capitalist motivated action, was above all governed by principles of utility and rationality, through what Tilley refers to as the disciplinary aims of institutions (1994:21). Most citrus was shipped to foreign markets, but a portion ("the ugly ones," as one worker specified) remained in local and national markets. Many of the cartons of clementines sold in American grocery stores in the winter are from the Sous plains, in competition with those from Spain. Landholdings of the rural population were by no means stable by the late 1990s, and they were decreasing. For Morocco as a whole, 34.5 percent of agriculturalists were landless in 1985; numbers were probably at least as high in the Sous plains. In Morocco in general, the number of rural dwellers who own their own land is diminishing, and among those who still have their own land, they increasingly have less of it. During the period 1970–80 alone, 10,000 recorded households became landless throughout Morocco, moving from 32.5 to 34.5 of rural households. The number of peasants who owned less than two hectares remained at around 650,000 for that period, but the proportion of lands this group owned fell from 7 percent to 3.7 percent of lands of one hectare or less, and from 9.3 percent to 6.4 percent for households with one to two hectares (El Khayari 1985; in CERED 1995:172–3). There was no similarly dramatic shift in land tenure in the Anti-Atlas mountains. Instead, twentieth-century economic changes there were due to decreasing rainfall, development of roadways, and an expansion of the availability of agricultural foodstuffs that led to a decline in gardening in the mountains.

The Protectorate period thus brought about a sweeping transformation of plains land with the introduction of commercial agriculture that in turn led to reliance on the state and to bilingualism and/or language shift away from Tashelhit to Arabic as Arab cultural practices more generally took hold. In the estimation of mountain dwellers, plains Ishelhin were working-class agriculturalists with few economic prospects. Plains Ishelhin could, however, garner cultural capital by participating publicly in Moroccan Arab expressive culture, thereby indexing their affiliation with a national citizenry whose unifying symbols were Islam, Arabic language, and urban Arab aesthetics. In the mountains, where the only Arabs were administrators, teachers, and doctors, Arabic and Arab aesthetics held little caché, and all verbal expressive genres were in Tashelhit.

Whereas Anti-Atlas men pursued upward mobility through urban commercial connections rather than agrarian work or civil service, plains parents relied on schooling rather than commerce as a means to their sons' (and increasingly, daughters') economic security. Plains dwellers were in more frequent and intensive contact with state policies that promoted Arabic. Simply speaking, being a native Tashelhit speaker was not enough for Ashelhi men from the plains to secure good jobs with Anti-Atlas merchants in the city, most of whom restricted employment to men from their tribal section whose character and roots they believed they could more easily assess. In contrast to men from the Anti-Atlas, many men from the plains could not say with certainty which tribe they belonged to; in the plains, tribe was no longer the central organizational concept that it remained in the Anti-Atlas. Members of a social network were not linked through native language, or ethnic group. Instead, laṣl and tribal affiliation were of utmost importance to Anti-Atlas men. Such a criterion fits uneasily with the "rational" capitalist motivation noted by Tilley.

Thus the economic and social systems in the plains and mountains were distinct by the end of the twentieth century, despite their populations' shared Tashelhit ethnolinguistic identity. Yet through the semiotic process of erasure (Irvine and Gal 2000), people attend to selected cultural practices and disregard others. In doing so, they emphasize particular bases of solidarity or, in contrast, justify their distinction, thus eliding significant social facts to better fit the desired ideal. Erasure operated when merchant Ishelhin from the mountains claimed that they preferred to hire fellow Ishelhin – but then erased plains Ishelhin from that category. From that perspective, Ishelhin did not include all Tashelhit speakers, but instead "hard Tashelhit speakers" (*išlḥiyn iqqurn*) or mountain people (ibudrarn) – but importantly, not plains Ishelhin. Similarly, erasure operates in French colonial and postcolonial writings on Morocco, where the Berber–Arab distinction is mapped spatially onto mountains and plains. Erasure operated, too, in lay people's linguistic ideologies that ibudrarn were the "real" Ishelhin. Yet as the Khouribga emigrant father in Chapter Five told me while videotaping his dancing daughter, and I later read in Protectorate archives, apparently Ishelhin "held tight" to Tashelhit, and were "very attached" to their customs. We should ask which Ishelhin were so inclined, and to which customs they were attached. More pointedly, it is unclear how assimilated customs fit into markers of authenticity, like those of plains Ishelhin who have adopted Arab practices. Wealthy (by relative standards) emigrant men and their families did continue to speak Tashelhit. It was the rural working class and poor who, upon emigrating to town, tended to raise monolingual Arabic-speaking children.

Ethnolinguistic categories like Arabs, Ishelhin, fellahin and ibudrarn hid, elided, and erased social and symbolic relations that were at times more important to constraining everyday action than the available categories. Agriculturalists, for one, fell into multiple economic classes that shaped their everyday actions and beliefs, as well as their marriage choices, access to and allocation of economic and social capital, residence patterns, etc. Otherwise put, the ideology that positions all Tashelhit speakers as Ishelhin erases their structural positions relative to modes of production, positions that distinguish among villagers and geographical regions of the Sous. Likewise, the ideology that posits an originary Arab–Ashelhi dichotomy erases patterns of social and class relations that may be more important than native language in shaping and constraining everyday action. In the late 1990s, at least, a shared working-class position reinforced solidarity between Arabs and Ishelhin in the plains. Yet this solidarity emerged only at periodic intervals, for instance when singing at life-cycle or religious festivities. Moreover, the ɛaṣabiyya (solidarity or group consciousness; Ibn Khaldûn 1967 [1377]) that Ishelhin felt with plains Arabs, despite their lack of tribal or kinship networks, receded when plains Ishelhin were faced with Arabic-speaking state bureaucracies. Schools and courts, for example, excluded Berber language, even if it was occasionally begrudgingly tolerated by some authorities. Plains Ishelhin shared such difficulties with mountain Ishelhin, even though mountain dwellers generally perceived little commonality with their co-ethnics in the plains, whether Arabic- or Tashelhit-speaking. Whether their ancestry traced to the plains or the mountains, Tashelhit speakers shared a common structural relationship vis-à-vis the state that largely disregarded the importance of native language. Official discourse instead emphasized shared Arabo-Islamic values, associating Morocco's Berber populations with the officially defunct social organizational unit: the tribe. In practice, the unity of the Moroccan nation as defined by Arab nationalists necessitated the erasure of Amazigh heritage, marginalizing Ishelhin and other Berberophones after Independence. Tashelhit-speaking residents of the plains fell between the gaps of these two discernible groups. Individuals may be keen on differentiating among themselves as a way of aligning the other (within their ethnic or linguistic group) with the external Other; ethnic slurs operate on this premise, policing the boundaries of community membership. Many plains Ishelhin downplayed the importance of native language to personal and collective subjectivities, allowing them to maintain social relations with Arabic-speaking neighbors and co-workers. Remaining mobile – socially and geographically – required the utmost ability to adapt to new situations; bilingualism was highly valued to that end. This ideology of sameness, at least outside of institutional contexts, facilitated the transition between ethnic groups.

Still, according to their co-ethnics in the mountains, plains Ishelhin were the most "Arab" of the Ishelhin because of iconic cultural practices they shared with plains Arabs: gender segregation and women's seclusion, singing in Arabic at life-cycle events, domestic architecture, and women's dress conventions (especially the lizar), all closely monitored given the micro-differences that indexed social identity. But plains Ishelhin decidedly were not Arabs by their own reckoning, or from the perspective of plains Arabs, because they used Tashelhit as their everyday vernacular. For plains Ishelhin, Arabic was closely associated with mobility – belied in actuality by the more effective mobility of mountain merchants. The class positioning of wage-laboring plains residents bound their fates more closely than did the shared ethnic membership with mountain residents. Not surprisingly, then, wage-laboring Ishelhin in the plains largely cast their lot with wage-laboring Arabs, and this helps to explain why plains-dwelling Tashelhit speakers have accommodated their Arabic-speaking neighbors to such an important extent. Hill and Hill (1986) discuss a similar dynamic across social classes of Mexicano- (i.e. Nahuatl-) speaking indigenous agriculturalists, a group whose political economy and social networks are intertwined with those of Spanish-speaking Mexicans and whose language practices exhibit both accommodation and differentiation.

The shared "structure of feeling" (Williams 1977) among wage-laboring plains agriculturalists may have occluded structural differences between Arab and Ashelhi communities in the plains, evident in their relative literacy and schooling rates, for instance (Table 6.1). Plains Ishelhin (iconically represented here by Arazan) were arguably more disadvantaged than Arabs in the plains (here represented in the village of Ait Dahman, officially known as Sidi Dahman), or Ishelhin in the mountains. Plains Ishelhin were more dependent on wage labor, and a smaller proportion of Razanis were literate than were Dahmanis, despite the presence of a primary school in Arazan and its absence in Ait Dahman. The table is arranged with Taroudant, the capital of the province, in the center; the Sous Valley locations on the left; and the Anti-Atlas locations, from most to least shaped by state institutions, on the right. Hence Walqadi is the market and bureaucratic center of the Ida ou Zeddout tribe; given its role as an administrative and educational center, its inhabitants tend to be more highly educated, literate, and employed as civil servants ("salaried") than those of any given Ida ou Zeddout village. The same holds true for Adar, the market and administrative center of Ida ou Naḍif. Statistics for individual Anti-Atlas villages, rather than commune centers, were not available, so the numbers are only suggestive.

The female-to-male ratio in the plains is approximately even, whereas women comprise two-thirds of the adult mountain population. Since these are administrative centers with salaried state jobs and some permanent stores, the number of salaried and employed there will be higher than in the villages. It is notable that in the plains villages, both Arab and Ashelhi, about half of the men were salaried, and 20–30 percent of men were

Table 6.1 Employment, literacy, and education in the Sous Valley and Anti-Atlas mountains

Location Type Tribe	Arazan (Tash plains) Arghen (%)	Ait Dahman (Arab plains) Menabha (%)	Taroudant (prov. capital) (%)	Igherm (admin. town) Ida ou Knsus (%)	Walqadi (market ctr) Ida ou Zeddout (%)	Adar (market ctr) Ida ou Naḍif (%)
Male salaried	47	49	52	27	15	8
Female salaried	0.7	4.5	13	2	3	2
Male indep. empl.	30	20	22	18	14	17
Female indep. empl.	1.2	0.9	2	20	23	27
Male literate	30	48	75	68	38	38
Female literate	7	20	44	12	6	2
Male schooled	55	78	89	89	89	67
Female schooled	20	48	78	46	32	6
Female : male ratio	49:51	49:51	51:49	55:44	61:39	65:35

Source: Adapted from Direction de la Statistique figures, Rabat, 1994

independently employed. The majority of men are thus accounted for. (Only around 5 percent of Arab plains women were employed, as were fewer than 2 percent of plains Tashelhit women.) In the mountains, in contrast, the percentages of salaried men were significantly lower, as were the independently employed rates. This is probably due to low reporting and a general suspicion of censuses. In regards to literacy and education, 70 percent of males and 93 percent of females in Arazan were illiterate, compared with illiteracy rates in Ait Dahman of 52 percent for males and 80 percent for females. Both males and females are schooled in higher percentages in Ait Dahman, too. Thus, whereas Ishelhin and Arabs in the plains have similar employment profiles, there is a greater discrepancy in participation in schooling and literacy activities. In comparison with Moroccan national statistics, it is unsurprising that literacy rates are also lower for women than for men. For Morocco as a whole, women's literacy is 40 percent, a largely meaningless figure given the disparity between the 52 percent of urban women who are literate, compared with the less than 5 percent of rural women who are (statistics in Sadiqi 2003:89 after Agnaou 2002). The economic marginalization of plains residents in the national economy, despite the area's agricultural wealth, and the virtual erasure of Ishelhin within the community of plains dwellers, is historically grounded in the transformation of land tenure and political economy under French administration.

Conclusion

Different political economic systems arose in the Sous plains and the Anti-Atlas mountains during the course of the twentieth century, shaping material and discursive constructions of community, individual subjectivity, class, ethnicity, and gender. The plains were home to a rural agricultural proletariat whose lands were expropriated by regional qayds and French colonists alike, then redistributed after Independence. Men worked for day wages in the nearby farms. The economic system of the mountains was entirely different than the plains; lands continued to be passed within a family from one generation to the other, but the barley harvests were rarely sufficient. An almost wholesale migration of post-pubescent males had not diminished men's ties to their lands, however, where women remained to work year-round. Given the different political, economic, and social histories of the plains and mountains, it would stand to reason that these topographical areas would be conceptually distinct in the scholar's eye. Yet the places I have been contrasting shared a common spoken communicative code, Tashelhit, which made them all Ishelhin by their own reckoning, even though plains dwellers were conceptually peripheral to the allegedly pure Ashelhi center in the mountains.

The chapter that follows considers musical productions and rehearsals by young women in Arazan that "point to junctures in the processes aimed at national integration" (Baumann 1987:29), as well as the failure of these processes to take hold as totalizing facts. Through expressive culture, we can begin to see the contours of hegemonic cultural forms attempting to anchor in collective practices, as well as alternative configurations of self and group. Plains people, and Ishelhin more generally, refer to musical productions as "playing." As I will demonstrate, the off-stage "play" in informal rehearsals rounds out a much fuller picture of the ethnolinguistic practices of Ishelhin in the late twentieth century, and complicates efforts to anchor a single people in a bounded territory with a unified, discrete language.

Chapter 7

Ishelhin into Arabs? Ethnolinguistic Differentiating Practices in the Periphery

> *. . . performances are not simply artful uses of language that stand apart both from day-to-day life and from larger questions of meaning, as a Kantian aesthetics would suggest. Performance rather provides a frame that invites critical reflection on communicative processes.*
>
> – Bauman and Briggs (1990:61)

"*Ḥḍramt!*" (Get ready!) Naima commanded the dozen other young women sitting in a circle in her mother's courtyard in Arazan, pounding a small frame drum (*ṭṭara* or bendir) for emphasis. The older married women chatted around the open stoves clustered in a corner of the courtyard, preparing a dinner of couscous with stewed vegetables and quince. In another courtyard off the corridor that ran the length of the groom's family's compound, men entertained themselves playing dqqa, Arab plains music. With the faint echo of the men's music in the background, younger girls warmed goatskin drums over the bonfire for their older peers. Naima started tapping a ganga rhythm characteristic of Houara (Arab) community song, with two heavy beats followed by a light one or a pause (- - _ - - _). Next to Naima, Aziza joined in the ganga on her hourglass-shaped drum (taɛrija). Khadija interrupted the rhythm on her own taɛrija; since these drums are always paired, this changed the beat, which then prompted Aziza to shift rhythms as well. Three more young women started humming a few lines of a commercial Tashelhit song that was popular that summer. Khadija changed rhythms again, this time to a familiar Houara song. Two young women sang the first verse in Moroccan Arabic; another called the response. As the young women laughed and brought the playing to a halt, Fadma pronounced, "Worthless (*walu*)!" Pragmatically, this assessment functioned more as a challenge to improve the next performance than as a reprimand. As a bivalent word (Woolard 1998a), equally integrated into both Moroccan Arabic (MA) and Tashelhit and not clearly a borrowing from one to the other, "walu" smoothed the transition between the sung Arabic and the spoken Tashelhit. The young women continued to intersperse singing in Arabic and assessing or taunting in Tashelhit until dinner was served.

The musical rehearsal opened an evening of festivities that culminated in the engagement of Naima's brother, from Arazan, to a woman from an Arabic-speaking village around 15 km away. Bilingual practices were common in community musical productions among Tashelhit-speaking plains people, including those of Arazan, in the late 1990s. In this chapter, I examine the intertextuality and iconicity of situated plains verbal expressive practices through which hegemony and marginalization are constituted, represented, and contested. Such practices challenge the catch-all characterization "bilingual" that oversimplifies expressive practices in the peripheries of the seemingly more homogeneous centers. In the linguistic hierarchy in post-Independence Morocco (Figure 1.3), vernacular Arabic was symbolically superior to vernacular Tashelhit not only for its perceived proximity to the classical Arabic of Islamic texts, but more importantly because of Arabic's alleged ability to unite the Moroccan nation. For native Tashelhit speakers in the plains, a mastery of colloquial Arabic afforded greater access to economic and symbolic capital. Additionally, and more frequently, MA allowed access to symbolic capital (such as diplomas) that could increase a person's access to economic capital in the form of civil service employment or an expanded pool of potential spouses. Scholars have scarcely attended to such in-between populations despite their relevance to the negotiation over ethnic and cultural heterogeneity that accompanies demographic and political economic changes.

The ethnographic material that follows draws into relief some of the dynamics through which community and marginality are created, maintained, and reproduced through language practices, not merely reflected in language practices. Members of marginalized groups themselves are active agents in framing and constructing their marginality through the control and manipulation of verbal expressive resources. This chapter is organized into two main parts. First, I detail the contours of the evening's transcript, focusing primarily on young women who figured centrally in both language maintenance and language shift, and were thus key language mediators. Secondly, I analyze the event and the broader phenomenon, including the process of learning to sing in a language one does not speak, and hypothesize as to how this practice might have come about. In conclusion, I raise methodological and theoretical directions for work on other marginalized language communities undergoing language shift.

Music in the Production of Ethnolinguistic Difference

> <u>lmɛllm maši bḥal lmutɛllm</u>
> The master isn't like the disciple.
> – Mbarka Mrat Lhaj, Roudani ššixa (professional performer) from the Hmar plains, Sous

In the late 1990s, Arab men rarely hesitated to marry Tashelhit women, but few Arab women were amenable to marrying Ashelhi men. The engagement party here was an exception, and the future bride's village was located about three-quarters of an hour away from Arazan by pickup truck off a dirt road. Arabic-speaking plains communities had no Tashelhit-language component in their expressive repertoires, leaving Ishelhin to accommodate their Arabic-speaking neighbors in song and, through bilingual mediators, in speech. The event analyzed in this chapter is an iconic representation of the mixed political economic situation of plains Ishelhin, according to Irvine and Gal's concept of iconization as involving a "transformation of the sign relationship between linguistic features (or varieties) and the social images with which they are linked" (Irvine and Gal 2000:37).

In examining the evening as a whole, I depart from the conventional ethnography of speaking approach that singles out a particular genre or performance particular to the course of an evening (Mills 1991). Scholars have conventionally analyzed language, song, and other verbal expressive genres in isolation from one another. Yet just as ethnographers of communication have insisted on collecting naturally occurring discourse rather than eliciting data or reconstructing "typical" exchanges, so too should our methodologies allow for analysis of overlapping, simultaneous, and juxtaposed modalities. Expanding the scope of an event in the transcripts – both verbal and musical – reveals both the patterning and spontaneity of verbal expressive practices in a bilingual community and captures a dynamic that links macro-social and political economic forces and the particular interactions that reflect, challenge, and refashion them.

My goals in excerpting from this linguistic transcript and musical notation are three-fold. First, I show how participants drew on Arabic and Tashelhit genres in ways that are constitutive of language ideologies and that demonstrate attention to prosody and phonology across verbal genres. Second, I suggest that the bilingual repertoire was compartmentalized by modality (song or talk, although the medial genre chant was alternatively in Arabic or Tashelhit). Third, I illustrate how Arabic song emerged as the focal point of the evening, conditioning individuals' unequal access to their community's expressive repertoire, and relegating Tashelhit to the sidelines.

Any transcript is a social construction shaped by the analytical goals of the compiler (Ochs 1979), although ideally a full and accurate representation of the speech event for the purposes at hand (Duranti 1997). Typically, a transcript captures a short excerpt of an event, its highlights, or particularly exemplary or iconic moments. Such a cursory pass would not suffice here, since my interest lies in the flow, order, and transition between expressive genres, languages, and spaces more than the referential content of song lyrics or participants' biographies. The transcript here captures the flavor of situated bilingualism, stretching across space and time, between places, and between multiple expressive genres and languages. It would be inappropriate to subdivide performance segments into overt and hidden performances after Scott's model (1990), for this would suggest that rehearsals and play, more broadly, should be deemphasized as the "hidden" transcript, since they are not intended to be seen outside the rehearsal space. Such an emphasis would inadvertently privilege the intended, "public" performance over the improvised, "private" performance – an arbitrary division indeed in a study of musical influence and linguistic practice.

A brief explanation of some pertinent qualities of the song genres introduced in Table 2.1 illustrates the young women's originality in moving between them. Plains people generically referred to their music under the umbrella term *lhḍṛt* (Ar. al haḍra). Here, the Arab genres consisted of ganga (called dqqa for men) and *lmizan* (Ar. mizan, lit. balance) during the second part of each song where the focus shifts from lyrics to rhythm and the dancing ensues. Tashelhit genres in the "off-stage" performance arenas in this evening were agwal, the women's collective song and dance performed in Anti-Atlas villages; tanḍḍamt (lit. arrangement or ordering); and rways, the commercially recorded popular music featuring a soloist, either a male rays or female raysa, with instrumental accompaniment.

In the plains, the Houari Arab genres were played by a circle of taεrija and tara drummers and one performer on the nqas (metal drumsticks tapped on a metal hubcap or a cylinder). One or more vocalists led the singing, and a chorus called the refrain, sometimes singing in unison with him or her. The tempo changed frequently and the rhythm periodically, and with these the intensity of the music shifted. A shift to a faster tempo and more closely spaced nqas strokes invited women to rise and dance. At this point, the drumming figured centrally. Dancing with plains music involved jumping high in the air, twisting and timing one's landing so as to match the tara. A talented dancer kept eye contact with the main tara drummer and timed his or her pounding feet to coincide with the drum's beat. Adolescent girls in the plains tended not to jump and stomp as vigorously as their older sisters, mothers and grandmothers. Instead, they moved between segments of stomping and others approximating Eastern Arab movements, in which they outstretched their arms and delicately fluttered their hands while showcasing their undulating hips with a scarf tied tight around the widest part.

The transcript below moves through three physical spaces over the course of several hours (Table 7.1 and Transcript 7.1): the groom's parents' courtyard (transcript lines 13–76), the road while atop a truck en route to the bride's village (lines 77–132), and the courtyard in the bride's parents' home (lines 136–end). Figure 7.1 plots shifts between modalities (where song is marked by quotation marks), between languages, and between rehearsals and performances. For analytical purposes here, rehearsals denote segments of musical play not intended to be heard outside the immediate peer group. Rehearsal segments contain more Tashelhit (especially lines 88–97 and 110–24), the informal "language of solidarity" (Hill 1985; Hill and Hill 1986), whereas public performances in the bride's family's courtyard (especially lines 147–75) were entirely in Arabic.

As the young women moved between languages, they remained attentive to phonological and prosodic parallels in ways that suggest that they considered both Arabic and Tashelhit components of the linguistic repertoire that could be mixed and fashioned to achieve a desired effect. This is evident in the opening utterances. In the transcript, Tashelhit is italicized, MA is underlined, bivalent words in both Tashelhit and MA are italicized and underlined, sung passages are marked with quotation marks, and spoken utterances are unmarked:

Transcript 7.1: Arazan Engagement Party

13	*Group:*	"wa allay, wa allay"	((vocables))
15	*Fadma:*	*wa:lu*	*Worthless!*
17	*Aisha:*	"wa laɛduwat"	"Oh my enemies"

The sound /wa/ was repeated in the initial position of these three utterances, the first and third sung (marked by quotation marks) and the second spoken; the first and second bivalent and the third in Arabic. The /wa/ in line 13 is a common vocable; in line 15 it is the first syllable of the word, and in line 17 it serves as a vocative morpheme that glosses as "Oh" in English. Despite pragmatic differences between these uses of the morpheme /wa/, and the additional uses of it in lines 27 and 29 below, there is a prosodic parallel that draws attention to the sound of the utterances – an acoustic tendency that recurs elsewhere in the evening's performances.

Also notable is the lack of code-switching within utterances, as evidenced in lines 21 to 44:

21	*Young woman:*	"wa hayia wa ah"	((vocables))
22	*Others:*	"lli bġa ḥbibu iṣbr ɛliha"	"The one who wants his lover waits patiently for her"
24	*Group:*	"ha, ha, ha . . ."	((vocables))
27	*Fadma:*	*wa:lu mayad*	This is *nothing/worthless*!
29	*Fadma:*	*ullah amk ibbi ha::*	I swear you broke [the drum] lo::ok
30	*Khadija:*	*ha ur ibbi ḥtta mani*	I didn't break anything
		is ka iṣmd ha!	it's just cold, look!
. . .			
43	*Latifa* (to KEH):	*nniġ am is gis illa lfḍl?*	Listen is it pleasing?
44	*Fadma* (to Latifa):	*ur a ta tšwi*	It's not good

Even between participant utterances, as was true in everyday plains speech, Tashelhit-Arabic inter-sentential and intra-sentential code-switching was infrequent. Bilingual speakers moved between languages to address monolinguals in a mixed sitting. But the kind of extended code-switching between French and Arabic typical of educated circles in Moroccan and other postcolonial cities is not predictive of multilingual language management by rural and non-elite groups. Here, singing in Arabic did not trigger a code switch to speaking in Arabic, in contrast to the single-modality code-switching in dialogue. Instead, participants used Tashelhit to offer assessments and commentary on the performance, their own states, and participants' behavior as it took place (cf. Goodwin and Goodwin 1992). More generally, however, speaking appropriately in Tashelhit sometimes required an Arabic loanword, assimilated or not; other times, the Arabic term carried different connotations than its Tashelhit correlate. Here, however, the song lyrics remained distinct from conversation, as if quotations, and were considered fixed forms whose phonological structures affected subsequent utterances but whose code did not.

After dinner, the villagers and I boarded atop one of three pickup trucks that followed the groom's family and friends to the future bride's village. Trucks were sex-segregated; my truck had mostly young women, a few mothers, and their children. It was a warm night, and the moon lit the fields as we drove the bumpy dirt path leading to the paved road. During the ride, the young women resumed their song. The truck ride – once again a liminal space between villages, homes, and kinship groups – allowed the young women to explore the breadth of their verbal expressive repertoire in ways that were invisible in subsequent "onstage" performance spaces. The participants did not qualify their playing (lɛab) in the truck as performance, since they devalued free improvisation practices as imperfect versions of finished performances.

This middle, liminal section of the evening contained the most Tashelhit and the most movement between song genres: rways → ganga → tanḍḍamt

Table 7.1 Shifts in language, genre, type, and modality across space (Sous plains engagement, September 1997)

Transcript line #	Notation page #	Performer(s)	Genre	Language	Type	Modality	Location
1	–	Mixed m	Dqqa	MA	Rehearsal	Song	Groom's courtyard
8–14	–	Yf	Ganga	MA	Rehearsal	Song	
15–16	–	Yf	–	Tash	Assessment	Talk	
17–26	–	Yf	Ganga	MA	Rehearsal	Song	
27–31	–	Yf	–	Tash	Assessment	Talk	
32–42	–	Yf	Ganga	MA	Rehearsal	Song	
43–44	–	Yf	–	Tash	Assessment	Talk	
46–56	–	Yf	Ganga	MA	Rehearsal	Song	
57–63	–	Yf	–	Tash	Assessment	Talk	
64–69	–	Yf	Ganga	MA	Rehearsal	Song	
70	–	Yf	–	Tash	Command	Talk	
77–83	–	Yf	Ganga	MA	Improvisation	Song	Pickup truck
85–87	–	Yf	–	Tash	Assessment/Q	Talk	
88–94	1	Aafaf / Yf	Rways	Tash	Adaptation	Song	
95–96	1	Aa / Kar	–	Tash	Metaling Q	Talk	
97	2	Kar / Yf	Rways	Tash	Adaptation	Song	
97–103	2–3	Kar / Yf	Rways/ ganga	Tash	Improvisation	Song	
105–108	4–6	Yf	Tanḍḍamt agwal	Tash	Improvisation	Song	
109	7	Yf	ṣalat ɛla nbi	MA	Praises to Md.	Chant	
111–112	7	Yf	Chant	Tash	Improvisation	Chant	

113	7	Yf	"Ahya"	Tash	Exclamation	Talk	
114–117	8	Yf	Rways/agwal	Tash	Adaptation	Song	
118–122	9	Yf	Tanḍḍamt	Tash	Improvisation	Song	
124	10	Yf	Rways	Tash	Adaptation	Song	
125		Fadma	–	Tash	Command	Talk	
126–127	11	Yf	Tanḍḍamt	Tash	Improvisation	Song	
128	12	Naima	–	Tash	Command	Talk	
130–132	12	Yf	Agwal	Tash	Improvisation	Song	
136–137	12–13	Yf	Ganga	MA	Performance	Song	Bride's village
144–163	–	Mixed age f	Ganga	MA	Performance	Song	Bride's courtyard
165	–	Yf	–	Tash	Apology	Talk	
166–176	–	Mixed age f	Ganga	MA	Performance	Song	
178–180	–	Adult m	Ganga	MA	Performance	Song	
181	–	Adult f	–	Tash	Command	Talk	
182–183	–	Adult m f	Ganga	MA	Performance	Song	
184	–	Adult f	–	Tash	Scolding	Talk	

Notes:
Ym: young unmarried male.
Adult: older or married.
MA: Moroccan Arabic.
Yf: young unmarried female.
Mixed: young unmarried or older married.
Tash: Tashelhit Berber.
Q: question.

Figure 7.1 Musical notation of engagement party, Arazan

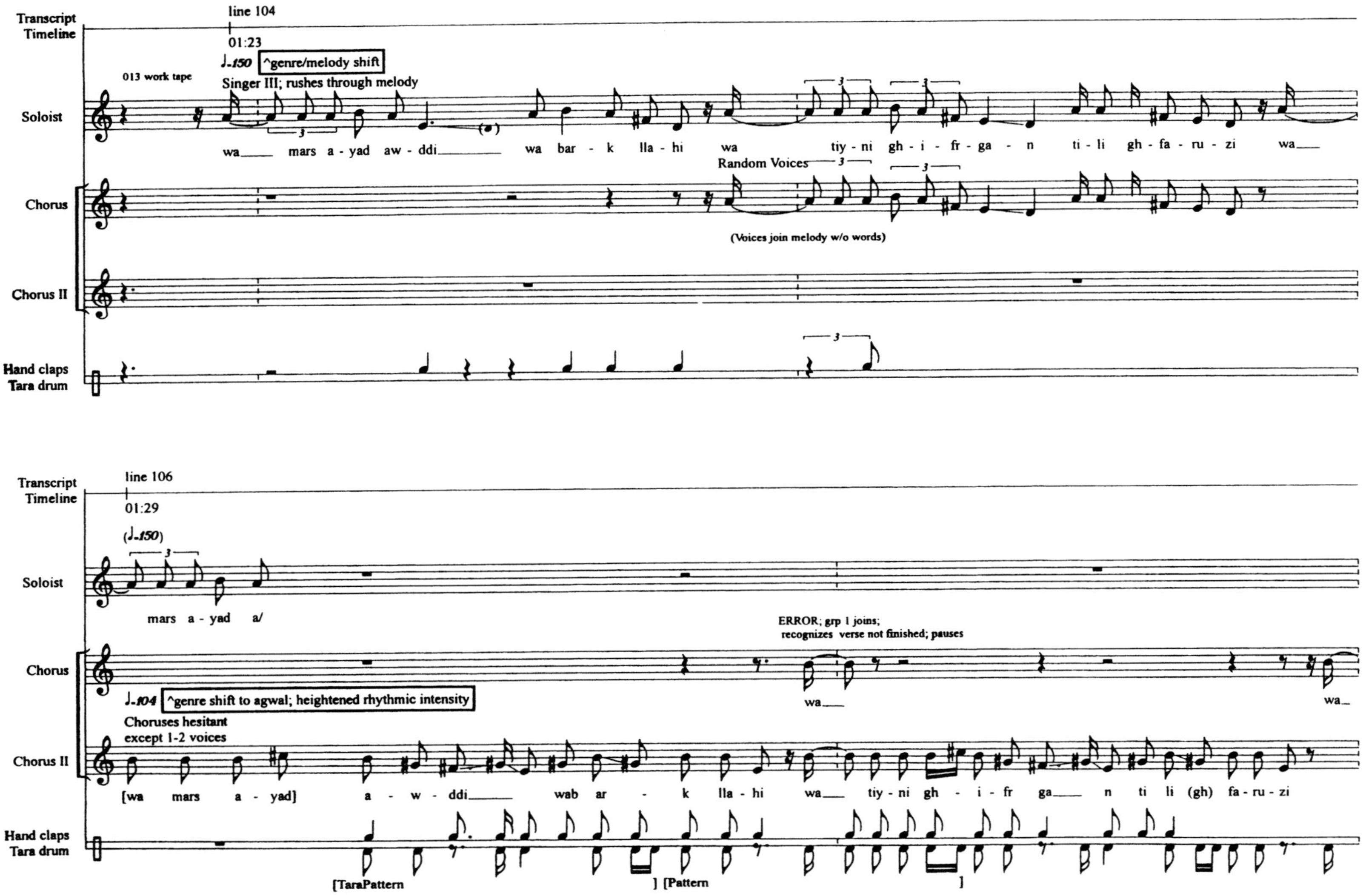

Figure 7.1 *Continued*

→ agwal (Table 7.1, from line 88). Each genre shift signaled a reframing of the context (Goodwin and Duranti 1992), opening up new possibilities for improvisation and inspiration. Genres are about boundary maintenance, as each genre has different indexical qualities and sources of authority; playing with genre entails playing with boundaries (Kapchan 1996:5). In the truck, the playing was more lighthearted, inspired, and playful than in the courtyard. In quick succession, the young women took up bits of song that they then abandoned; one melody or rhythm trailed into another. Commercial and community song was interspersed, as were genres and languages, with no apparent pattern. The pace of the rhythmic and melodic shifts was dizzying, as evidenced in Figure 7.1. As in much of the Muslim world, women's musical instruments were limited to frame drums, affording portability and flexibility (Doubleday 1999). It was unclear who owned them; they exchanged hands frequently according to whim and will. The transitional space and moment of the truck ride opened up possibilities for the innovation and change that are characteristic of liminal spaces (Kapchan 1996). Moreover, it invited participation by non-Arabic speakers whose participation in on-stage performances was limited. In the on-stage performances that would take place later in the evening, Razani women who did not know Arabic lyrics drummed, danced, and sometimes sang the refrain's vocables, but they did not take up the central verses that commented on the festivities.

Young women like the monolingual 15-year-old Aafaf, then, played a central role during rehearsal, but receded to the background during the on-stage performances. In the truck, she took up a popular commercial Tashelhit song, and the others joined in (lines 88–96).

88	*Aafaf and Chorus:*	*"a igan iġ ifulki ssaɛd n yan*	"We say he has good luck
		u iwin d yan ira"	when he marries the one he wants"
91	*Singer II:*	*"da da da dam"*	(vocables)
92	*Aafaf and Chorus:*	*"Allah t awddi ma ira ujdaɛ tawada*	"The horse no longer needs to trot
		a ttaksi n ljdid ar ka tẓẓad aġaras"	The new taxi beats the pavement"
93	*Singer II:*	*"da da dam da da dum"*	(vocables)
94	*Aafaf:*	*"wa ili awa nkki d bariz ad nmun"*	"My dear, Paris and me go together"
95	*Karima:*	*illa lmal? dars lmal?*	There is wealth? He has wealth?
96	*Aafaf:*	*a nddu s bariz illa lmal*	Let's go to Paris there is wealth.

With a commercially recorded song in Aafaf's repertoire, it appears that what Schuyler (1979) calls the community's "repertory of ideas" was for these young women much more variegated than what Caton (1990) calls the "repertoire of means" passed down from adults to young adults and adolescents. That is, the young women in the truck innovated musically by using their parents' songs as part, but not all, of their stock. Aafaf had little knowledge of Arabic, but she was a favorite drummer and dancer among her peers, singing only during refrains to Arabic ganga songs in public performances. In the liminal space of the truck, she was able to take the floor with a Tashelhit-language song that organized the subsequent participation of her peers. Questioning Aafaf's lyrics, Karima posed a metadiscursive query in Tashelhit, then shifted the melody and sang a rways verse, the chorus of which the other young women took up for several repetitions (see Figure 7.1). Simultaneous speech or overlap is marked by [:

97	*Karima:*	*"afrux ur igi lflus*	"A boy is not money
		yawi d agudi n [lflus	bring back a ton of money"
98	*Chorus II:*	*// ["wa iġ ira [aḍar] a muddu*	// "If my [leg] wants to travel
		s ġilli ur ixalid wa la ili"//	to an unknown land" //

A tanḍḍamt then immediately followed the rways song above:

101	*Chorus:*	*"istahl yan ifulkin lluz awa*	"The good one deserves an *almond*
		istahl tifilit n umgard	he deserves a necklace
		istahl yan ifulkin lluz awa"	the good one deserves an *almond*"
104	*Young woman* ((shouting)):	*wa Nayma! Nayma!*	Hey Naima! Naima!

After one young woman interrupted the performance to beckon Naima, another picked up a drum and transformed the Tashelhit tanḍḍamt into an Arabic ganga. This move brought about a genre shift as well as a linguistic code-switch. Still another genre shift followed soon after when a young woman hurriedly produced a tanḍḍamt melody that the group then took up, easing the pace into the typically heavy and slower agwal Tashelhit genre (see Figure 7.1):

105 *Singer III* ((quickly)) *then Chorus* ((slowly at first; then rapidly repeated)):

// wa mars ayad awddi wa barkllahi	//"It's March, my dear, and may it be blessed
wa tiyni ġ ifrgan tili ġ faruzi" //	they say that dates on the branch are
	[like sweets] on porcelain [platters]"//

The agwal performance segment is notable because Razanis repeatedly insisted to me that they did not know this Tashelhit genre that they characterized as *lhḍṛt n udrar*, mountain music. Indeed, in three years of attending plains festivities, I had never seen agwal performed there. Perhaps the young women had heard it on Tashelhit radio, or a group of them had attended a wedding in the mountains. Regardless, the genre was firmly entrenched in these young women's repertoire – since the whole group participated – although it remained restricted to the off-stage context, one of the many verbal expressive repertoire components absent from representations of Ashelhi popular culture.

Soon thereafter, Singer I initiated generic praise chanting (ṣalat ɛla nbi) then common at life-cycle celebrations throughout Morocco (except the Berber mountains):

109	*Singer I/random*:	wa sidi tbarak allah wallah allah	Oh Sidi blessings of God

Retaining the cadence and prosody of this Arabic chant, Singer II immediately offered an improvised chant in Tashelhit:

111	*Singer II*:	*wa immi wa immi ha*	Oh mother oh my mother
		(1.0)	(1.0)
		wa nniġ am tiwwi myya	I told you (f) take a hundred

Attention to prosody was again evident in the exasperated "*ahya!*" (Oh!) that sparked a commercial Tashelhit (rways) song opening with a prosodic parallel between the emphasized /h/ and the subsequent /ɛ/ of *iɛyalin*:

113	*Young woman*:	*ahya!*	Oh well!
114	*Singer I* ((softly)):	*iɛyyaln ula tiɛyyalin"*	"Oh boys and girls"
	((8.0))		
116	*Sing II/Chor II*:	*"iɛyyaln ula tiɛyyalin*	"Boys and girls
		ad tili lmḥabba ngra tun"	may there be *love* between you"

In lines 118–24, the young women again improvised, moving between Tashelhit tanḍḍamt and rways genres. The sequence opened with a generic introductory melody with falling intonation and then a rising /u/ repeated twice (see Figure 7.1):

118	*Singer I*:	*"u: ullah ra ndu"*	"I swear we're going"
119	*Singer II*:	*"ullah a myya u: a myya u:"*	"I swear a hundred"

The singers then moved between genres in quick succession as follows:

– tanḍḍamt:

120	*Choruses I/II*:	*// "annz ttaksi n Trudant*	//"Let's take a taxi to Taroudant,
		ššur ukan a nmun"//	slow down we're coming along"//

– rways (from Fatima Tabaamrant):

124	*Chorus II*:	*"wa ddunit tga ġikad"*	"That's the way the world is"

– spoken command:

125	*Fadma*:	*tlaq i rriḥ xay i rriḥ*	Cut out the talking pick up a song

– tanḍḍamt with ganga drumming:

126	*Singer I/Chorus:*	*// "wa iġ ira aḍaṛ a muddu*	//"And if my leg wants to travel
		s ġilli ur ixalid wa la ili"	//to an unknown land"//

– spoken command to a young girl:

128	*Naima:*	*gyyur s ṛgg ka ur s ṛgg*	Sit down just sit down.

Two or three other young women then initiated songs that the group did not take up before one melody stuck. The soloist started with one line that the group then took up as a slow and heavy agwal:

130	*Singer I:*	*"atbir umlil atbir umlil*	"White dove, white dove"
		bbrk allah a tawnza zund lɛid lɛrš	Good for you, oh bangs [girls] like Throne Day
		ay atbir umlil"	oh white dove"

Throughout this improvisation session, the young women's linguistic agility instantiated a prevalent Tashelhit language ideology, namely that "having language" (*illa dars wawal*) was a virtue worthy of others' admiration, respect, and reverence. To "have language" means to be able to adapt one's speech to one's interlocutors, to be subtle, clever, witty, or pious through word choice, metaphor, allusion, riddle, rhyme, intonation, and timbre that depart from the more mundane, referential function of language. Young plains women applied this mastery to song texts and musical genres as they moved agiley between the plains community's poetic traditions and mass mediated commercial expressive forms. In informal settings, individuals and small groups experimented musically with stock items, adjusting lyrics, melodies, and drumming patterns to create new sounds. This was true for Arab and Ashelhi communities alike, and for their use of Arabic and Tashelhit musical genres. In the truck ride with only intimates present, all of this could be accomplished in Tashelhit. But in the public performance spaces, the same skills needed to be deployed in Arabic. These community song performances – what others have called folk or traditional music (Bauman 1977; Bauman and Briggs 1990; Bohlman 1988; Caraveli 1982; Herzog 1950) – both reproduce and expand the community's repertoire of lyrics, music, and rhythm. Each performance segment was enhanced by new influences, individual inspiration, context, and musicians' and audience members' biographies.

Once the women arrived in the bride's village (line 141), they resumed singing in Arabic through the end of the festivities. Yet they continued to offer metadiscursive commentary in Tashelhit, as when an embarrassed young woman apologized to another for her aunt who was dancing too enthusiastically (line 157); and where the hostess attempted to expel a man who had just entered the women's performance circle, usurping the floor from the women who continued to play (from line 178):

178	*Man*:	"wa ya lɛris ḍwwi b šmaɛ lbldi	"Oh groom, light with candles
		wa ila jak ez-zin ḍwwi b trisinti	and when the beautiful one [bride] arrives
			light with electricity
		wa galt lik mmak wa sir allah irḍi ɛlik"	Your mother told you, 'Go,
			may God look after you'"
181	*Hostess* ((yelling at man)):		
		ffuġ! ffuġ akk!	Get out! Just get out!
182	*Man* ((ignoring her)):		
		ṣlat allah ɛlik	"God's prayers on you
		ṣlat allah ɛlik wa rasul allah"	God's prayers on you oh prophet of God"
184	*Hostess* ((scolding)):		
		ḥšuma aq waḥaq ṛbbi a bla ḥšuma	Shame on you, I swear, shame on you

The "on-stage" performances in this final public space – the bride's parents' courtyard – were the most polished, with the fewest aborted starts. The patterning of multiple expressive genres and two languages in this evening's events reinforced the hierarchical superiority of Arabic over Tashelhit. Tashelhit talk framed the center-stage Arabic-language performances where identities associated with Arab-ness – and thus plains-ness – were strengthened and validated. Tashelhit, for its part, was used for directives and assessments, but remained relegated to the off-stage performance, an index of informality and solidarity. Yet there was strength in the covert prestige (Trudgill 1983) of speaking a marginalized language that suggested an "alternative hegemony" (Gal 1995a).

The young women here alternated between languages rather than using hybrid forms. As Kapchan explains in her study of the marketplace oratory of Moroccan women in the Middle Atlas town of Beni Mellal, hybridity "express[es] not an agglutinative process, or one that cuts and pastes, but an actual *mixing and blending* of forms" (Kapchan 1996:7, italics in the original; see also 20–4). During the plains engagement festivities, there was an integration of multiple genres across two languages, with only slight hybridization within specific sung genres, and only in moments of transition, as we will see shortly. Genres, or what Pratt (1987) calls stylistic registers, might be seen instead as group-internal fault lines that individuals use to include and exclude others, and to levy critique in ways that, as Kuipers writes, "fracture, divide, and rearrange groups and sub-groups in new ways" (Kuipers 1998:7). Although not hybridized, these performances push the boundaries of the genres in play and thus challenge the institutions and traditions associated with them. Genres are no longer understood to be "sets of discourse features" but instead are "orienting frameworks, interpretive procedures, and sets of expectations" (Schieffelin and Woolard 1994:59). While each genre here has distinctive formal features, more important to our discussion are the orienting frameworks each entails and the ways in which these frameworks establish expectations for subsequent performances and interactions. The improvisation responded at each turn to what preceded it, stringing together genres and shifting expectations, a fluid assumption and then abandonment of multiple identificatory frames, all playfully keyed. The relationship between genres and languages here involves the device Bakhtin identifies as the dialogized interrelation of languages, distinct from hybridization and what he calls "pure dialogues" (Bakhtin 1981:358). In his formulation, these encounters may be intentional or unintentional, whether at the level of the individual utterance or from a wider purview. The evening presented here was heteroglossic as a whole: multi-voiced, in Bakhtin's sense, with authoritative, prior "speech," if we extend "speech" metaphorically to include sung voicings.

Participants' code-switching here cannot be accounted for simply by individual choices shaped by interlocutor, topic, setting, function, or psychological associations with each language (Bentahila 1983). Nor can code-switching be explained merely as a colonial legacy (cf. Swigart 1992, 1994) or as evidence of cultural assimilation into the nation (Suleiman 1994, 2003; Taifi 1995). The bilingual patterning is entrenched in the plains, although distinct from the relatively stable Arabic diglossia that characterizes the Arabic-speaking world more broadly (Ferguson 1959; Haeri 2003; Hannaoui 1987; Heath 1989), and from the French-Arabic diglossia of twentieth-century North Africa (Boukous 1995; El Gherbi 1993; Holt 1994; Pleines 1990).

In exploring the patterning – and idiosyncrasies – of bilingualism in a peripheral place, we can better understand both the sources and the social consequences of multiple language use. In the Sous, mountain dwellers are positioned – and position themselves – as more faithful to their cultural heritage than plains dwellers who literally and figuratively dance around the periphery of a core Ashelhi homeland. Native Tashelhit speakers in the mountains see their co-ethnics in the plains as "giving in to Arabs" since they have incorporated Arabic-language elements into their expressive repertoires. In this way, fractal recursivity (Irvine and Gal 2000) displaces the Arab–Berber distinction evident at one level onto another level, positioning some Tashelhit speakers as more Ashelhi than others, and perpetuating the distinction between what French Protectorate officials called "Arabized Berbers" and "pure Berbers." Yet these Tashelhit speakers consider themselves Ishelhin, as do their Arabic-speaking neighbors. Still, they are largely absent from the scholarly record, from popular consciousness, and from state language policies. The fluidity of the expressive practices here destabilizes recursion for both rural Moroccans and the scholars who write about them.

The matter of learning to sing in an unfamiliar language raises certain logistical questions. The Arabic used in ḥḍṛt song genres differed from everyday MA in meter and intonation. Plains men learned to speak MA at an earlier age than did females through schooling, through interactions with Arabic speakers in the fields and towns, and according to a plains ideology that speaking Arabic was a male-gendered practice. Men thus transferred their spoken familiarity with MA to singing. But Tashelhit-speaking plains women and girls did not transfer spoken knowledge onto their sung productions. If that had been the case, schooled young women would have been best positioned to sing these songs, and that was not typically so. Caton argues that the conventions of everyday talk ground the bases of what Hymes (1972) calls communicative competence in song and poetry (Caton 1990). Caton is right to emphasize – drawing on Friedrich (1979) Sapir (1921, 1995 [1933]), and Jakobson (1987) – that "poetry is ubiquitous in everyday conversation," and that the poet either intensifies or foregrounds "the aesthetics of communication in the production of verse" (Caton 1990:50). Tashelhit poetic language, however, was only one element of musical competence required to participate in Tashelhit community song. Musical competence extended beyond talk to attention to non-linguistic sonic phenomena, particularly rhythm and meter, as well as a deft grasp of social context, most notably familiarity with the individuals who were implicated in the success or failure of a sung poetic performance.

Young Tashelhit-speaking women in the plains learned intonation, rhythm, and melody prior to Arabic lyrics; this was clearest in moments when performers erred in their calculations or hesitated to join the chorus (cf. Hoffman 2002a regarding Anti-Atlas song). To learn lyrics, young women first discerned syllable pitch and length, only later matching phonological and morphological elements to these syllables. Melody and rhythm carried the song a certain distance, to the refrain, at which point the only lyrics were the vocables "whoa, whoa," semantically void utterances that functioned pragmatically like the English-language "yeah, yeah." At that moment, the lyrics upheld a meter that emphasized the song's focal point: the drumming and dancing segments of the mizan. Musical form predominated over lyrical and semantic content, but outside of their immediate communities, these musical productions were subject to more criticism. In an interview with a professional entertainer and songwriter (šši̱xa) in Taroudant named Mbarka Mrat Lhaj, I played a recording of Arazan ganga community music, asking Mbarka what she thought. She responded diplomatically but pointedly: "The master isn't like the disciple (lmɛllm maši bḥal lmutɛllm)." Yet for young women in the plains, participation in hḍṛt productions offered amusement and catharsis, and it hardly mattered who was the master. The university student Halima, one of Arazan's strong young women musicians, told me, "If I'm under pressure, I have to sing. It's something I can't control, but I'm not happy without it. It's a part of me; it's part of who I am, even if I don't live in the village any more."

She felt an attachment to singing in Arabic that she did not feel when speaking Arabic, and indeed she loathed speaking Arabic with anyone who understood Tashelhit. Clearly, the modalities of talk and song were dissociated in her mind and practice; there was a correct domain for each language. I turn now to consider how this state of affairs may have arisen and its implications for the plains community specifically, for Ishelhin and Imazighen more broadly, and for speakers of contracting languages writ large.

Semiotic-ideological Representations of Linguistic Difference

> *The borderlands have no typical citizens; experiences there undermine the safe ground of cultural certainty and essential identity.*
>
> –Tsing 1993:225

Irvine and Gal (2000) identify a useful set of semiotic processes that they argue inform ideological representations of linguistic difference: *iconization*, *fractal recursivity*, and *erasure*. These processes stem from and shape "the ideas with which participants and observers frame their understandings of linguistic varieties and map those understandings onto people, events, and activities that are significant to them." They are ideological in that they are "suffused with the political and moral issues pervading the particular sociolinguistic field and are subject to the interests of their bearers' social position" (2000:35). They have concrete consequences for the ways individuals and groups draw boundaries, and they condition individuals' access to symbolic, social, and economic capital. I want to consider each of these processes as they illuminate expressive repertoires generally and plains Ashelhi repertoires specifically.

Through the semiotic process of *iconization*, "linguistic features that index social groups or activities appear to be iconic representations of them." A linguistic feature that would normally point to the speaker's social identity instead appears somehow to depict or display a social group's inherent nature or essence (Irvine and Gal 2000:37). Broadly speaking, singing in Arabic indexed a plains-wide social identity. Yet to mountain dwellers and to urbanites, this practice was suggestive of plains Ishelhin's tendency to "give in" to Arabs and Arabic, and to "turn away from" their Ashelhi heritage, irrespective of the density of the Tashelhit-speaker's social network (Milroy 1987), or their everyday speaking practices. Accents tend to operate as iconic: for example, to many American northerners, the phonological and prosodic features of an American southern accent iconize the southerner's essence as backward, slow, and circuitous. The accent thus can seem to embody or iconize its speaker. Similarly, the nasal quality that many Midwestern Americans associate with both East Coast Americans and with the French iconizes a snobbish, uptight character. Iconization operates with lexical items as well as phonic qualities, as with the Soussi Arab's use of Tashelhit words such as *ašku* (because, in the place of northern MA terms laḥqaš or ḥit), *awddi* (my dear, instead of the MA bniti or wldi; lit. my daughter and my son), or *uhu* (no, for the MA le or southern MA la:weḥ). These lexical items iconized not only a region, but also the qualities of peasantness (according to many northerners and urbanites): stubbornness, closed-mindedness, parochialism, and limited intellectual ability. Yet in the Sous plains, Arabs used these Tashelhit words as a matter of course, not as a regional marker; still, the practice indexed them as somehow apart from other rural and urban speakers of Arabic.

A second semiotic process, *fractal recursivity*, involves the projection of an opposition relevant at some level onto another level of opposition, so that for instance out-group relations are projected onto in-group relations. Both French Protectorate officials in the first half of the twentieth century and mountain Ishelhin in the late 1990s projected an Arab–Berber opposition onto a plains–mountain opposition. Paradoxically, the Arab–Berber dichotomy seemed to organize distinctions among Ishelhin, projected in a fractally recursive way, by providing two categories of Berbers: Arabized Berbers and what we might call Berber Berbers. An underlying discourse of linguistic and ethnic purity informed this semiotic process, and it emerged in face-to-face metalinguistics and metapragmatics, much as it did on widely disseminated radio Tashelhit.

Through *erasure*, the third semiotic process, people highlight some cultural or linguistic practices while backgrounding others so as to emphasize bases of solidarity or, in contrast, to justify their distinction. In doing so, they elide significant social facts to better fit the ideal at hand. Anthropologists are as guilty as laypeople of erasure each time they represent cultural practices emphasizing certain salient elements over others, overlooking pesky inconsistencies. The ethnolinguistic differentiating practices iconized by the terms Arab, Ashelhi, fellah, and abudrar hide, elide, and erase social and symbolic relations that are at times more important in constraining everyday action than the categories themselves. Thus, for instance, erasure highlights the agricultural component of the category fellah and erases the individual's relationship to the means of production, effectively lumping together owners and wage laborers.

Similarly, erasure operated in denying an Ashelhi identity to the young plains women who sang in Arabic, despite their use of Tashelhit in the speaking modality. While they did not erase themselves from the category of Ishelhin – and indeed, neither did plains Arabic speakers who were acutely aware of linguistic difference – the mountain dwellers (ibudrarn) or "hard Ishelhin" (išlḥiyn iqqurn), as well as the city dwellers, tended to brush plains Ishelhin away from the "real Berber" category and into the symbolic margins. It is little wonder that many plains women, once they emigrated to towns like Taroudant, disowned their Ashelhi heritage, maintained a primarily Arabic-speaking household, and attempted to integrate into the larger Arabic-speaking speech community from which they did not risk erasure, and into which assimilation was considered the norm. Plains Ishelhin could more easily become "Arabs" than "hard Ishelhin." The residency and linguacultural (Friedrich 1989) requirements of being Ashelhi remained outside the possibilities of most plains dwellers, making Khadduj's decision to marry a man from Arghen in the mountains (Chapter 6) particularly daring.

Why Sing in Arabic? An Historical Perspective

In seeking an explanation for the phenomenon that plains Ishelhin sing in Arabic, we might examine both the historical contact between people – and their languages – and the circulation of musical genres more generally. Verbal expression in part constructs social identities, and particularly ethnic, local, and gendered identities. In the broader picture, this practice seems to underscore cultural Arabization and linguistic Arabicization. When asking why the practice has endured, the experience of the Miri Nuba people undergoing Arabicization in Sudan is suggestive.

> Customs, practices, and ideas may well be taken up initially for ulterior motives, such as a desire for respectability, a temptation to conform, or simply a fleeting interest in novelty. But they seldom persist on the strength of their original appeal alone. As their novelty or prestige value wear off in the course of general acceptance, so they are endowed with more elaborate meanings and granted a deeper commitment; they may begin to be taken seriously for their own sake. (Baumann 1987:131)

Baumann's argument here links Islamic religion and Arabicization such that identification with these values led to important changes in Miri Nuba material culture like the adoption of clothes and new norms around modesty (or, more to the point, the rejection of nudity). That said, the material and ideological manifestations of cultural change shift over time and can only be understood through the meanings local people grant to them.

To understand why plains Ishelhin sang in Arabic at festive events, I want to consider two contrasting just-so stories and then venture three additional hypotheses suggested by the archival record. Here we can see the tension between, on the one hand, the structural position of these communities in a political economic system and, on the other hand, the ideologies that mediate and make meaningful the practices that are co-constructed with political economies. Ideologies – in the neutral, non-motivated sense (cf. Eagleton 1991; Schieffelin and Woolard 1994) – emerge through narratives that weave together threads of history in a causal chain.

Just-so stories show how fractal recursion can work in a narrator's favor to construct contrasting histories. Diglossic compartmentalization dates to at least World War II, and possibly much further back; none of the elderly plains Ishelhin I spoke with recalled singing in Tashelhit at life-cycle events as youths. In the nearby plains village of Tazzemourt, in the Guettioua, a school administrator named Lahsen, married to a Houari Arab who spoke some Tashelhit, told me:

> With so much going back and forth between Arabs and Ishelhin, at some point people [read: Ishelhin] just dropped their Tashelhit song and took up the Houara song. But it doesn't matter really, Arab or Ashelhi, it's all the same.

In Lahsen's just-so story, plains Ishelhin (or more specifically, the Guettaouia of Tazzemourt) used to sing in Tashelhit, but eventually accommodated their Arab neighbors by adopting their musical practices, including their Arabic lyrics. This may simply reflect what Friedman calls the "relation between that which supposedly occurred in the past and the present state of affairs" (1992:837) – where people explained shifts in musical practices according to spoken language shift (from Tashelhit to Arabic). But the account may also be historically accurate, raising the question of why Tashelhit speakers rather than Arabic speakers dropped their ancestral singing practices. The accommodation may have gone one way, surprising given the relative hierarchical equality of the two vernaculars in the pre-Independence period.

A second just-so story contends quite the opposite, since for Razanis the question of expressive culture's origins did not even arise, given that the practice was so taken for granted. Si Hmed, the rural administrator in Arazan, was amused at my query, but patiently responded:

> We just do as our ancestors did. We are Ishelhin here. But the only time aḥwaš and agwal gets played in the village is when ibudrarn come down from Arghen. The Arazan people do not know that kind of music.

Yet the transcript from the truck ride indicates that some of the young women *did* know agwal, even though they would never perform it in front of a man like Si Hmed. Plains Ishelhin listened to radio programming in Tashelhit, so they knew that many other Ishelhin sang in Tashelhit at community festivities. If the ancestors of valley dwellers came from the mountains, they may well have adopted Arabic in order to assimilate. Moroccans reminded me periodically that the Prophet Mohammed enjoined those who live away from their ancestral land for three years to take up the customs of their adoptive people.

In that regard, it is possible that the ancestors of Arazan came from elsewhere, and this is the view Fatima Mhammd offered me. A native of Arazan who moved to Taroudant when she married, twenty years before I moved in next door, Fatima explained linguistic shift more generally as a concession of the destitute:

> Back in the early days (*zikk*), people didn't stay put! It's not like these days when you can say "this is a person's tamazirt" or "that is their tamazirt." You ask whether people stayed attached to the land? What land?! Back when there was hunger, my aunt [from Indouzal] used to tell us, people moved from place to place, wherever they could find to live and work. They left their fields and their lands; they didn't care, they just wanted to flee the hunger. They used to say that back when there was hunger, they used to drink a glass of tea while nibbling a single date; they couldn't afford sugar. That was a long time ago, before I was born, while the French were still here. At that time people didn't stay put. Whatever the people spoke in the land where they found themselves, they spoke it too.

We might say, too, that whatever the people sang in the land where they found themselves, they sang it too. Or as the tazrrart opening Part I advises, "If you arrive at the edge of a land, watch discreetly/Whatever the people of that land do, follow their lead" (*iġ ilkum yan imi n tmazirt imiyys iqqiys/anna d salan ayt tmazirt lhun d isn*). Interestingly for the Sous plains, once again speaking and singing – as modalities that might require different communicative codes – remain below the surface of consciousness even for those whose expressive repertoires exhibit this multiplicity. Historically there has been extensive displacement of villages and families due to drought, hunger, natural disaster, and, during the French Protectorate, the large-scale appropriation of land by the Moroccan officials appointed to serve the French. How do we characterize the musical repertoire of a social group, community, or place so as to make individual contributions, quirks, and proclivities expected rather than exceptions? For at least some observers, the widespread history of displacement that Fatima Mhammd describes makes it impossible to distinguish between Arabs and Berbers in any absolute sense. But note that even when people move across the borders, changing linguistic practices and group allegiances, the categories remain. Many individuals also remain attached to the group with which they ally despite the apparent malleability of not only the ethnic group's boundaries but also "the stuff it encloses" (Barth 1969:15).

There are at least three other possible explanations for this arrangement, two of which involve emigration and a third motivated by a generalized reverence for Arabic.

A first hypothesis is informed by the language ideology that maps verbal expressive genres onto places, very locally circumscribed, an ideology that precluded the possibility of one group appropriating an expressive form from another group. Arazan's residents claimed ancestry from multiple mountain tribes and tribal sections, many of whom had distinctive enough Tashelhit-language singing traditions that they may have adopted the Houari neighbors' musical repertoire rather than privileging one Tashelhit form over another. They certainly could have altered the genres and repertoires to fit their new circumstances, mixing song texts, melodies, and performance conventions, for example. But given the prevailing language ideology that a person should only sing about something appropriate to his or her experience, as I explained in Chapter Five, these emigrants might have been reluctant to take up another group's lyrics. People in each small cluster of hamlets considered their Tashelhit song repertoire unique, marking place and group cohesion. Yet authorship in Arabic song was understood to be less locality-specific than Tashelhit song, so the same rules perhaps did not need to apply.

A second hypothesis also concerns emigration, but posits that a considerable number of immigrants to Arazan may have spoken neither MA nor Tashelhit but instead the Tamazight Berber vernacular. Military records from the Igherm Native Affairs post established in 1928 document the large influx of nomadic Imazighen, Tamazight-speaking Berbers from the Eastern High Atlas tribes of the Ait Atta and the Ait Khebbash, in the 1920s and 1930s. These Imazighen, called Beraber in the Protectorate record, fled the French occupation and moved through a number of still-dissident lands of the Anti-Atlas mountains and pre-Saharan plains. It is possible that some of them settled further north during the final stages of submission, in the Sous Valley, and took on local customs. This would also account for Lahsen's comment that, in his youth, it was common to perform Tamazight community music in neighboring Tazzemourt, although later generations did not learn it; like he and his peers, they were allegedly too "tired" (*narmiġ*) to sustain it.

A third hypothesis is grounded in the Arabic language's cultural capital stemming from its perceived indissociability with the Islamic religion. Plains Ishelhin could index their identification with a broader Moroccan citizenry by participating publicly in Moroccan Arab cultural traditions whose unifying symbols have been Islam and Arabic language since the beginning of the nationalist movement. The tribe of Arghen to which Arazan belongs, at least its "mountain fraction," as French records called it, has particular cultural capital; one of the most influential Muslim reformers in Moroccan history, Ibn Toumart (b. 1092), is believed by locals to have come from the Anti-Atlas village of Tighmart, from which his name may have derived. Ibn Toumart was the fierce salafi (purist) leader who founded the Almohad Empire by defeating the vainglorious Almoravids in Marrakesh and rallying large sections of the High Atlas and Anti-Atlas to his cause. He settled in the Nfis Valley of the High Atlas where he founded the Tinmal mosque, recently restored as a UNESCO world heritage site. With its austere design, the mosque contrasts sharply with elaborately decorated contemporary architecture in Marrakesh. Ibn Toumart allegedly sponsored the study of the Quran in Tashelhit, in order to reach rural populations overlooked by the Almoravids. Arabic language thus clearly was not central to early Islamic identity; the religious Islamization of the Moroccan countryside preceded its linguistic Arabicization by several hundred years. Despite this linguistically diverse and tolerant past, however, Morocco has been marked since the beginning of the Protectorate in 1912 by the symbolic importance of Arabic (Figure 1.3) to the point where Razanis in the late 1990s, like many Moroccans, associated Arabic language with religious piety. It is possible that this reverence conditioned expressive culture in important ways.

Historically, then, it is difficult to pinpoint how and when plains Ishelhin came to sing in Arabic. One would think that French tribal reports would help here, but they do not characterize expressive practices beyond noting a tribe's "language" or "bilingualism." The otherwise detailed colonial ethnographic accounts do not get at the specific *social and spatial patterning of bilingual practices* (cf. Hoffman n.d.). The cross-cultural ethnographic record on verbal expression contains few accounts of multiple language management across expressive genres. Ethnomusicologist Anthony Seeger (1987) documented a similar situation among the Suya Indians of Brazil who sing in several languages other than their spoken language; what mattered to them, Seeger said, was rendering the songs accurately. Like the Suya, plains Ishelhin closely associate each genre with a language. Yet unlike the Suya, Ashelhi improvisations take one element, such as a drumming pattern, and apply it to lyrics conventionally not associated with it. Also unlike the Suya is the lack of integration of Ashelhi songs into the performance repertoire as seamless parts of a now "traditional" expressive repertoire. As Chernela (2003) details, multilingualism is integral to funereal wailing, a seemingly intimate life-cycle ritual, among Brazilian Indians. Baumann (1987) notes that among the Miri people of the southern Nuba mountains of Sudan, certain musical and dance styles have entered their repertoire whose lyrics use colloquial Arabic, but whose performance forms resemble the genre already in place, for instance with stomping dances. Miri "moonlight dances" that sing of an urban lifestyle and desire for consumer goods are among the most favored genres, and they are sung in Arabic. Yet unlike most Moroccan Sous plains women, most Sudanese Miri are bilingual with Arabic. While Arabic genres were certainly imported into Miri communities, they are accessible to even the unschooled, and are yet another instance of the reach and influence of northern Arab aesthetics.

Ultimately, what may all of this matter, especially if, as Lahsen the school administrator said, "Arab and Ashelhi are the same"? Indeed, it might be disingenuous to compare an imagined originary society with its seemingly bastardized contemporary form. We can only catch glimpses of earlier manifestations of cultural practices; it is unlike the nature of culture to remain constant in its multiple iterations over time and space.

Still, the language of sung expression is meaningful on at least two fronts. First, it marks commonality with other communities whose members sing the same genres but are not of the same language group, so that communication – even marriage – between Arab and Ashelhi becomes possible. Second, the musical genre itself conditions modes of human participation, shaping which individuals sing, what is voiced, and how music fits into a broader verbal expressive repertoire. For example, in the plains, musical specialization has become more widespread, so that some communities have begun to bring in professional musicians rather than perform collectively (Hoffman 2000a:272–95). Still, women and men in the plains derived so much pleasure from performing these Arabic genres that it is difficult to imagine them abandoning music-making entirely to the professionals.

Conclusion

Pratt posits that "dominant and dominated groups are not comprehensible apart from each other" and that "speech practices are organized to enact their difference and their hierarchy" (1987:59). The process of hierarchicization emerged clearly in community music performances, exhibiting the semiotic process of recursion that Irvine and Gal (2000) argue compels groups to displace differences evident on one level onto another level. Tashelhit speakers of the Ashelhi periphery treated the modalities of song, talk, and chant as elements of an expressive repertoire that, because of its Arabic component, differed from that of their co-ethnics up in the mountain homeland, but also linked them to a plains-wide bilingual speech community that shared a political economy and land tenure system grounded in Protectorate-era land expropriation and subsequent transformation of the plains from pastoral use to commercial agriculture. At weddings, engagement parties, saints' festivals, and national holidays, Tashelhit speakers in the plains marked their peripheral positioning to an idealized Ashelhi community, privileging their solidarity with neighboring Arab communities. Although the region was bilingual, individual bilingualism in the plains only went one way. Arabs rarely learned Tashelhit due to the widespread conviction that Tashelhit was hard (ṣaεb/*išqa*), virtually impossible for a non-native speaker to acquire, and that its speakers were "hard," too, whereas Moroccan Arabic was allegedly easy (sahl/*irġa*) to learn, and light (xafif/*tfsus*). Despite its positive valence here, the term light is also used derogatively by both Ishelhin and Arabs as an insult to an immodest or fun-loving, irresponsible woman. MA was also considered prestigious within a local political economy of language that differed sharply from the one more frequently noted by scholars who position literacy languages (Standard Arabic and French) as high-status in contrast to the low-status vernaculars (whether MA or Berber) (Sadiqi 2003:200). This seemingly broader generalization simply did not hold for Tashelhit women in the plains and towns who associated MA with prestige and what they called *ššiki* (Fr. *chic*): status-consciousness.

Tashelhit speakers living in the Sous plains called themselves Ishelhin in the late 1990s, but as I have demonstrated here, that taxonomic category included practitioners of a wide range of verbal expressive practices. Tashelhit was the shared vernacular of the home, gardens, and public village spaces such as the market. Yet plains Ishelhin sang and danced – with great relish at engagements, weddings, circumcisions, seventh-day infant naming festivities, and the new bride's annual return to her parental home – in Arabic. In the plains, mothers whispered to their babies in Tashelhit; but when those babies moved into adulthood, the community sang to them and about them – publicly at least – in Arabic. This chapter has attempted to understand this paradox: how it may have arisen, why it was maintained, and why it might matter both to the people involved and to the broader global process of language shift away from indigenous languages and towards state languages.

Although not linguistically uniform, the plains community was economically interlinked: Arabs and Ishelhin alike worked as seasonal agricultural wage laborers. They attended each other's festivities, socialized with neighboring villagers, celebrated life-cycle rituals and ventured on pilgrimages to saints' shrines, and married their children to one another. Social ties were forged through shared labor and friendship as often as blood – rather than through shared language. Ethnic groups, as Barth reminds us, emerge from the maintenance of borders based on differentiation patterns by those who monitor them. For that reason, we need to examine particular interactions, encounters, spaces, in which ethnolinguistic differentiation is constructed, challenged, and reinforced.

The practices I have described in this chapter challenge essentialist or purist understandings of ethnicity predicated on a single expressive vernacular. Moreover, they require that we query the relationship between linguistic practices and language ideologies, forcing us to ask which *part* of expressive practices matter to ethnic group classifications and to whom: an insider, a Protectorate official, or a state administrator. The bilingual practices I have discussed here disrupt the essentialist, purist dichotomy of Ashelhi and Arab, but they do not render these categories irrelevant. People "categorize back" (Malkki 1995:8) through heterogeneous, often patterned, everyday practices in ways that complicate efforts by indigenous activists to identify, codify, and promote a purified, essentialized, ancestral Amazigh identity. In practice, if not in theory, cultural and linguistic syncretism characterized much of rural Morocco even in the period of ethnic marginalization and Arabocentrism that I am documenting in this book. The fact that plains Ishelhin sang in Arabic during crucial life-cycle rituals suggested their abiding membership in a plains-wide community, a community characterized by a domain-specific distribution of languages and genres. *Speaking* Tashelhit or Arabic acted as a boundary-marking practice between subsections of plains society. But *singing* – in what we might call a *musica franca* – reinforced their connection.

Life-cycle events are intimate sites for the reproduction of expressive metaculture. The prominence of Arabic in the collective performances of plains Ishelhin would seem to suggest that a language shift was taking place away from Tashelhit and towards Moroccan Arabic in the plains. Yet the opposite may be argued if we attend to participants' interactions in the in-between spaces around their performances in MA. In liminal and interstitial moments of talk, in musical and prosodic innovation, and in improvisation and play, Tashelhit emerges as not only central to the linguistic repertoires of these plains women, but vibrant. Young women such as the ones singing and drumming at the engagement festivities shouldered the responsibility of language socialization for the future generation of plains Ishelhin. If young women's practices were shifting towards Arabic, the plains as a whole arguably would shift, as have scattered plains communities elsewhere, not only in the Sous but also in the Haouz plains around Marrakesh, the arid plains around Ouarzazate, and the pre-Saharan Tafilalt to the southeast.

The situation I have described here does not suggest that a widespread language shift was in process in the Sous plains, at least in Arazan. In this sense, it contrasts with Weber's classic analysis of "peasants into Frenchman" (Weber 1976) and Frye's subsequent study of how "Indians" became "Mexicans" (Frye 1996). In the Ashelhi case, the fact that young women chose to use Tashelhit with each other, in speaking, singing, and listening to commercial Tashelhit music, suggests that Tashelhit was alive and well – but in its place. Arabic, too, was restricted to particular domains, but that did not mean that it was poised to replace Tashelhit wholesale.

What do we make of those communities of Ishelhin who publicly avoided reproducing the sung Tashelhit poetry that many of them believed represents "good speech," and instead adopted the singing practices of their Arab neighbors? Do we even know that they did abandon Tashelhit expressive culture, given that at least some of their ancestors may have spoken and sung in even a third language, Tamazight? A serious look at the evening's "hidden transcripts" in the form of musical rehearsals and play segments – but as literal transcripts, as Gal has stressed in a critique of Scott's loose terminology – foregrounds the central role of Tashelhit language and cultural forms in innovation and spontaneous performances. Even hidden transcripts have publics, as Gal reminds us. This is despite Arabic's centrality in key moments of heightened attention, suggesting the presence of what Gal calls "alternative publics" and "alternative hegemonies" (Gal 1995a:417). Metaphors of resistance and submission operate uneasily here. Language maintenance strategies may usefully include accommodation of the dominant language, a process that fits uncomfortably into narratives of linguistic and ethnic purity.

Perhaps if we attend more closely to hidden transcripts, to rehearsal and improvisation rather than formal and reconstructed performances, and to the liminal spaces between recognized places, then we can understand more fully how social and linguistic hierarchies are constructed and maintained in the mundane, the quotidian, the messy, and the unclassifiable. While Scott conceived his concept of "transcript" metaphorically, he ignored the methodologies that require scholars of discourse to work with actual transcripts (Gal 1995a). His call should be taken literally, for the unkempt transcripts around communicative events reveal entrenched language ideologies and complex intertextualities (Bauman and Briggs 1992; Coplan 1988) with iterations of multiple verbal genres across languages. As for Sous Valley Ishelhin themselves, many were aware of their linguistic distinctiveness, living in what Clifford terms "a pervasive condition of off-centeredness in a world of distinct meaning systems, a state of being in culture while looking at culture" (1988:9). It is this synchronic experience-near and experience-distant positioning that Geertz argues makes for good anthropology (1983:57–8). It also made plains Ishelhin reflective philosophers on their condition, practical negotiators of their fates, and decidedly un-nostalgic perpetrators of their own symbolic domination.

Part V

Resonance

The construction and maintenance of a body of ideological communications is therefore a social process and cannot be explained merely as the formal working out of an internal cultural logic.

– Wolf (1982:388)

akšš̌ud iqqurn ijdrn ġwad lli izgzawn
Dry wood burns green wood.
– Tashelhit aphorism

Chapter 8

Mediating the Countryside: Purists and Pundits on Tashelhit Radio

. . . *hegemony can never be singular . . . it does not just passively exist as a form of dominance. It has continually to be renewed, recreated, defended, and modified.*

– Williams (1977:112–13)

. . . *language presents the picture of a ceaseless flow of becoming.*

– Vološinov (1973 [1929]:66)

While listening to a riddle program on Radio Agadir, cutting onion for the midday stew, I asked Fatima Mhammd the meaning of a word the programmer used. She responded, "I don't know, that's the way the ibudrarn (mountain people) talk; they know the hard [real] Tashelhit (*tašlḥiyt iqqurn*). You have to go to the mountains to get real Tashelhit." Echoing Sadiqi's argument that "urban Berbers consider the rural Berber way of speaking as their reference" (Sadiqi 2003:167), this native of rural Arazan seemed oblivious to the irony of her comment, given that the radio announcer was an urban language broker, a professional, and decidedly not a tabudrart. In Fatima Mhammd's depiction, the announcer was a transparent medium through which "real" Tashelhit was delivered to the listening audience that took for granted its authenticity and authoritativeness. The Tashelhit that Fatima Mhammd associated with the mountains – but also the radio – was ostensibly free of Arabic interference. Although a native Tashelhit speaker herself, Fatima considered her familiarity with the language to be limited, due to her childhood spent in the Sous plains rather than the mountains. The Tashelhit-language radio programs were as much intended for adult rural–urban emigrants like Fatima as for the monolingual mountain residents who relied on the programs for news and entertainment. Yet listeners were not only attentive to the radio program's referential content, but also to its iconic representations of Tashelhit language that, I argue in this chapter, were inspired by an idealization of the rural homeland

and a purist language ideology. Calvet (2000) has referred to language purity as a "desire to protect" that "illustrates a thoughtless fear of change, of borrowing words and expressions from other languages. It is as if only stability could somehow guarantee identity." Tashelhit radio language replicated a nostalgic discourse about the homeland not so much by presenting rural speech as by advocating a purified Modern Standard Tashelhit (MST) modeled pragmatically after Modern Standard Arabic, using an expanded lexicon of neologisms and agriculturally inspired metaphor.

Foundations of Moroccan Radio

Radio programming in Morocco began in Rabat under the French Protectorate in the 1920s. Originally the languages of diffusion were French and Classical Arabic. The beginning of programming in the Amazigh vernaculars was coextensive with the 16 May 1930 dahir (decree) that recognized customary law for those Amazigh tribes following it (rather than Islamic law) prior to submission to the French Protectorate. Vernacular radio was ostensibly intended to disseminate the Protectorate's political agenda. Despite its foundation in colonial propaganda, radio programming in the Independence period became a primary medium for the state to disseminate information to its citizens. As in the case of India, in Morocco, "Colonial and independent national radio policy has confronted the same demographic diversity" and "its goals have been shaped by political and cultural parameters" (Manuel 1993:39). Unlike rural India, rural Morocco was well-supplied with radios. While the poorest families did not own radios, or later, televisions, people listened collectively with fellow villagers.

Tashelhit radio faced a task similar to that of other postcolonial nation-states: to strengthen national identity while acknowledging national diversity (cf. Spitulnik 1998). Radio in the Moroccan vernaculars was situated in the political economy of language similarly to what Spitulnik describes for Zambia's multiethnic population. In Zambia, she notes, by allocating radio programming in selected language varieties, the state officially recognized ethnicities as

> *equally different* – that is, different in the same way – in terms of their presumably harmless, apolitical "cultural" differences. Amounting to a virtual *culturalization of ethnicity*, each ethnic group is said to have its own unique traditions, dances, songs and history, which it is encouraged to preserve and promote for the sake of the youth, tourism, and national identity. (Spitulnik 1998:167; italics in the original)

Tashelhit radio served essentially the same purpose vis-à-vis the state – but the Amazigh language community reflected in radio programming was far from homogeneous. Since the early 1970s, in addition to the programming diffused from Rabat, regional radio centers have operated with programming in both Arabic and the Tamazight regional geolects (Tarifit, Tamazight, and Tashelhit). In the Sous, Radio Agadir programming broadcast in both Arabic and Tashelhit. Tashelhit programming typically consisted of a few hours a day during the week, except during the forty-day mourning period following Hassan II's death in 1999. At that time, Amazigh music and news was replaced by Arabic-language programming throughout Morocco, including Quranic chanting and classical Andalusian music, precluding the dissemination of information about the political transition in the Amazigh language varieties.

The emergence of purism in radio with the expansion of Tashelhit into public domains, especially media, is a historically situated process. In some ways, it could only have happened at the end of the twentieth century. The broader sociopolitical context then had at least three notable dimensions:

1 An opening in the political system increased freedom of expression, including the implied freedom to speak one's native language in public places.
2 Widespread recognition that Arabicization policies failed to solve the country's education woes; Arabicization was aimed at replacing French with classical Arabic in the country's classrooms as a means of unifying expression and national identity.
3 Mass media and commercial cassette culture increasingly reached into the country's rural areas.

Substantively, radio programming informed Tashelhit speakers about the places and practices of the vernacular's other speakers. By suggesting commonality between Tashelhit-speaking places, and by association, the individuals in those places who would never meet, radio programming has been central to an ongoing shift in the basis of Ashelhi identity from one rooted in a specific *place* (and the social relations that that implied) to an identity grounded in the decentralized *practice* of speaking Tashelhit. Radio was uniquely situated in this process at the turn of the twenty-first century, for unlike print or video, it was accessible to the unschooled and literate alike. Radio messages bore the government's stamp of approval; programming was self-censored, and the listener could be confident that the programming was not subversive. Given the close monitoring of public representations of the Tamazight vernaculars under Hassan II, and the widespread marginalization of its speakers, Imazighen were attentive to their intuition about the appropriateness of using Tamazight in writing or speaking outside their homes and villages.

A Political Economy of Radio Language

Radio representations of language I collected between 1996 and 1999 were implicated in a rich political economy in which lexical items, phonology, genre, and language ideologies were produced, circulated, consumed, and negotiated in ways that indexed the differently situated individuals and groups of the broader Tashelhit language community. Notions of the homeland and the countryside were central to this political economy, constantly forcing the issue of individuals' commitment to their homelands and native language, and activating fractal recursion in which the Arab-Ashelhi distinction was projected onto individual Tashelhit speakers.

In the collective intercity taxi conversation I discussed in Chapter 3, the father complained that his daughter's teacher faulted the Tashelhit-speaking home environment for preventing the girl from mastering Arabic. The father exclaimed that this was not entirely true. "Look how much Arabic we already use," he said. "Why do we say *lblast*" [Fr. *place*], punching his taxi seat, "that's Arabic, or French or whatever. We should say *taskkiwst* [Tash. lit. small sitting thing]. Or *farmasi*. Do you know what 'pharmacy' is in Tashelhit?" The taxi driver responded, "*tgmmi n isafarn*," meaning literally "the medicine house."

It is notable that neologisms for "small sitting thing" and "medicine house" entered conversational Tashelhit, given the pervasive use of functional antecedents. Those mainly took the form of assimilated borrowings from French and Arabic like lblast and farmasi, and might be considered bivalent (Woolard 1998a), meaning they were fully integrated in both Tashelhit and Moroccan Arabic. The only place I had heard these neologisms before was on Tashelhit radio programming. Indeed, the taxi driver later confirmed to me that he had learned such terms from the radio.

Arguably, the word a Tashelhit speaker used to refer to a taxi seat mattered little. Yet the tenacity some Ishelhin displayed in seeking out the "right" or "authentic" way of representing objects and concepts with sounds and symbols was part of a larger shift in consciousness about the relationship between language and social identity. The utterance is, after all, "the most sensitive index of social changes" (Vološinov 1973 [1929]:19). As Sapir wrote, "'He talks like us' is equivalent to saying 'He is one of us'" (1995 [1933]:51). For Ishelhin, indexes included lexicon, intonation, register, and use of frozen genres such as proverbs and religious invocations.

The purified Tashelhit register used in radio programming presented a dilemma: it was prescriptive rather than descriptive of everyday linguistic practices, and thus not immediately comprehensible to all Tashelhit speakers.

Berberist linguists and lay people have faulted schools for Arabizing everyday Berber speech by encouraging lexical borrowings and advocating Arabic use in domains where speakers previously spoke only Berber. However, radio discourse presented an antidote, inspiring the use of Tashelhit neologisms grounded in other Tamazight varieties. This enhanced Tashelhit or what I am calling MST proved adequate to discuss even current affairs and religion – as well as rural concerns like farming – without resorting to borrowing or code-switching into Arabic or French. By establishing a purified Tashelhit code, a distinction emerged between vigilant insiders who made an effort to speak "pure" or "real" Tashelhit and those purportedly lax outsiders who permitted Arabic to infiltrate their spoken Tashelhit. Purist ideology suggested that verbal hygiene bolstered Tashelhit linguistic cohesion, and thus Ashelhi community, autonomy and authenticity. The monolingual (usually female) Tashelhit speaker who was idealized in purist and activist discourse remained, ironically, precisely the one with the least facility to eliminate Arabic loanwords and assimilated terms whose etymologies she may not have known at all. She tended to consider bivalent and borrowed words as Tashelhit, including most notably the prevalent religious invocations embedded in Tashelhit syntax and lexicon, as I discuss later in this chapter.

Ishelhin of all walks of life engaged in metalinguistic and metapragmatic discourse, whether they were monolinguals discussing politeness norms about talking and keeping silent, or bilinguals who assessed code-switching into MA as šširi (acting chic, or putting on airs). As people moved between village and town, or came into contact with others who did, and as they listened to the radio, cassettes, and to their neighbors, metalanguage mediated evaluations of difference, only in part in reference to urban, national language ideologies. Urban and Arabic influences raised particular concerns among those Ishelhin who associated Arabic influence on Tashelhit with a desertion of Ashelhi identity. The question then became how this contracting language should be represented when the "control of representations of reality" constituted "not only a source of social power" but also "a likely locus of conflict and struggle" (Gal 1989:348).

Listeners implicitly and explicitly challenged radio programmers to display fluency in a range of Tashelhit genres with all their attendant complexity; particularly valued were obsolete turns of phrase, metaphor, and allusion that required familiarity with oral poetry and regional history. Professors and amateur documentarians of Amazigh popular culture participated in programs and call-in shows, for example, in which they tried to outwit each other by decoding antiquated riddles and obscure proverbs. While listeners remarked that they were pleased to hear "their" language on the radio, not all listeners wanted to hear speech that resembled their own; they sought better versions of it.

Talk is never just about words, of course, and listeners paid more attention to the truth value of what they heard than its linguistic form. As Vološinov notes,

> Only in abnormal and special cases do we apply the criterion of correctness to an utterance . . . Normally, the criterion of linguistic correctness is submerged by a purely ideological criterion: an utterance's correctness is eclipsed by its truthfulness or falsity, its poeticalness or banality. (1973 [1929]:70)

Yet there are moments when attention to linguistic form is heightened, and the perceived correctness or purity of language draws listeners' attention. Language ideologies inform perceptions people have of themselves and others, not only as speakers, but as members of groups distinguished by systemic behavioral, aesthetic, affective, and moral characteristics. People see linguistic features as reflecting broader cultural aspects of people and activities (Irvine and Gal 2000:37).

Contest over evaluations of "good" Tashelhit took place during events in which the community expressed itself most powerfully, as in the songs of the life-cycle celebrations described in Chapters Five and Seven. But such evaluations extended to Tashelhit radio as well. This chapter discusses the place of broadcast representations of Tashelhit in the political economy of language in the Sous and Anti-Atlas. Political economy, as I intend it here, comprises "the generic economic processes of the production, distribution, and consumption of goods, including 'non-material' ones, and the patterns and culture of power that control or influence these processes" (Friedrich 1989:298). The chapter is organized by the vectors of this political economy: production, distribution, consumption, and circulation.

The political economic approach to language practices that I have been developing throughout this ethnography is intended as a corrective to the idealist/materialist divide between research on language use on the one hand and social hierarchy and inequality on the other hand (Irvine 1985). I am not referring to the commoditization of Tashelhit per se, as in monetary exchange for words that Irvine describes among Senegalese Wolof praise singers and their clients (Irvine 1989). My concern instead is with the ways people produce and circulate purist and mixed (xalḍn) language forms, how they represent them to imagined audiences, and how these language forms circulate between the airwaves and evaluative conversations in remote mountain hamlets as people make sense of their own lives. In the distribution of these "goods," as Bourdieu aptly describes,

> What circulates on the linguistic market is not "language" as such, but rather discourses that are stylistically marked both in their production, in so far as each speaker fashions an idiolect from the common language, and in their reception, in so far as each recipient helps to *produce* the message which he perceives and appreciates by bringing to it everything that makes up his singular and collective experience. (1991:39)

In the final years before the governmental recognition of Amazigh language and heritage that led to the first steps towards its integration into public spheres, Tashelhit radio proposed an alternative to the prevailing national linguistic market otherwise represented on government-sponsored radio programming. In this alternative market, Tashelhit was not in explicit competition with Arabic, and the standards for evaluation and exchange were internal to the Tashelhit language community.

If holding onto an Ashelhi identity simply meant speaking Tashelhit, the matter would be straightforward enough: the language options would appear to be MA and Tashelhit. But what distinguished the two? There is considerable lexical and pragmatic crossover between the language varieties – idiomatic expressions, intonation and prosody, narrative conventions, and bivalent lexical items particularly regarding religion. Any language bears the imprint of the history of contact between its speakers and speakers of other languages. MA syntax and lexicon have been heavily shaped by contact with Tamazight varieties since seventh-century Eastern Arab invaders arrived in Morocco. The Tamazight geolects shared many conventions of communicative competence with the Arabic-speaking communities who lived alongside Ishelhin in the south. Speaking appropriately in Tashelhit sometimes required a switch into Arabic; in other instances, an Arabic term carried different connotations than its closest Tashelhit correlate.

Even if Ishelhin in the plains did not consider it a problem to use MA, many Ishelhin in the mountains and towns claimed that cultural and linguistic assimilation inevitably led to language shift away from Tashelhit. This is a practical matter, but also a symbolic one: negative associations constitute a major factor in language shift for all the Tamazight varieties. In contrast to the positive valuations the French Protectorate administrators and officials espoused for Berbers, many Moroccans since Independence have distanced themselves from the Tamazight language and its rural connotations. Paradoxically, the close association between Tashelhit and the countryside has led some Ishelhin to endow their native language with positive qualities that challenge Arab and Arabic hegemony.

As Tashelhit expanded from strictly inter-personal oral communication into mass media and print, people with conflicting conceptions of history and divergent visions for the future have reimagined their temporal association with Tashelhit.[1] Some Tashelhit speakers I knew referred to their language as old-fashioned mountain talk unsuited to urban life, and MA as the key to a more prosperous future. Yet other Tashelhit speakers considered Arabic language and Arab identity to be inadequate purveyors of their Amazigh history and experience. When purged and rejuvenated, Tashelhit constituted a rich interactive medium that linked groups in mountains, plains, and cities. Like the indigenous Mexican population described by Frye, Ishelhin actively refuted the idea that they had to choose between continuing "unchanged" (in fact or in essence) or being "lost" (Frye 1996:9). The Tashelhit radio register elaborated this theme while meditating on the land, family, religion, honesty, eloquence, and amarg (music, mood). These themes tugged at the heartstrings of emigrants who placed the burden of maintaining the Tashelhit moral economy on the countryside's population and on speaking the Tashelhit language.

Expressive practices in the media, as Spitulnik states, "are both a source and a result of certain language valuations" (1998:181). The most notable linguistic valuation regarding Tashelhit was purism: a conscious effort to purge Arabic and French lexical borrowings and assimilations from Tashelhit. Lexical purism was integral to the constellation of efforts by Amazigh intellectuals, linguists, activists, poets, musicians, and amateur documentarians of Amazigh popular culture (al fanun aš-šaɛbiya al amaziġiya) whose intellectual and political agendas intersected and nourished each other's efforts. Nostalgia was only part of the appeal, however, since purist language ideologies tended to be more about social relations than language per se: individuals adopted purism to bolster claims of discrimination in Moroccan society. As a linguistic practice, purism was iconic of the self-sufficiency, strength, and rootedness of this marginalized group.

Reflecting the Countryside

Tashelhit broadcast discourse reflected the countryside through agricultural metaphor and the valorization of rural verbal and musical expression, but its speech forms departed from everyday rural speech in significant respects that mirrored the difference between scripted and conversational speech.

In scripted radio monologues (including news programming and poetry), extensive linguistic innovation and self-monitoring was possible – much more than in on-air conversations, interviews, and extemporaneous commentary. To illustrate this point, below are four examples of scripted monologues and one unscripted dialogue taped on Tashelhit radio programming, focusing on linguistic innovation, assimilation, and recontextualization. The first three examples are notable for lexicon and syntax common to MST, and the fourth mixes agricultural imagery with commonplace Arabic borrowings to aid listener comprehension. The fifth example is a dialogue in which interlocutors experimented with speech forms resembling everyday Tashelhit, replete with Arabic borrowings, but they are juxtaposed with Tashelhit neologisms, meaning new, revived, or recontextualized words or phrases (cf. El Moujahid 1994; Tilmatine 1992). In each example, the semantic value of Tashelhit lexical items was extended to suit urban demands, more specifically to announce community meetings, advertise housing developments, and raise public health awareness.

The strategy used by radio announcers to introduce and normalize neologisms was threefold: (1) repetition, (2) juxtaposition with more commonly used terms and phrases, especially MA borrowings and (3) careful syntactic placement, embedding the neologisms in readily understandable contexts. If we are tempted to see the grammatical constructions in what follows as mere idiosyncrasy, we might recall Vološinov's observation that "*everything that becomes a fact of grammar had once been a fact of style*" (1973 [1929]:51; italics in original).

Production

Example 1: Lexical innovation – lexical recontextualization
The first example opened a news segment:

tizi	*n*	*inġmisn*	*n*	*tsggiwin*
time	of	news	of	region

It's time for regional news.

Each of the nouns here was commonly replaced in everyday speech with other terms in both the rural and urban milieux: *luqt* for "time" (as in Example 5, line 1 below); <u>*laxbar*</u> for "news," and *tamazirt* for "region." The term *tizi* was used by Tashelhit speakers occasionally to mean "in the time of," "era," or "a long-ago time," as in the English "in the days of yore." As such, Tashelhit speakers were familiar with it from folk tales, but in the context of talking about a time slot of a few minutes, speakers commonly used the assimilated loan word luqt from the Arabic al waqt, according to the assimilation conventions of clipping the definite article /al/ to /l/. *Inġmisn* comes from the Tashelhit root *isn*, "to know." The *inġm* means literally "if one" or "if that," making this an innovation that means "that which is known" or "news." More commonly, rural Ishelhin used the assimilated Arabic borrowing laxbar. *Tsggiwin* is a peculiar usage here, because urban Ishelhin used the Arabic borrowing al mantaqa, and rural Ishelhin, especially those who were not schooled, tended to use the term for land or countryside, tamazirt, with the implied meaning "our [rural Ashelhi] homeland." The resulting phrase, *tizi n inġmisn n tsggiwin*, recontextualized unfamiliar lexical items in familiar syntax, using the connector /n/. Pragmatically, the phrase was understandable in that it marked off the musical program that preceded and followed it.

Example 2: Borrowed time

The second example concerns time which is marked differently in urban and rural contexts. In towns and cities, Ishelhin used Arabic cardinal numbers and some used Arabic ordinals as well, rather than Tashelhit. Likewise, they used Arabic to mark hours in the day and days of the week. Mountain residents, instead, used Tashelhit ordinal numbers, and all but the youngest school children used Tashelhit cardinal numbers as well. On the radio, however, announcers used Tashelhit cardinal numbers to mark time where lay people used Arabic borrowings or non-numerical time markers. Here the announcer stated that a local association meeting would be held at 8:30 pm:

tmi	*n*	*ssaεt*	*tiss*	*tamt*	*d*	*uẓgn*
beginning	of	hour	[f. possessive]	8	and	half
starting at 8:30						

Tmi is a neologism for the pervasive Arabic borrowing men, lit. "from," followed by the morphologically assimilated Arabic loan word *ssaεt* (Ar. saε) whose final /t/ feminine marker is realized upon assimilation into Tashelhit. *Tiss* is the conventional feminine marker of belonging in Tashelhit, followed by the Tashelhit cardinal number, the standard conjunction /d/, and then an archaic Berber term for "half": *uẓgn*. The term *uẓgn* typically means half of a material object like a parcel of land or a loaf of bread, rather than a concept such as an hour. Tashelhit speakers who counted clock time used Arabic with a slight allowance for the connector between eight and half: Arabic tamaniya wa nuṣ became the Tashelhit assimilated phrase *tamaniya u nuṣ*. That is, whereas the grammar of the radio phrase was technically correct, communicative competence, extending beyond knowledge of grammar and lexicon, required a code switch into Arabic to refer to clock times. But a Tashelhit speaker familiar with the term uẓgn most likely marked time relative to the five daily prayers, four meals, or the sun's placement in the sky – all seasonally variable – rather than the abstract principle of standard time. Rural women, for example, conveyed the concept of approximately 8:30 pm by reference to the day's last prayer, *dar tinyiḍs* (lit. belonging to sleep; Ar. aɛša).

Example 3: Counting the days

The third example concerns the broadcaster's announcement that an event would take place on February 1. The announcer said *yan ġ fbrayr*, lit. "one in February." This usage was unconventional on several fronts. The first day of the month was typically referred to by the ordinal number "first" rather than the cardinal "one." Moreover, there were three calendars in use among Tashelhit speakers: the lunar Muslim Hejri calendar; the solar Gregorian ("French") calendar; and the solar Julian agricultural (*fllaḥi*) calendar. The same word, *fbrayr*, was used to designate February in the two solar calendars, but their corresponding dates differed by thirteen days. The "first of February," then, might refer to either the Gregorian February 1 or instead the Julian or agricultural February 1 (the Gregorian February 14). Since all three calendars were in concurrent use in southwestern Morocco, and since individuals did not mention a calendar when referring to dates, the only way to determine the relevant calendar was to consider the speaker's social identity and the event context. For instance, if a rural school teacher gave a school holiday as being the fifteenth of *mars*, she would mean the administrative (Gregorian) March 15. When her student's mother invited her to the village *lmɛruf* (collective commemorative meal for a saint) to be held on the fifteenth of *mars*, she would mean either the agricultural March 15 or the Gregorian March 28. Not surprisingly, this can lead to a good deal of confusion, at least among state officials and foreign anthropologists trying to keep track of dates; even official bulletins indiscriminately record Julian and Gregorian dates for saints' festivals. Thus, the radio announcer's *yan ġ fbrayr* was contextually incongruous. The radio medium and the topic suggested that *fbrayr* referred to the Western solar calendar. As such, the conventional way of referring to February 1 was with the Arabic borrowing lluwl febṛayyer (lit. first [of] February) or the Tashelhit *isizwar n fbrayr* (lit. first of February).

Example 4: Mediating the countryside

Rural imagery and nostalgia for the homeland saturated radio discourse. Yet the audience for Tashelhit programming extended beyond farmers and students to the emigrant Ishelhin who sought their livelihoods in the cities, sent their children to school, and yet continued to consider the countryside their laṣl. Through the semiotic process of iconization inherent to purist ideology, linguistic features of rural speech depicted or displayed the social group's nature or essence (Irvine and Gal 2000:37). Through the complementary process of fractal recursivity, the urban–rural spatial opposition and Arab–Ashelhi ethnic opposition were projected onto linguistic difference, so that each term "was" Tashelhit or Arabic, and bivalent and assimilated terms indicative of contamination, deviation, or weakness; this language ideology is rooted in French colonial discourse on linguistic purity (Hoffman under review). Purified linguistic forms offered reassurance through covert prestige (Trudgill 1983), challenging the ethnolinguistic hierarchy in Morocco that disfavored Ishelhin relative to Arabs as well as their language.

There was extensive overlap between the work of Berber linguists, poets, documentarians of popular culture, and radio broadcasters involved in preserving, standardizing, and representing Berber language and promoting its use in public domains in the 1980s and 1990s. The radio register paralleled contemporary Tashelhit oral poetry that Berberists have demonstrated tends to be grounded in traditional sung poetry (Lakhsassi 1986; El Moujahid 1994). The jingle for Radio Agadir, a catchy ditty broadcast periodically throughout the day in the late 1990s, advertised Tashelhit programming by evoking nostalgia for the homeland:

Agadir inu	*Agadir inu*	*tlla gis immi nu*	*illa gis baba nu*	*Agadir inu*
My Agadir	my Agadir	my mother is there	my father is there	my Agadir

The jingle is from a commercially recorded 1981 song performed by the popular Tashelhit band Issafarn whose name means "medicine" or "remedies." The term has experienced a revival despite the increased use of Arabic loan words for medicine, as we will see in Example 5. Lyrics were penned by Mohamed Moustaoui, a contemporary Anti-Atlas poet, folklorist, and then-local political representative from the Nihit area of Ida ou Zeddout in the Anti-Atlas mountains.

Agricultural imagery was even used to sell urban real estate. The advertisement in Transcript 8.1 was for a government-sponsored housing association called IRAC in a new development called Wifaq outside of the coastal city of Agadir, in a subdivision called Ben Sargaou. The advertisement aired in the summer of 1997. Arabic lexical borrowings are underlined and bivalent and assimilated Arabic terms are both underlined and italicized, as elsewhere in this book.

Transcript 8.1: Radio Advertisement for Real Estate

1	*Agadir*	*lmdint*	*n*	*wafulki*	*d*	lbḥr	*d*	*tafukt*	
	Agadir	*city*	of	goodness	and	sea	and	sun	
	Agadir the city of goodness, and the coast, and sun								
	((Music))								
2	lmu'assasa	tajihawit	*n*	ttajhiz	*d*	lbnna	*n*	*iffus*	*IRAC*
	association	tools	of	tool	and	building	of	South (lit. right)	IRAC
	The Building Tools Association of the South, IRAC,								
3	*tṛẓm*	*awn*	*aġaras*						
	opens	for you (pl.)	path						
	opens up a path for you								
4	*s*	*tirgg^{w}in*	*n*	*wakal*	*maġa*	*tbnnam*	lεimarat		
	to	gardens	of	land	where	you (m.pl.) build	buildings		
	to plots of land where you can build								
5	*ġ*	lmšruε	*n*	*lWifaq*	*n*	*Ben Sargaw*			
	in	project	of	Wifaq	of	Ben Sargaou			
	in the Wifaq development in Ben Sargaou.								
	((Music))								
6	lmakan	*ifijijn*	*ad*	*dawn*	*ittustayn*	*ġ*	lmšruε	*lWifaq*	
	place	cool	pres.	for you (m.pl.)	chosen	in	project	Wifaq	
	The cool[2] place chosen for you in the Wifaq development								
7	*ġ Ben Sargaw*								
	in Ben Sargaou.								
	((Music))								
8	lmu'assasa	tajihawit	*n*	ttajhiz	*d*	lbnna	*tmmaġ*	*bidda*	
	association	tools	of	tool	and	building	fights	always	
	The Building Tools Association always endeavors								
9	*ad*	*awn d*	*tawi*	*tazduġt*	*ifulkin*				
	pres. contin.	on you (m.pl.)	bring	living	good (pl.)				
	to find you a good place to live.								
	((Music resumes))								

Two land phrases are notable in the advertisement: "opens up a path for you" (line 3) and "plots of land"/"gardens" (line 4). The first metaphor is used here to mean "gives you the chance," announcing an opportunity. The use of "path" (*aġaras*) in line 3 connotes a rural setting, as in a path through the fields, but with the moral connotation of the Straight Path that many Muslims believe God enjoins them to follow. The term had additional connotations for Ishelhin, whom both Ishelhin and Arabs said lived according to the maxim *aġaras aġaras*, "the road is the road," rather than following the zigzag of the morally and spiritually corrupt. This path leads to the *tirgg^{w}in n wakal* (line 4), the plots of land on which the buyer could build a home or building. In agricultural milieux, there were a number of terms for a plot of land, depending on its size, irrigation system, and contents. The word *tirgin* was usually reserved for irrigated vegetable plots, or gardens, small but carefully cultivated. Mountain farmers with only rainfed barley fields did not call these fields *tirgg*^{w}*in*, but rather *igran* or *lbur*. In areas of the Sous Valley where farmers planted in both rainfed lbur and irrigated vegetable gardens, the latter were also called igran to distinguish fertile land from the more arid rainfed lands. By using tirgin here, the advertiser avoided the potential confusion over the fertility or productivity of these development plots by choosing the word that was not multivalent and regionally variable in its meaning, but instead referred only to fertile land. By using common Arabic terms for association, tools, and buildings, as well as the sea, the advertiser not only conveyed the official name of the builders' association, which presumably served Moroccans regardless of native language, but also assured the comprehensibility of the message, a more important goal than enriching the audience's lexicon with Tashelhit neologisms.

Merely hearing a neologism did not prompt a listener to use it, but some MST words did catch on within some social groups. For example, the conventional evening greeting "good evening" in Tashelhit in the late 1990s was the Arabic loan phrase msa u lxir condensed as *msa lxir*, and when departing, for "goodnight," it was tsbaḥ ɛla xir. The term *timinsiwin* was resuscitated for both purposes through a popular evening call-in radio show of the same name (broadcast out of Rabat rather than Agadir). Most callers to the show were emigrant men in the cities, and they sent their greetings and messages to friends and family in both countryside and city. In that program, the term timinsiwin was used for both "hello"/"good evening" when people met or, here, picked up the phone, and for "goodbye"/"goodnight" as when people parted or, here, when they hung up. Through this program, Tashelhit-speaking listeners became familiar with the expression. Some Swasa used the term occasionally to mean "good night." Interestingly, timinsiwin was only picked up in casual speech for "good night" upon parting; thus its semantic value and pragmatics contracted to only one of its two meanings outside the radio context. I should note here, however, that a person's use of timinsiwin had indexical as well as phatic value – it indexed a concern with the influence of Arabic on Tashelhit speech and an awareness of lexical alternatives to loan words, and therein lay the appeal for the young men and women who used it for rhetorical flair, always self-consciously. I also heard urban women use it when departing from a language-mixed speech event where there had already been heightened attention to code choice among participants. The term timinsiwin most likely will not replace tsbaḥ ɛla xir entirely among Ishelhin, but it has begun circulating in the political economy of language in the Sous, and increased in use after government openings towards Amazigh matters under Mohamed VI. This process mirrors that of Arabization in education. Primary school students, for example, used the MSA term siyara (lit. carriage) in their textbooks and classrooms to refer to what their parents more commonly called *tumubil* after the French assimilated term *automobile.* School seemed a more powerful medium than radio for effecting lexical shift among the population as a whole, especially given the widespread resistance to Berber language revival efforts in Moroccan pubic discourse.

The extent of a new form's influence depends on the authority of the innovator, the prestige or influence of the social group associated with the innovation, and the means and breadth of the new item's dissemination. For this reason, it was significant that Tashelhit programming was state-run. Irrespective of individual political stances, state sanctioning lent its authority to a medium that otherwise could have been construed as marginal or potentially subversive. In consequence, the topics and linguistic forms aired on the radio were implicitly endorsed by state officials. This suggested that, adapted in moderation by lay people, neologisms would not raise the suspicions of Ministry of the Interior officials, then increasingly vigilant about Amazigh activism in the wake of the ethnic conflict in neighboring Algeria's Kabyle Berber region.

Example 5: Dialogue on Ramadan fasting

The radio monologues in Examples 1–4 above were prepared in advance, offering the broadcaster an ideal opportunity to use neologisms. In dialogue, in contrast, the interlocutor is more constrained in using neologisms because of the need to maintain the conversational flow. Dialogue permits fewer opportunities for the micro-structuring that linguistic purism demands. Radio dialogues in my sample exhibited a higher frequency of Arabic borrowings and code-switches into MA than did prepared monologues. It was not uncommon, however, for the rate of Arabic influence to increase or decrease throughout the dialogue, as speakers relaxed their self-monitoring or, on the contrary, heightened their attention to borrowings.

The goal of promoting an enriched MST was, at times, incongruent with the widespread language ideology that Arabic and French were better suited to discuss medical, scientific, and other learned subjects. This ideology seemingly was at odds with one of the station's public service functions: to disseminate health advisories. To this end, interviews with medical specialists and generalists discussed health concerns, including health constraints on fasting during Ramadan. Radio announcements were the only consistent public health messages that reached many rural communities, and as such, audience comprehension was of utmost importance. The discussion that follows concerns diabetes, the "sugar illness" affecting growing numbers of

Moroccans who consume high levels of refined sugar and lead increasingly sedentary lives. The brief interview from December 1997 follows in Transcript 8.2, between the program host and Dr. Saad Eddin El Otmani, professor of medicine in Casablanca, editor of a medical journal, and author of the newspaper column "Your Health and Self." These two publications were well-known Islamist journals in the 1990s. Dr. Otmani later became the secretary-general of the Islamist Moroccan PJD, the Justice and Development Party, that made significant parliamentary gains under Mohamed VI. Both host and guest employed strategies for introducing medical neologisms while ensuring comprehension in a range of communities. In the literal translation of each word or morpheme (second line of each three-line segment), abbreviations include pres. (present tense), fut. (future tense), cont. (continuous), neg. (negation), poss. (possessive), s. (singular), and pl. (plural).

Transcript 8.2: Radio Interview on Fasting During Ramadan

Host:

1	*imssflidn*	*nġ*	*iɛzzan*	*a*	*ig*	*rbbi*	*luqt*	*nnun*	*d*	*timbarkkiwin*
	listeners	our	dear	pres.	be	please	time	your (m.pl.)	and	blessings

Dear listeners please give your time and blessings

2	*hayyaḥ*	*nmaggar*	*d*	*idun*	*ġ*	*igiwr*	*n*	*ġass*	*ad*
	we	meet	with	you	in	interview	of	day	this

We meet for today's interview.

3	nrju	*ad*	*did*	*nġ*	*tġwim*	*kigan*	*d*	*lfayt*
	we plead	pres.	from	us	take	much	of	benefit

We hope that you find it useful.

The host opens with a conventional radio greeting in line 1, addressing her listeners, and evoking God's blessings. In line 2, she introduces a neologism for interview, *igiwr*, literally "meeting," by first using the better-known verb form of the same root, "to meet" or "to gather": *maggr*. Line 3 opens with an assimilated borrowing for "we plead" used in the sense of "we hope" following the pragmatic construction used in Arabic media programming. The phrase for "useful," *kigan d lfayt*, is comprised of the term *kigan* which usually refers to a large quantity of material, such as hay, with the conjunction /d/ and the assimilated borrowing al fayt → *lfayt*. Next the host introduces her guest (lines 4–13).

Host:

4	*igiwr*	*n*	*ġass*	*ad*	*aytma*	*d*	*istma*	*sul*	*ukan*	*ra*	*ndfur*
	meeting	of	day	this	brothers	and	sisters	still	intensifier	fut.	cont.

Today's interview, Brothers and Sisters, will be

5	*d*	*g^wmatnġ*	dduktur	*Saad Eddin El Otmani*
	of	brother our	Dr.	Saad Eddin El Otmani

with Dr. Saad Eddin El Otmani

6 *lli snniġ igan yan udbib izlin ġ tmuḍan timukras ns ġ*
that I knew is (cont.) one doctor apart in illnesses problems/knots his in
who is known as an exceptional medical doctor

7 *ġ lmdint n Barršid ġik lli iga yan lusted ġ tiġri yattuyn*
in city of Barshid here that is one *professor* in education higher
in the city of Barshid, a university professor

8 *ġ* lkuliya al adab *ġ lmdint n Dar Bayḍa*
in college of arts in city of Casablanca
in the College of Arts in the city of Casablanca.

9 *iga nit* lmudir lmajalla *n Furqan ġiklli ittara yan iġmart ġ* ljarida *Raya*
is also director Journal of Furqan thus writes one column in newspaper Raya
He is also the director of the journal Furqan and writes a column in the journal Raya

10 *lli d ittffuġn kra igat imalas ismm as niġd issaġ as ṣṣaḥt nk n* unfus
that appears every each week name its or called its health your of self
that appears every week called "Your Health in Hand."

11 *igiwr n ġass ad rad t nzli d* dduktur *SEO lli snniġ tiklit yaḍnin*
meeting of day this fut. we separate with Dr. SEO who I knew once other
In today's meeting, we have Dr. SEO to ourselves, who also

12 *iga yan n imsggarn* lmu'assasa *n* Hassan Ettani *n ušnubbš* f *ṣṣaḥt d Rmḍan*
is one in partner association of Hassan II of research in health and Ramadan
is a partner in the Hassan II Association for Research on Health and Ramadan

13 *niġd* ɛuḍw ġ lmu'assasa Hassan Ettani lil bhaat aṭṭibiya ḥawl al ṣṣiḥa wa Ramaḍan
or partner in association Hassan II in research medical about health of Ramadan
or a partner in the Hassan II Association for Medical Research on Health and Ramadan.

Neologisms in this interviewer's introduction include *ndfur* (continue) in line 4, and *tiġri yattuyn* (higher education) in line 7. *Tiġri* means both reading and schooling in Tashelhit. Recontextualized Tashelhit terms include *izlin* (apart) in line 6 that usually refers to the physical separation of one thing or concept from others, but here is used to mean exceptional, since the doctor clearly does not work alone. In line 6 as well, the host juxtaposes two terms for illnesses: *tmuḍan,* which the interlocutors will use repeatedly throughout the interview, and a more general term for problems of any nature, *timukras* (sing. *tamukrist*), literally "knots" or by extension "problems." Arabic borrowings include "College of Arts" (line 8) and line 9's "director," "journal," and "newspaper." Morphologically assimilated Arabic borrowings include *lmdint* (lines 7 and 8) (Ar. al madina).

There are two juxtapositions of utterances with the same referent that deserve our attention here. First, line 10 contains two contiguous words for "named:" *ismm as* "its name" and *issaġ as* "it is called" (with the double /s/ marking the passive), joined by "or" (*niġd*) that serves pragmatically in conversation to signal a rephrasing of a previous utterance. Next, in line 12, the host uses *imsggarn* (partner),[3] a term more frequently used to mean companion, and then follows with the Arabic term εuḍw in line 13. In the first part of this utterance, the host refers to the doctor's association using the morphologically assimilated Arabic noun lmu'assasa (association) + /*n*/ + Hassan Ettani, followed by a neologism for research, *ušnubbš*, from the Tashelhit verb "to search for" (*šnubbš*) + /f̱/ (in) + (assimilated Arabic) *ṣṣaḥt* (Ar. ṣṣiḥa as in line 13) + /*d*/ (and) + Ramadan. Thus in line 13, the host announces Dr. Otmani's title, in the original Arabic form in circulation. By then, even a listener who was unfamiliar with Arabic terms for "research" and "medical" would have understood the kind of institution that employed Dr. Otmani.

The host next introduces the topic of diabetes (lines 14–28). A borrowed Arabic religious invocation pronounced without the glottal stop, as inšallah (line 14), becomes its Tashelhit counterpart in the interview closing (line 52), *iġ t inna ṛbbi*, literally "if God said it."

Host:

14	al	dduktur	*SEO*	*ġass*	*ad*	inšallah	*rad*	*aġ*	*isawl*	*f*	*tmaḍunt*	*n skkar*
	def. art.	doctor	SEO	day	this	God willing	fut.	to us	talk	on	illness	of sugar

Today, Dr. SEO, God willing, will talk to us about diabetes

15	*d*	*man*	*anaw*	*n*	*imuḍan*	*n*	*skkar*	*lli*	*rad*	*ittazum*
	and	what	kinds	of	diabetics	of	sugar	that	fut.	fast

and which kinds of diabetics will fast

16	*d*	*man*	*anaw*	*nna*	*ur*	*iẓḍarn*	*ad*	*t*	*ittazum*
	and	how	many	he said	neg.	he is able	pres.	it	fast

and also those who cannot fast.

17	*nra*	*a*	*k*^{w}*n*	*najj*	*d*	dduktur	*SEO*
	we want	to	you	present	with	doctor	SEO

We would like to introduce Dr. SEO.

Dr. Otmani:

18	*yat*	*tmaḍunt*	*yaḍnin*	*lli*	*ġ*	*ixaṣṣa*	*bnadm*	*illa*	*imik*	*n*	lḥraj
	one	illness	other	that	in	must	*person*	there	little	of	caution

One other illness that people must be cautious about

19	*ġ*	*willi*	*ra*	*yazum*	*iga at*	*tmaḍunt*	*ad*	*n*	*skkar*
	in	those	fut.	fast	is	illness	that	of	sugar

for those who fast is diabetes.

20	*tmaḍunt*	*n*	*sukkar*	*gis*	lanwaε	*illa*	nnawε	*lliġ*	*imkn*	*i*	*bnadm*	*a*	*yazum*
	illness	of	sugar	is	kinds	is	kind	that	possible	to	person	pres.	fast

One kind of diabetes is the kind that allows a person to fast.

21	*illa*	lanwaε	*yaḍnin*	*lli*	*ur*	*imkn*	*i*	*bnadm*	*a*	*yazum*
	there is	kinds	other	that	neg.	possible	to	person	pres.	fast

There are other kinds that do not allow a person to fast.

22 nnawɛ *lli izwarn llig ur imkn i bnadm a gis yazum?*
kind that first when neg. possible to *person* pres. is fast?
The first kind that does not allow a person to fast

23 *tmaḍunt ad n skkar lli ittɛalaj lli ittdawa bnadm bnadm s tissgnit n linsulin*
illness this of sugar that treats that medicates *person person* with shot of insulin
This is the kind of diabetes that a person treats with insulin shots.

24 *ġwad lli ittgan tisgnin linsulin ġwad ixaṣṣat ad ur yazum*
that one who does shots insulin that one must pres. neg. fast
The one who gets insulin shots should not fast.

25 *bnadm amaḍun n skkar lli dar illa kra n* lmaraḍ *yaḍnin*
person ill of sugar that poss. is some of illness other
A diabetic who has another illness

26 *ġ* ddat *ns kra n* lmaraḍ *yaḍnin zund ġwalli yuḍn tigzal*
in body his some of illness other like the one suffers kidneys
in his body, some other illness like kidney stones

27 *ula tmaḍunt n wul ula kra n tmaḍunt zund ġikad ?*
or illness of heart or some of illness like this
or heart trouble or a similar illness,

28 *timuḍan ad kullu ar skrnt i umaḍun ad ur imkn a yazum*
illnesses these all pres. make to diabetic this neg. must pres. fast
all of these illnesses make it impossible for the diabetic to fast.

From line 18, a bivalent term, *bnadm*, or person (lit. Arabic ibn + Adam or "son of Adam," but pragmatically functioning as gender-neutral; cf. Kapchan 1996) appears throughout. Dr. Otmani borrows "kind" in singular (nnuwɛ) and plural (lanwaɛ) from Arabic (lines 20, 21, and 22), rather than using the widespread assimilated French borrowing *markat* for types or kinds (Hoffman 2002a:537). Other Arabic borrowings here include lḥraj (caution, line 18), the morphologically assimilated *ittɛalaj* (treat or relieve, line 23) followed by a synonym borrowing, *ittdawa* (medicate), and by ddat (body, from CA that) and lmaraḍ (illness) in line 26. The doctor uses the Tashelhit terms for kidney (line 26) and heart (line 27), notable because they are common in poetry but more commonly replaced by Arabic or French terms when discussing anatomy.

Not all borrowings from Arabic are semantically and pragmatically identical in Tashelhit. The Arabic borrowing for child, drri (line 31), seems odd at first glance given its numerous Tashelhit equivalents. However, here the doctor uses it to emphasize the age of a weaned child older than a toddler. This distinction is not possible using the Tashelhit terms for a child (m.) (*araw*, *afṛux*, and *aḥšmi*) from birth through adulthood.

Dr. Otmani:

31 drri *ixaṣṣat tamġart ar lliġ tlla tmadunt n skkar ixaṣṣa ad ur tazum*
child must woman until is there illness of sugar must pres. neg. fast
Until [the infant is] a child, a diabetic woman should not fast.

32 *amaḍun n skkar lli imqqurn bahra lli dar ila kraḍ ida ɛšrin d mraw n usgg^was*
diabetic who old very that poss. there 3 times 20 and 10 of years
Diabetics who are very old, 70 years [old]

33 *d uggar awa amḍun n skkar ixaṣṣa ad ur yaẓum aški ntta imqqur d gis tamaḍunt n skkar*
and over well diabetic should pres. neg. fast because he old and in him diabetes
or over diabetic shouldn't fast, because an elderly person who is diabetic

34 *iġ yaẓum rad t idr u* laken *ma igan amaḍun n sukkar lli imkn a yaẓum*
if he fasts fut. fall and but what is diabetic who possible pres. fast
if he fasts he is going to fall [sick] but who is the diabetic who may fast

35 *amaḍun n sukkar ġilad d lli išttan* ddwa
diabetic now and who eating medication
the diabetic now the one who takes medication

36 *ar išta ur a ittga tissgnit n lansulin d ar išta* ddwa
pres. eats neg. pres. does shots of insulin and pres. eats medication
he eats he doesn't take insulin shots and he takes medication

37 *ula ar ka iskar rijim ur a išta skkar*
or pres. just does diet neg. pres. eats sugar
or who just diets or doesn't eat sugar

38 *dar s skkar ns iga nit* mutawazzin
poss. his sugar his is even steady
whose sugar [level] is steady

39 mutawazzn *d ur dar s illa kra n tmaḍunt yaḍnin ġwad imkn*
steady and neg. poss. his there some of illness other this one possible
steady and who has no other illness this one may

40 *as a yaẓum u* laken *iġd ikka dar uḍbib ns aški=*
to him pres. fast and but if he visits house doctor his because=
that one may fast but only if he visits his doctor. Because=

In lines 34 and 40, the doctor borrows the term "but" from Arabic (laken), preceding it with the Tashelhit *u* "and" in the place of the Arabic wa which together functions like the Tashelhit *mš* "but." In line 32, the doctor uses the Tashelhit numerical system based on units of ten and twenty. Thus *kraḍ ida ɛšrin d mraw* translates as "three times twenty and ten," or seventy. This system of counting was used by Anti-Atlas women I knew, but no longer among schooled Ishelhin or even many men. Counting this way thus iconized Tashelhit knowledge and indexed the abudrar/tabudrart social identity. Line 37 contains the French borrowing for diet (*rijim*, Fr. *régime*), whose definition immediately follows in Tashelhit: avoiding sugar (and often salt).

The following section (lines 41–45) contains the embedding of Arabic borrowings from line 38, "steady," "even," or "balanced" (mutawazzin). The host interrupts Dr. Otmani and restates his point in line 41 with another morphologically adopted Arabic term, *inggada*, for balanced, which Dr. Otmani then transforms into "balanced" (*mi inggada*) in line 42. The host defines this word's meaning further in line 43 with the phrase "stable, that doesn't rise or fall," repeated by the doctor in line 44, and finally paraphrased by the host in line 45 ("it is at one number and remains steady"). Throughout, the two overlap each other's utterances, marked here as [and indicating moments of heightened interest rather than impoliteness or impatience. Latching utterances are indicated by =.

Host:

41 = *ar* *ttinin* *a* dduktur *aḍbib* *amaḍun n skkar* *lli mu* *inggada* *su* [*kkar* *ns*
= pres. they say vocative doctor doctor diabetic who balanced su [gar his
= Doctor, they say that the diabetic who keeps his su [gar under control

Dr. Otmani:

42 [*lli* *mi inggada* *skkar* *ns* *s* lfanid *waḥ* [*dat*
[who balanced sugar his by pills a [lone
[The one who stabilizes his sugar through medication a [lone

Host:

43 [*is itbt* *ur* *ad* *itzayyad* *ur* *a* *inaq* [*ṣ*
[is stable neg. pres. increase neg. pres. lowers
[that's stable, that doesn't rise or f [all

Dr. Otmani:

44 [*ur* *a* *itnaqaṣ* =
[*neg.* *pres.* lowers =
[doesn't fall=

Host:

45 = *illa* *ġ* *yan* rraqm *ibqqa* *gis*
= there is in one number remains there
= It's at one number and remains steady.

Ibqqa gis (line 45) is an example of what Youssi calls conjoined Arabic and Berber lexicon (1990:276), in which one word is morphologically adapted from Arabic and the other word remains in its original Berber form. An example he offers is *takurt n uḍar*, in which *takurt* is a Berber assimilation of the Arabic kura (ball) with the added preposition /*n*/ to *aḍar* (foot/leg) → foot-ball. Here, ibqqa comes from the Arabic verb bqqa (to remain), morphologically adapted into the Tashelhit verb conjugation for third person singular (initial /i/) and, here, used with the Tashelhit present tense of the verb "to be" (*gis*) making it semantically redundant: if something remains, its presence is implied.

Dr. Otmani:

46 *yna d ur dars tlla kra n tmaḍunt yaḍnin*
one and neg. poss. is some of illness other
The one who does not have another illness

47 *ġwad imkn as a yaẓum u* lakin *ad zwar ikk dar uḍbib*
this one possible can pres. fast and but pres. precede visit poss. doctor
he can fast but first he should visit the doctor.

48 *nttan ar ad as inna izd* lxir *ad nit is dars illa is dars ur illi kra n tmaḍunt yaḍnin*
that one pres. to him says if goodness this just if poss. be if poss. neg. be some of illness other
He'll tell that one that if he is in good shape, just be sure that he has no other illness

49 *niġd kra n* lmuškil *yaḍnin lli ra t yaj ixaṣṣat ad ur yaẓum*
or some of problem other that fut. prevent must pres. neg. fast
or other problem that should prevent him from not fasting

Host:

50 *ḥaqqan aytma d istma ġnšk ad a ila igiwr ġass ad*
maybe brothers and sisters amount this pres. is meeting day this
I think, Brothers and Sisters, that that's all [the time] we have for today's interview

51 narju *ad gis tawim kigan d lfayt*
we plead pres. there gather much of benefit
we hope you benefited greatly.

52 *ix ar askka iġ t inna ṛbbi u* salamu ɛlaykum *u* raḥmat allah
if until tomorrow if it said Lord and peace upon you (pl.) and mercy God
Until tomorrow, God willing, and may peace and God's mercy be upon you.

In Tashelhit colloquial usage, diabetes was often referred to by its MA name, mrḍ as-skkar literally the sugar disease/illness, that becomes *mrḍ n sskar* when embedded in Tashelhit morphology. In the previous conversation, neither of these phrases was used, and the Tashelhit term *tmaḍunt* stood in for *mrḍ*. For the term medicine, the interlocutors alternated between the Arabic ddwa (medicine) and fanid (pills), rather than the Tashelhit *isafarn* (remedies) used for physical but also emotional or spiritual ailments, and used metaphorically in rural sung poetry as a cure for heartache, longing, or spiritual impurity (Hoffman 2002a). Isafarn was a favorite term among standardization advocates as the umbrella term for medicine, just as *tmaḍunt* was preferred for illness. For doctor, the speakers used the French term as well as two pronunciations of the phonologically assimilated Arabic term *aḍbib* (line 47); as is characteristic of Tashelhit, the Arabic */th/* becomes Tashelhit */ḍ/*. Among Tashelhit-speaking monolinguals, the second pronunciation with the */ḍ/* phoneme is standard. Finally, both Tashelhit and Arabic speakers in Morocco used the Arabic formula "If God wills" (inšallah) (line 14), or a Tashelhit equivalent "If God says it" (*iġ t inna ṛbbi*) (line 52) whenever referring to a future event; the host here used both forms. She marked the close of the program segment with a classical

Arabic formula wishing the peace and God's mercy upon her listeners, salamu ɛlaykum *u* raḥmat allah (line 52) – but guarding the Tashelhit /*u*/ for the conjunction "and" rather than the Arabic /wa/.

Translating Islam into the vernaculars

Borrowing from Arabic into Tashelhit was most prevalent in the radio register when discussing religion, a particularly sensitive issue for purity advocates. There were two kinds of Arabic borrowings in conversational speech that reflected religion. The first were borrowings of Arabic roots grammatically adapted into Tashelhit verb forms (e.g. May God repay you, allah yaxlf in MA becomes *a ixlf ṛbbi* in Tashelhit). The second were direct quotations from the Quran, a book generally considered untranslatable from the original Classical Arabic.[4] Lexical borrowings for religious concepts were numerous (e.g. ḥisab, judgment [day]); jjnun, spirits; dunub, sins; kafir, unbeliever, non-Muslim; and mu'minin, believers or Muslims). These terms can be considered borrowings when there is no preferred term used in their place among monolingual Tashelhit speakers. In addition to these borrowed terms for discussing religious themes, both Arabic and Tashelhit speech in Morocco was full of formulaic speech conventions that invoked the name of God (either allah or *ṛbbi*). Thus Arabic was invariably present in one form or another, regardless of the vernacular or register interlocutors used. The use of this emerging Modern Standard Tashelhit served an *indexical* as well as a *referential* function. Listeners expected it simultaneously to reflect the speech and interests of rural Ishelhin while linking them to modern urban institutions and the Moroccan nation-state.

Circulation and consumption

Attention to language used on the radio is highest in news programs when, as Jaffe notes for Corsica, the focus is on language as symbol rather than language as tool. When listeners focus on newscasters' speech, "familiar notions of purity and boundedness make their way to the top of people's consciousness" (Jaffe 1999:270). In Morocco as in Corsica, many people commented that purified speech was preferable, but that it was difficult to practice and enforce. So while Ishelhin highly valued "pure" Tashelhit in theory, their everyday conversational practices showed an appreciation for language mixing as a means of accommodation and context-appropriateness. Metalinguistic commentary by monolinguals revealed patterned norms, genre use, and silence; a person's code-switch into MA was marked as ššiki to many Ishelhin, a particularity of women who *ataššiyyik* (put on airs) in their self-presentations.

Walking in the late morning through the streets of a market town such as Taroudant or Igherm, or down paths in rural villages, the sound of Radio Agadir streamed from stores and homes. Women listened to it while cleaning or preparing the midday meal. At the time of my fieldwork, even in town, the familiar drone of Moroccan television programming did not begin until lunch time; instead people listened to the radio. Many Ishelhin had favorite weekly or nightly programs, especially the riddles, as one person told me, "those mεani [sayings] that only our grandmothers and the mountain people still know."

Call-in programs were popular, as they allowed city dwellers to greet rural-dwelling family and friends who lacked telephone access but had access to a radio, as well as other emigrants in other Moroccan cities. This program in particular suggests the intimacy listeners presumed between people the show reached, because many callers, who were almost without exception men, announced their home telephone numbers and addresses to encourage their friends around the country to contact them. Although women rarely called in, rural and urban women listened regularly and attentively. Women as well as men served as program hosts, as in Example 5 above, and professors, doctors and other specialists offered their expertise to variety programs.

Program segments followed a seasonal schedule. During Ramadan, programming was primarily religious, and included Quaranic recitation (tajwid),

Figure 8.1 Sifting barley into flour and couscous and listening to Tashelhit radio, Ida ou Zeddout

Figure 8.2 Young women mimicking a shrouded bride and companions, Ida ou Zeddout. Note the radio/cassette player displayed for the photograph.

Figure 8.3 Fatima Mhammd prepares couscous and listens to Tashelhit radio.

presentations by religious scholars on Islamic matters such as fasting, and hadith explanations. During the spring/summer season, musical programming and light entertainment segments predominated to entertain listeners during their summer vacations, the periods when children were out of school. The fall/winter season had a larger proportion of cultural and information programming, including presentations by professors on subjects of local historical and geographical interest, local journalists and specialists of popular culture on local culture, as well as poetry, short stories, and human interest stories. In all seasons, local, national and international news together constituted a regular feature of the daily programming.

Radio programming kept rural dwellers informed about world events by delivering news and commentary in a language they understood, for few understood Arabic or French. Their appreciation of the programming, as they commented to me, had several angles. First, monolingual speakers, in particular women, noted to me that the programming validated Tashelhit language simply by using it, rather than using Arabic. Second, many Tashelhit speakers found pleasure in hearing words and music intended for their consumption, rather than the mass media (in Arabic) targeted at the entire country. Third, some appreciated the recognition that they, too, wanted information to participate in current debates on topics like health, politics, education reform, and regional history.

If we are tempted to believe the language ideology that held that unschooled rural dwellers spoke a more Arabic-free Tashelhit register than urban dwellers, consider the following interaction from my February 1997 fieldnotes from Ida ou Zeddout. Two men in their thirties sat among unmarried young women outside in the cool evening air. One was Mbarek, a shepherd's son, married with two daughters, from one of the poorest but most beloved families in the village. Mbarek planned to take the fifteen-hour overnight bus ride to Casablanca the next day to return to his job stocking bottles in a liquor store. He began asking the young women what "the words are in Tashelhit" for a number of things – bicycle, airplane, airport. For bicycle he used the common Soussi MA word picala in his question. Nadia responded "*bisklit*," using the French assimilated borrowing into both MA and Tashelhit. Mbarek told Nadia that her suggestion was French (*tafransist*). For airport, which he referred to as *laropor*, borrowing from the French *l'aeroport*, Nadia suggested the Arabic maṭar; Mbarek pointed out that this was Arabic (*taεrabt*). When none of the other girls could come up with another term, Mbarek revealed that the authentic Tashelhit term for airport was *asays n taylalin*, literally "place of flying things." Ftuma remarked, "I don't know what the word is in Arabic or French or English for that matter, but I can tell you that in Tashelhit, that's not our word." Like Hill's (1987) findings among Mexicano (Nahuatl) speakers in Mexico who do not mark all terms as *castellano* that the linguist would mark as Spanish, Ftuma identifies some assimilated borrowings – especially for borrowed material objects – as Tashelhit.

Mbarek's and Ftuma's remarks raised a pertinent question: who is the authority on "correct" speech in oral-dominant societies: monolingual native speakers, purist speech activists, or historical linguists? Hill notes that among Mexicano speakers, "for some usages where self-conscious purism in speaking *mexicano* has stimulated male avoidance of *castellano* elements, women are 'more Spanish' (or 'less Mexicano') than men" (Hill 1987:121). Similarly, according to Mbarek's formulation and purist conventions, Ftuma (as well as the other village women) would be more "Arab" or less "Tashelhit" than their self-conscious male peers. This was a recurring paradox in mountain communities that should make us revisit the scholarly literature that claims that women are simultaneously more conservative than men in their speech in situations of stability, and more innovative than men in contexts of change (Labov 1978; cf. Hill 1987).

The double paradox here is that conservatism may mean syncretism with Arabic, lexically speaking, by monolingual speakers such as Anti-Atlas women, as with the bilingual Mexicanos. Some advocates of Tashelhit purism I knew suggested that rural dwellers were trapped by a kind of false consciousness that deafened them to the impurity of their own speech. After overhearing Mbarek's comments about the impurity of monolingual young women's Tashelhit, I suggested to him that the words he called "real" might be borrowings or new terms, since items such as bicycles and airports were nonexistent in the imagined yesteryear (zikk) when Tashelhit was purer. (Somewhat self-consciously, Mbarek used the Arabic term haqiqi for "real.") Mbarek's response to my suggestion that even "authentic" words might be borrowings was that yes, the words he advocated were "made from other words." Still, he said, they were the "correct" (*ṣḥin*) words since they were not rooted in Arabic or French. Here Mbarek used the grammatically embedded Arabic lexical item for correct (ṣaḥiḥ). The proof he offered was that these Tashelhit terms were used on the radio. Just as radio interviewers use exemplary classical Arabic in state Arabic programming, and schoolhouse French in the French programming, Mbarek's expectation was that Tashelhit radio programming similarly employed skilled practitioners of the language. Mbarek described how he systematically used Tashelhit radio to purify his Tashelhit:

> After the Arabic news on Médi Un [a Tangiers-based bilingual Arabic-French radio station], I turn to the news in Tashelhit. It's the same news stories, so if you hear "airport" in Arabic in the first broadcast you can listen for the word used in the second broadcast in Tashelhit. The stories on the news are the same, so you can just substitute the words.

Mbarek's concern with lexical purity, like that of some other young urban-dwelling migrant men, led him to critique the lexical choices monolingual speakers conventionally used in his native village. Indeed, as Mbarek explained how best to speak Tashelhit, Nadia and the other young women did not embellish his argument as they tended to do in conversation. They did not press him for more details, nor did they suggest that he was right or wrong. A few of the young women repeated the phrases he introduced, but without comment. The conversation remained hypothetical anyway, since most of the young women had never seen a bicycle or an airplane.

In this purist ideology, each language is complete in itself and independent of other communicative codes. Recourse to another language to borrow terms reflected a lack of diligence on the part of its speakers, both a moral and an intellectual critique. In discussion with Mbarek, I attempted to introduce a temporal element. Rather than seeing that some borrowings from Arabic resulted from the introduction of new concepts and goods, Mbarek's stance presumed the other condition for lexical borrowing: that "real" Tashelhit words fell out of use as Arabic or French words replaced them. Indeed, this had been the case with many other words for everyday items in Tashelhit. In those instances, a purist strategy aimed to recuperate the "lost" terms and put them back into circulation.

Underlying the preoccupation of Tashelhit lexical purists with Arabic borrowings, whether these advocates were primary-school-educated migrant wage laborers, like Mbarek, or university professors, was a social struggle about who must accommodate whom in Moroccan society. Amazigh activists insisted that Arabic words and the Arabic-speaking sector of the Moroccan population were inseparable; using Arabic amounted to admitting cultural and social dependence on Arabs. It was not necessarily that purists harbored animosity towards particular Arabic speakers. It was more that many of them saw the domination of Arabic language over Tashelhit as unjustified and reinforced by the social denigration of things Amazigh in public domains. For Mbarek, Tashelhit's staying power signaled collective resilience to adversity and linguistic and social devaluation in the wider nation-state. An emigrant urban dweller, Mbarek had a metalanguage to handle the concept that certain words were not "Tashelhit" and that there were instead lexical items that were more proper to Tashelhit and thus more authentic than the common borrowings.

The mountain-dwelling young women participating in this conversation considered the words they used simply as *winaġ*, "ours," and their language as *awal nġ*, "our talk." Their reasoning was that since they only spoke Tashelhit, the terms they used must have been Tashelhit terms. These young women spent negligible if any time outside the village, did not speak or understand colloquial or classical Arabic, and only the few who had been through a few years of schooling understood some colloquial and perhaps a bit of standard Arabic. It would seem, then, that they were the closest thing to speakers of "pure" Tashelhit, if such a thing indeed existed. How was it that Mbarek suggested that perhaps "their" Tashelhit was not "real" Tashelhit? These future mothers already spoke quite differently than did their mothers and grandmothers, as villagers readily acknowledged (Hoffman 2002a).[5] In Mbarek's view, the old woman in the village remained the quintessential Tashelhit speaker, the repository of social values reflected in the mεani she could produce as the situation required, thus, the real "(T)ashelhi(t)" person. The difference was much more complex than that of whether they referred to a soup bowl as a *tazlaft* (Ar. zlafa) or a *timkilt* (Tash. meal vessel). Paradoxically, younger women and men in the mountains borrowed more frequently from Arabic than did their elders and Ishelhin in the plains, who had greater access to Arabic, especially with regard to numbers and colors. Yet mountain women's metalinguistic standards did not evaluate speech for language purity; they did not reprimand each other when they used Arabic loan words as was common in the plains, where a Tashelhit speaker could be heard to tell another who spoke MA with an outsider, "Speak Tashelhit! Why are you speaking Arabic?"[6] While young purists may have pointed to older Tashelhit speakers as superior manipulators of Tashelhit, they tended to have difficulty identifying particular elements characterizing superior speech, like the pragmatically appropriate use of fixed forms like proverbs and rhetorical strategies like irony – and they were unable to reproduce this speech themselves.

The differing goals of radio announcers affected the extent to which they eliminated Arabic from the Tashelhit they used on the air. One Amazigh poet and renowned Berber folklorist, Omar Amarir, who was familiar with radio broadcasting personalities over several decades, made the following distinction during an interview at his home in 1999. Some radio personalities, he said, take the approach that speaking as simply as possible, with heavy borrowing from Arabic, can encourage listeners to tune in even when they have a less than native level of comprehension of Tashelhit. It also facilitates comprehension for Arabic speakers who listen to radio programming to learn Tashelhit. Other radio announcers, Amarir remarked, draw on the broadest possible familiarity with Tashelhit. Such announcers give listeners the opportunity to hear a kind of lexically purified and expanded Tashelhit that is less commonly displayed outside of oral poetry. Among the elderly rural woman whose speech this register most closely resembled, there were none of the neologisms of the radio register as far as I could discern.

This second kind of announcer, as I suggested in Examples 1–4 above, employed Tashelhit terms that had fallen out of use in an attempt to enrich a shared Tashelhit lexicon with neologisms. Youssi states that the Berber radio register was characterized by (1) Arabic lexical items morphologically "nativized" into Berber (Hill 1985:315), and (2) re-conceptualization of what he calls "native vocabulary," which he does not define but we may consider to characterize the re-contextualization of lexical items in Example 1 (Youssi 1990:269, using data from Berdi 1988). One consistency of MST, I would add, is that it draws from other Moroccan varieties of Berber (especially Tamazight from the Middle Atlas) as well as non-Moroccan varieties of Berber. Regardless of the explicit language ideology of radio programmers, however, in practice the Tashelhit that was diffused varied more according to whether it was studiously prepared in advance and read aloud or instead produced live in the studio. A more purified Tashelhit characterized prepared segments, such as news programming, poetry, and advertisements as in Examples 1–4 above, whereas live studio conversations that were less consistently monitored tended to employ more lexical borrowings and code-switching as rhetorical strategies, as in Example 5.

Listeners rationalized the modified Tashelhit radio register within the same frame in which they made sense of radio and, increasingly, television programming in other languages. Speakers could use what they heard as a gauge against which to measure the correctness of their own speech – as Omar the taxi driver did when he asked his passengers for the correct Tashelhit word for pharmacy, or as Mbarek did when asking the village young women for the Tashelhit words for bicycle and airport. The most notable correction this super-Tashelhit made of everyday Tashelhit use was to replace Arabic borrowings with neologisms – which was also a primary goal of the Amazigh cultural and linguistic rights movement under Hassan II (cf. Crawford and Hoffman 2000; El Moujahid 1994; Tilmatine 1992). Although some unschooled Moroccans understood the SA of radio and television programming after years of listening and watching, most did not. This was particularly true for rural Tashelhit speakers, many of whom were accustomed to understanding little of the Arabic radio broadcasting they heard around them. With the emerging MST, on the other hand, the same ideology was presumed by many listeners for Tashelhit as for Arabic and French – that what radio announcers spoke was "good" speech and "real" language – purer versions of their native tongue.

Listeners were also keen to note regional variations in broadcasters' lexicon, phonology, intonation, and rhetorical style, reacting either of two ways when they heard Tashelhit that differed from their own. Some remarked with the Tashelhit aphorism *kra igat tamazirt d wawal ns*, literally "Every land and its talk," or "Every place has its own way of speaking." When I asked one Ida ou Zeddout woman where she thought a radio announcer was from, given the difference between the cadence of his speech and hers, she exclaimed, "Who knows! Every place has its way of saying things. But now with the radio, it's all mixed up and people want to talk like they hear on the radio." She suggested that the broadcaster may have altered her speech to suit the medium and audience expectations. Indeed some listeners aesthetically preferred one pronunciation over another (for instance the verb-final voiced uvular fricative /ġ/ of the Igherm region for the first person singular conjugation, rather than the aspirated /ḥ/ of the Tiznit region or the voiceless uvular fricative /x/ of the Western High Atlas, in, for example, the word *sfldġ* /*sfldḥ*/ *sfldx* (I listened). Ishelhin understood that /ġ/, /ḥ/, and /x/ were regional phonetic variations on the same morpheme, making them mutually comprehensible.[7] Radio broadcasters tempered their speech so as not to isolate listeners by sounding as though they were from outside the region; Ishelhin tended to circumscribe the boundaries of community close to home.

Other assessments of radio discourse were more loaded with social evaluations. Some listeners responded to difference by asking themselves and each other what "real" Tashelhit sounded like – that is, which groups of people spoke Tashelhit free of Arabic and whose speech was mixed (xlḍn) with Arabic. In contrast to the linguistic relativist listeners, these listeners ranked speech on a continuum from purity to contamination. Contaminated speech was curable with willpower, self-discipline, and the tools to make alternative lexical and stylistic choices.[8]

Conclusion

Is lexical purism a "losing battle," as Hill claims (1987:130)? Perhaps the answer depends on what the war is about. If the goal of purism is to rid spoken language of borrowed and assimilated terms – lexical "impurities" – then surely Hill is right. However, the goal instead may be to encourage the development of neologisms and break the cycle of dependence on the dominant language. Many Ishelhin considered a reliance on Arabic and French as destructive not only to their language, but also to their individual and collective esteem. In this respect, purism may not achieve its expressed purpose, but it may succeed at a larger goal that is unarguably worthwhile and utterly achievable.

I have attempted to demonstrate in this chapter that Tashelhit language ideologies favored lexical purism as a normative move across oral genres in radio programming, but that radio speech exhibited more flexibility with ample code mixing, assimilated borrowings, and bivalent terms in Tashelhit, colloquial and classical Arabic, and to some extent French. Seemingly contradictory language ideologies stemmed from deeply rooted understandings of the inherent dissimilarity between speaking and writing. Most pointedly, in the view of many in the Tashelhit radio audience, radio language should not reflect lay people's talk since it tended to be inadequately pure. This language ideology bears a striking resemblance to Saussure's langue-parole distinction, as well as to Chomsky's competence-performance dichotomy. Neither Saussure nor Chomsky provide models for understanding the discrepancy between competence and performed linguistic practice, particularly given linguistic flux as integral to social transformation. As a practical matter, radio listeners looked to radio to reflect a higher standard that the average speaker or writer could attain. The expectation seemed to be that everyday speech was a bastardized *parole* of a yet-to-be-defined collective *langue*, after Saussure's classic formulation. Yet the production and circulation of poetry, proverbs, stories, and social histories in radio format simultaneously preserved and expanded the lexical and genre repertoires of Tashelhit speakers.

Rural speech in the region as I heard it, taped it, and transcribed it was far from "pure," if purity meant an absence of borrowings, assimilated lexical items, and unique communicative conventions. The radio register allegedly based on rural speech promoted an ideology of purism: an elimination of extra-ethnic (especially Arabic) elements, and an emphasis on agricultural imagery and other markers of a rural connection. Tashelhit radio discourse did not simply mimic the speech practices of its target audience, for that community has been marked, to varying degrees, by the Arabizing influences of urbanization, schooling, and increased interaction with both actual and media Arabic speakers. The case instead illustrates how media speech offered models not only for correct speech but also for social identities attached to particular speech styles. Even when an audience is only implied, speaking is a social act. Intentional decisions about lexical choice and pronunciation, and even habitual behaviors reflecting a person's social experience, enter into a linguistic political economy bound up in issues of ideology, power, agency, and structure.

Appadurai is right to emphasize that "many lives are now inextricably linked with representations, and thus we need to incorporate the complexities of expressive representation (film, novels, travel accounts) into our ethnographies, not only as technical adjuncts but as primary material with which to construct and interrogate our own representations" (1996:64). Yet for many of the world's people, especially those without access to films and television and those who do not read, radio and other audio media are even more important sites for ethnolinguistic representations. Sounds travel further than sights. I have discussed ways that Tashelhit-speaking lay people talked about, reacted to, and critiqued verbal representations of "their" language in social interactions in order to argue that, sometimes, it matters which word a person uses for taxi seat or bicycle. Lexical choice, like code choice, can index key facets of social identities and collective aspirations.

Metalinguistic commentary circulated between the airwaves, newspapers, and conversations in remote Anti-Atlas mountain hamlets, not just in urban streets and Amazigh activist association meetings. Because of their wide dissemination, they are illustrative for our understandings of the connections between social changes that were taking place in both rural and urban places at the end of the twentieth century. Although Ishelhin were most consciously attentive to lexical use, radio's most pervasive effect was its role in encouraging tolerance for linguistic and cultural pluralism in Morocco. The purist language strategy that characterized the radio register represented an attempt to cope with the fragmentation that modernization brings about through migration, urbanization, language shift, and the changing aspirations that accompany these processes for both those who move and those who remain in the countryside.

Chapter 9
Conclusion

> *Is it possible to locate oneself historically, to tell a coherent global story, when historical reality is understood to be an unfinished series of encounters?*
>
> – Clifford (1997:13)

A transnational, universalizing rhetoric of endangered or contracting languages is found in many societies today. This rhetoric posits that each language is equally valuable and worthy of presentation; that its loss diminishes the richness of all humanity, not just that of native speakers; that languages are disappearing at an alarming and historically unprecedented rate that should shock and move us to action; and that stopping language loss is an imperative on par with conservation of the world's forests, oceans, and skies. Hill (2002) offers an important critique of such approaches to endangered languages, arguing that they dismiss the particularistic, private attachment that speakers of small languages often have to their vernaculars, and downplay the real economic and political conditions that encourage or discourage the use of certain languages.

The problem, too, is that such universalizing rhetoric fails to take stock of the ways that speakers of these languages experience language themselves, and the variety of constraints on verbal expression that people face. Moreover, it disregards the diversity internal to the communities concerned, diversity that situates some people to benefit from language maintenance or language loss. This internal heterogeneity in indigenous or endangered language communities is largely swept under the rug in an effort to represent groups as unified and steadfast in their demands to an often less than receptive state law-making body (Hoffman 2006). As I have been arguing, some groups – like plains Ishelhin – get erased from the category of Ishelhin because they are seemingly tainted by Arab cultural practices and language.

It is not so much that the Tamazight language varieties, like many other minority and indigenous languages, have been "lost" as they have been "subordinated, enabling their return as hegemony is overturned" (Friedman 2003:744). To this end, recent efforts by the Moroccan government to incorporate Tamazight language and Berber heritage into public domains are laudable, particularly for the symbolic value they grant this heretofore marginalized population and scorned indigenous language. But research institutes and educational policy should not distract our attention from the abiding foundation of Berber language maintenance: rural women, usually monolingual, almost always unschooled, and overwhelmingly alone in their mountain villages with each other. These rural hamlets are the real language institutes of Morocco. They are the sites of richness in Tashelhit expressive genres, in lexicon, in storytelling and song, in religious and quasi-religious rituals that all take place in Tashelhit. In the mountains, Arabic is restricted to the classroom and to solar- or increasingly electric-powered television that tells children that their ancestors were the Arabs who gathered about the Prophet Mohammed in the Persian Gulf. Schoolchildren are taught that Islam is their shared religion, and Arabic is their shared language. These messages further distance children from their households where the other family members, who labor manually, eat two midday meals at 10 am and 3 pm rather than the single midday meal at noon mandated by the Moroccan curriculum, a curriculum oriented towards the parents of urban schoolchildren, parents who may work outside the home. It is unclear whether Tamazight instruction in primary schools will succeed either in teaching Tamazight to Arabs (as well as Imazighen) or increase its symbolic value as integral to Moroccan heritage.

The language instructors of the mountain language institutes – namely, illiterate, monolingual mountain women – ascribe to a language ideology that is at odds with that of the (largely male) policy-makers and activists. Rural women's ideologies are grounded in experiences much closer to home, rather than the universalist rhetoric of the fetishizing culture-preserver. Different life experiences have led to conflicting metapragmatics of language, language ideologies, and ideas around language socialization. For the mountain women, there is no choice of language to be made; they only know one. Yet universalizing rhetoric calls on individuals to make careful communicative choices; even Fatima Tabaamrant sings about the need for women to be vigilant lest they "lose" their Tashelhit to Arabic. This message seems more appropriately directed at urban and peri-urban native Berber speakers. The problem is that language maintenance largely rests on the shoulders of women who are kept, by husbands and fathers, in the mountains and illiterate, to tend their homesteads and fields, to reproduce both children and culture, and to ensure their men's prosperity. The universalizing rhetoric of language maintenance romanticizes an authentic linguistic community as parallel to actual face-to-face communities, confusing imagined communities built around speaking practices of a single idiom with more conventional communities grounded in patriline, tribal and tribal section membership, and local political economy. What is the difference, we might ask, and why might it matter?

The difference is largely that a kind of homogeneity of experience and expression is expected of members or participants in the first kind of imagined linguistic community, as well as a uniformity of language ideologies about the nature of language and means for its correct use. This is the imagined community that governmental officials invoke since introducing the Amazigh language into the primary school curriculum for a few hours each week. This is the imagined community of the perceived radio audience of Tashelhit-language broadcasting, whether out of Agadir in Berber-speaking lands or in the capital Rabat.

While we hear about the cultural diversity *within* this imagined linguistic community, with the idiomatic expressions or community music particular to this tribe or village or that one, what we rarely hear is discussion of the political economic forces that have shaped some of the crucial variance in language use and attitudes. In Morocco in the Protectorate and Independence periods, differing land tenure systems have been most crucial, for they either have brought some Amazigh communities closer to their Arabic-speaking neighbors or instead have kept them at a distance. We can characterize these strategies as accommodation and resistance; these processes operate not just at the level of ethnic contact, but also at the level of linguistic relations. In the Anti-Atlas mountains, men are landowners even though they emigrate to the cities and leave their wives and children to farm the fields and process the harvest. Performances of all verbal expressive modalities – talking, singing, chanting, storytelling, orating, bargaining, etc. – are conducted in Tashelhit.

In both sub-regions of the Sous – the plains where people accommodate their Arabic-speaking neighbors by taking on certain parts of their verbal expressive repertoire, and the mountains where Tashelhit is the lingua franca and expressive idiom – Tashelhit speaking women socialize children into the Tashelhit language. The vast majority of these women are not literate; a larger percentage of men are literate in both places, but the number is still not as elevated as in towns and cities. So while women continue to teach their children their ancestral language, the ways they use language vary between the mountains and the plains, a significant difference that has not been acknowledged in recent changes in language policy laws. More attention to local performances – and less attention to transnational, universalizing rhetorics – would better serve both public policy and the minority communities whose interests they are designed to protect. Transnational rhetorics stress the insularity and particularity of each language, set of cultural practices, and system of beliefs. Yet metaculture is evaluated in individual instantiations, through situated performances, and in relative terms.

This study raises a number of questions that may be instructive for research on language practices and ideologies amongst other indigenous groups. I have investigated ways in which practices, discursive and material, are associated with one ethnicity or gender or the other, and in which they are made convincing and consequential to neighboring speech communities that consider themselves – and are considered by outsiders – as a coherent group. I have attempted to explore some of the implications for women when language and labor are gendered as female, and the ways in which individuals challenge, reinvigorate, and reproduce this relationship between land, language, and gender.

In conclusion, I would like to return to the monolingual Ftuma in Ida ou Zeddout, who as a future mother will pass on the Tashelhit language but whose lexicon the emigrant merchant found too tainted with Arabic for his liking. In contrast, we have the singer-songwriter and recording artist Tabaamrant, friend of the Amazigh movement, who urges women to maintain their ancestral language and keep their community strong. Similarly, we have the ethnographer who documents gendered contributions to the making of an Ashelhi homeland – and the maintenance of the Tashelhit language – and who is engaged in a potentially indefensible endeavor. Both activists and scholars effectively bolster a status quo in which an inextricable relationship is forged between rural women, indigenous language, and hard agricultural labor. Both Tabaamrant and many Tashelhit-speaking laypeople are concerned about the cultural assimilation of Ishelhin into an Arab-dominant Moroccan society and homogenized narrative, and the loss of history and heritage that accompany assimilation.

It is crucial to offer other descriptions, and interpretations of social life and language in the mountains and plains, since the ones that we have at present simply will not do. Take, for instance, Marthelot, who may not have been alone in his failure to acknowledge the multiple forms of "modernity" in the rural Moroccan hinterlands. He wrote in 1973 that the Berber mountains were a "mountain sanctuary," but warned that, and I translate from the French,

> mountain sanctuary does not mean living region! Is the region, more specifically, still capable of supporting the ethnic group (*éthnie*) that assembles there? The mountain is not entirely depopulated, but it risks becoming nothing other than a museum of bones and customs, including language, a museum where the main object on display, other than the traces on the ground of an obsolete settlement, partly in ruins, would be nothing other than a population comprised of *old wise men*, entirely unfamiliar with the course of history. (Marthelot 1973:473; italics added)

Contrary to Marthelot's depiction, even thirty years on there were old sages in the villages, but they were women more often than men. Yet there were also babies, young women, and teachers from the cities. The Tashelhit homeland is no museum – it is a living, breathing, and changing place always understood and defined (in part only) through the city. People engage with the countryside for material or moral sustenance. Some want out, others get out. Some want in, others invest through marriage and home-building, and settle down to start families away from urban hassles. Marthelot, like the French Native Affairs officers writing tribal reports in the first half of the twentieth century, forgot the women in the homeland – even though women have long been the majority of its residents.

The countryside is made, as Williams argues, through the exploitation by some of others – and here we find a gendered distribution of practices and movements whose dynamic grants women almost sole responsibility for the social and linguistic reproduction of their community. The dichotomy of city/human : country/nature is persistent, he writes, but when we look at the history of countrysides, we see that the dichotomy does not hold. Contrary to its discursive representation, the country is not a fact of nature. Indigenous people further complicate this scenario because, from an urban perspective, they are deeply rooted in the earth. A dilemma of representation ensues: indigenous to the land, they have the moral prerogative to remain there, and this forms the ethical basis of indigenous rights movements. Their indigeneity, however, should not obscure their histories, and the history of rural Moroccans and their homelands is indeed a history of conquest, land seizures, domination, and ultimately reliance on market and urban centers. French Protectorate writings on *le pays berbère* characterized its population as attached to the land yet incompetent at tending it, and the Berber as attached to his [*sic*] patrimony, guarded about his women [*sic*]. The Berber in these writings was unequivocally male – yet already men were leaving the countryside in droves for the cities. The women, while present, were absent from Protectorate accounts, and their contributions to the making of the countryside – and the "Berber lands" – were disregarded. But it is not so clear what exploitation looks like in the context of a (materially and ideologically) mutually dependent system. It raises the question of whether a sub-group needs to be exploited to reproduce a minority language like Tashelhit and keep it vital and vibrant.

The methodological and human rights dilemma I am proposing is how activists and anthropologists alike can ethically encourage the same language practices and ideologies that, while helping perpetuate an endangered language, also gender space, restrict women's movements, and confine women to lives of hard labor. Social and geographic marginality of some groups may be the surest safeguards against language shift for the collective, but it is difficult to advocate that some groups be denied equal access to resources. One wonders what would happen if these rural women left language maintenance to the emigrant men, to radio announcers, and to intellectuals and policy-makers with their idealized notions of linguistic purity. Perhaps instead of increasing the visibility of these same men, the Amazigh language rights movement will be a catalyst for converting rural women's cultural capital to economic forms given their centrality in, albeit unreflexiveness about, language preservation.

In his final book, Wolf attempts to mediate once and for all between the competing anthropological theories of class and cultural systems as explanatory models. He theorizes how culture and political economy are collectively implicated in the production and imposition of power. He writes,

> the advocates of "class" assumed that a common position, long a gradient of control over the means of production entails a common interest shared by all members of the class, and hence common propensities for action. Yet class and classness are better understood in terms of relations that develop historically within a social field . . . a class may be "unmade" and its members scattered and reallocated to different groupings and strata.
>
> The advocates of "culture," for their part, have generally thought that whatever underlies cultural commonalties – be it language, upbringing, customs, traditions, race – will produce sentiments of identity, social solidarity, love of country, and aversion to cultural "others." Yet, as with class, the forces postulated as generating culture were never strong enough in and of themselves to produce the envisioned unifying effects. Historically, both classness and culturehood needed to be mobilized and reinforced to come to fruition: in many cases, the requisite energies emerged from the turmoil of politics and war. (Wolf 1999:65)

Maybe the Ida ou Zeddout father in the collective taxi ride was getting at something deeper than his fellow passengers acknowledged when he stated that "we're not like Ait Tafraout." If I hadn't visited Tafraout and the Ammeln Valley myself several times, I probably would not have agreed with him so quickly. According to the terms I have laid out in this book, it would seem that Ait Ida ou Zeddout and Ait Tafraout n Ammeln are somewhat "the same." Their communities are both characterized by heavy male migration to Casablanca with women staying behind to harvest barley and almonds. Although they may share the same kind of allegiance to the tamazirt, the specific tamazirt to which each group is loyal differs. Divided by the mountains of the Ait Abdallah whom the French succeeded in conquering only in 1934, among the last dissident tribes, links between the Ida ou Zeddout and the people of the Ammeln have been minimal. People from these places are more likely to meet in Agadir, or in Casablanca. Now with a new road linking Igherm and Tafraout, and with urban schooling of these merchants' sons, new possibilities open for conceiving of another basis of community, one grounded in the fact of being native Tashelhit speakers. This was the vision of the young rural development leader who challenged the Ida ou Zeddout father's pessimism. The tension between these different conceptions of social group formation and behavior remains, and with Ishelhin constantly moving between rural and urban places, it is likely that the tension will persist.

What has emerged from contact between peoples and languages is a simultaneous accommodation and differentiation, through sung and spoken practices, respectively. In some places, this has led inadvertently to a language shift that many today are concerned with reversing. While purist strategies are a common reaction to language loss, purism is not the most efficacious strategy for offsetting the language shift that often accompanies state expansion into rural areas, as earlier scholars have documented in a variety of locales (Anderson 1991; Burnham 1996; Ferguson 1999; Kroskrity 1993; Kuipers 1998; Kulick 1992).

If we consider Tamazight in general and Tashelhit in particular to be contracting languages – a fair premise given the accelerating shift from Tamazight towards Arabic, especially since the massive urbanization of the 1970s, and the contraction in its domains of use – then we would do well to examine the ethnolinguistic organization of expressive culture as well as the domains of use for what Nettle and Romaine (2000) call metropolitan and peripheral languages. Tashelhit is a peripheral language by any account: peripheral to MA within Morocco, virtually unacknowledged outside of state boundaries and, as an oral language, entirely absent from world affairs, despite the presence of some native Tashelhit speakers in high governmental, business, and policy-making positions (where they are obliged to speak Arabic, French, English or another non-native language). Following Nettle and Romaine's paradigm, prior to Independence, Moroccan rural economies operated nearer to the level of subsistence (Nettle and Romaine 2000:130). The Arabic-speaking elites in the northern Moroccan cities may not have been influential enough to cause language shift among the general population, even though Arabic clearly remained the predominant language in governmental and religious affairs as it had been since the Berber empires of the medieval period, for which we have limited textual evidence (Shatzmiller 2000). The situation is different today: metropolitan languages are advancing quickly at the expense of peripheral ones throughout the world, largely because of the economic expansion in a few of the world's societies, with the resulting significant difference in the economic power of metropolitan and peripheral societies (Nettle and Romaine 2000:133). Economic development may indeed provide some ordinary individuals with "unprecedented opportunities for domination by providing people with technologies and institutions that they can use to promote their own influence and control" (Nettle and Romaine 2000:139).

Yet as Friedman (2003) cautions, such resources may only be available to minority elites who, across the globe, are the visible instantiations of globalization. Globalization, with the decline of nationalist hegemonies, is leading to new forms of fragmentation within societies. For Morocco, it remains to be seen where the new fault lines will appear, given the twenty-first-century political opening towards the Amazigh component of the country's heritage and present, and given the preexisting but widely unacknowledged group-internal fractures. These fractures have made the contours of both Tashelhit language and Amazigh identification constantly open to negotiation not only by urban intellectuals, wordsmiths, and activists but also, as I have endeavored to demonstrate in this book, by rural laypeople as they go about their everyday lives.

Notes

Chapter 1

1 An example of what I am calling postnationalism is the phenomenon found among some groups of Tamazight speakers who bypass Arabic altogether in adopting a European language alongside the heritage vernacular. Mokhtar Ghambou has remarked this among Tarifit speakers in his native Al Hoceima in the Rif region; heavily marked by emigration to Holland and Spain, multilinguals there speak in Tarifit and Dutch or Spanish, and find Arabic irrelevant. By the fourth generation of emigrants, however, Tarifit disappears (Mokhtar Ghambou, personal communication, Rabat, March 16, 2005).

2 I have two qualifications concerning this division of Berber vernaculars into three geolects. First, the terms that Berber speakers use for these varieties vary by region. For example, people in the Errachidia region (southeast Morocco) distinguish between Tarifit, Tamazight, Tasoussit (in the Sous region) and their own *tašlḥit*. Many Riffis call both their language variety and that of the Middle and Eastern High Atlas *tamaziġt* instead of differentiating between Tarifit and Tamazight as do many people of other regions. The term *tazayanit* was used by Swasa more frequently than the term *tamaziġt* to refer to the vernacular of the Zayan people, who are also called Imazighen in much ethnographic and historical literature. The second qualification is that vernaculars can be placed on a continuum in which the standard three varieties are only the most widely recognized varieties. The variety spoken in the Errachidia region lexically and phonetically combines what they call *tasusit* and Tamazight traits. The variety spoken in the Taza region north of Fes, for instance, combines Tarifit and Tamazight lexical and phonetic elements.

3 The Moroccan Jewish population dwindled to around 5,000 after significant emigration to Israel especially after 1967. Earlier, Jews lived among rural Berbers as well (Levin 1999). For more on the remaining Jewish population, concentrated primarily in Casablanca, see Kosansky (2002, 2003), Levy (1999), and Weingrod (1990).

4 The tiwizi (collective laboring) system was in place in some Ashelhi mountain communities such as Ida ou Finis neighboring Ida ou Zeddout, some Western High Atlas villages such as Riyad and Had Imoulas, and some Sous plains villages

near the foothills, such as Touraght. Village girls and women collectively harvested the fields of one household or those owned by the village, usually considered the property of the mosque. The host household fed the workers for the duration of the harvest and then on completion thanked them with a special meal. The women maintained a festive atmosphere throughout these periods of collective labor, often drumming and singing during meal breaks, which several told me helped them to turn the work into a celebration. Under tiwizi, some lands were not harvested until fall; by procuring outside workers, in contrast, people in Ida ou Zeddout finished harvesting by mid-summer. European and American Berberists have emphasized collective laboring as a quality of Berber society, generalizing primarily from evidence from the Eastern High Atlas (e.g. Hart 1984). Comparative documentation from the Anti-Atlas or other parts of the Sous is needed, but my observation is that collective laboring is more prevalent among land-owning people in the Western High Atlas and Sous plains than in the Anti-Atlas. For a discussion of tiwizi in the Ziz Valley of southeastern Morocco, see Ilahiane (2004). Montagne (1973) and Lortat-Jacob (1981) also contain brief discussions of tiwizi.

5 David Crawford called my attention to this important taxonomic distinction.

6 Haeri (2003) documents a similar phenomenon in Egypt, although Egyptian Arabic is more prevalent in Egyptian media than MA is in Moroccan media.

7 An assessment of the overall impact of these shifts on Imazighen would require attention to High Atlas Ishelhin as well as speakers of the other Amazigh varieties (Tamazight and Tarifit). High Atlas speakers of Tashelhit and Tamazight are outside the scope of the present ethnography. They have been extensively written about in both the Protectorate and post-Protectorate periods; their political economies differ in important ways from the Anti-Atlas and Sous plains, especially due to greater resources for subsistence farming. For ethnographic treatments of High Atlas Berbers, see Amahan (1998), Crawford (2001), and Miller (1984).

Chapter 2

1 Hart (2000:25) notes that he was warmly received among Berbers of Ait Atta of Saghru and Aith Waryaghar of the Rif mountains, with openness and frankness. In contrast, he encountered extreme suspicion among nomadic Arabic-speaking Rgaybat informants in the Western Sahara.

Chapter 3

1 I am grateful to Neal Durando for drawing my attention to this poem.

2 In societies where feminine domains are more clearly valued, such as Iceland, women are crucial agents in the reproduction of national ideologies as well as the reproduction of the family (Koester 1995).

3 Tafraout, also called Tafraout n Wammeln for the Ammeln (aka Ammiln) Valley it borders, is a market town southwest of Taroudant. It is the home region for the first wave of Soussi merchants to Casablanca at the beginning of the twentieth century, and still the largest pool of Anti-Atlas emigrants to Moroccan and European cities. Many merchants from that area have made tremendous fortunes. Because of their prosperity, some other Ishelhin see them as a model for balancing migrant and homeland lives.

4 Popularly called "the Tashelhit writing" (*tiġra n tšlḥit* / kitaba diyal šilḥa) by schooled young people, Tifinagh is an alphabet of 39 letters, written left to right, that is believed to be indigenous to North and West Africa among Berber-speaking people. A small proportion of Moroccans overall recognized Tifinagh in the late 1990s, fewer could read it, and even fewer could write it. In Morocco, its use was largely restricted to artistic and poetic domains; now it is used for Tamazight language instruction in primary schools. The letter yaz (ⵣ) in particular is frequently used in Amazigh movement imagery as a symbol of Amazigh identity. The alphabet is currently used in United Nations-sponsored literacy programs in Mali and Mauritania among the Kel Tamasheq or Touareg people. The current alphabet promoted by Amazigh activists and used in UN programs is a two decade-old standardization of multiple Lybico-Berber alphabets.

5 The liver, rather than the heart, may have been the center of affect in Arab as well as Berber culture until recently, tracing back to Ibn Sina. This concept of liver as "the seat of the natural faculty and the baser human appetites" (Good 1977:36) has also been traced to Iran, and to parts of South and Southeast Asia (cf. Wilce 1998:266–7).

6 Tifawt can also refer to people, as when a girl suggested, "Let's go outside and see what tifawt the night has brought."

7 See Goodman (1996) for an account of public hand-holding in rural Kabylia, Algeria, as a conscious attempt on the part of young Amazigh activists to change people's mentality concerning mixed-sex interaction.

8 I regret not having caught this moment on film. Hassan wore the tamlḥaft I had specially made in Taroudant, with its understated decoration contrasting with the young women's flashier wraps. I had loaned it to Ftuma to wear the day before, while she washed her own; I was wearing a tamlḥaft borrowed from someone else. Was Hassan mimicking a Tashelhit woman, or was he mocking my own appropriation of their dress?

Chapter 4

1 *tasa ṣbri nit*
. . . *a yat tguḍi ka giti iġaman*
. . . *a kkiġ timizar ula tiqbilini*
. . . *tammara aġ llan mddn aḍan d ussani*
. . . *man srsn yuggan mad d akk*^{w} *hmmani*
. . . *mad issn lxir n willi zrinini*
. . . *willi ḍinin aṛumi s tiddi d wawali*
. . .

. . . awal f ufla luqt ad t id yiwini
. . . han lmdayn ġass ad ka ġa thallani
. . . imma timizar n udrar nḥgr tnti
. . . ur anniġ iġarasn ad aġd lkmni . . .

2 Nation-wide, employed emigrant men worked most frequently in commerce (25.97 percent), in industry (17.18 percent), and in construction and public works (13.34 percent). Women worked most significantly in industry (49.86 percent) and in personal and domestic services (21.98 percent) (CERED 1995:169).

3 The Ait Tafraout are one of four tribal sections of the Ida ou Zeddout, the others being Ait Musi, Ait Ourgummi, and Ait Nihit. Ait Tafraout n Ida ou Zeddout should not be confused with the town of Tafraout, located further southwest, whose tribe is Ida ou Gniḍif. The latter are highly represented in Casablanca and other northern cities. Their remittances have initiated a major architectural and infrastructural overhaul of the Sous region, replacing stone with massive cinder block homes, colorfully painted pink and tallow, and extending electricity and running water to remote villages. The Ida ou Gniḍif are perhaps the most visible and wealthy of the emigrant Ishelhin.

4 I am grateful to an anonymous reviewer of Hoffman 2002b for directing my attention more squarely to the gendered connections between nostalgia and modernity. Nostalgia has been elaborated as a product of modernity and late capitalism in recent ethnography and cultural criticism (Ivy 1995, especially pp. 55–8; Jameson 1984, 1989; Stewart 1996).

5 Division de la Statistique, Population Rurale par Fraction et Douar. *Recensement générale de la population et de l'habitat du 1994*. Ministère de la Prévision Economique et du Plan.

6 See Hoffman 2000b for more on the politics around Moroccan identity cards and the state's registration of rural bodies.

7 In local taxonomies, land ownership and land use were important indexes of group membership; the same terms had regionally distinct meanings. In the rainfed Anti-Atlas agricultural fields were called *igran*. Irrigated vegetable plots, in contrast, were *tartib*, of which the Ida ou Zeddout had few. In the Sous Valley, in contrast, rainfed fields are called by the Arabic lbur. Irrigated lands for produce were called igran. The variability of agricultural terminology presents a challenge to the ethnographer concerned with land ownership. A plains dweller, for example, may state that she has no igran, but she may neglect to mention the lbur she owns which, in local practices, is insignificant and tended only twice a year for planting and a modest harvest. A mountain dweller, in contrast, considered her igran those rainfed barley fields that she tended, owned by her husband or father.

8 I am indebted to M.E. Combs-Schilling for pointing out the relevance of this phrase to my discussion of "full" places as positively endowed, in contrast to a Western idealization of peaceful (and thus uncrowded) places (personal communication, March 1999).

9 Tashelhit sung poetry commonly shifts between first person singular and plural pronouns (here, me and we). Euphony supercedes strict adherence to grammar rules governing conversational speech (Hoffman 2002a). In verses such as this one, the singer took the voice of the bride: she simultaneously spoke for the

particular and the collective, and her shift reflected this move. I translate burial literally because Ishelhin compared moving with dying, as we saw in an earlier tazrrart. This theme recurred in other expressive domains because, they said, you could no longer count on a woman who married outside the village or a person who emigrated.

10 *Safi* is used in both Tashelhit and Moroccan Arabic as a marker of agreement, signaling the end of a discussion or concurring with a point just made. It can also mean "that's all." For example, a woman might respond to the question, "How many children do you have?" with "I have one, safi." Here, Saadia signaled that she recognized that this was the end of her days of being on her own.

11 "S/He said to you" is a rhetorical phrase or discourse marker (Schiffrin 1988) that precedes reported speech in both Moroccan Arabic (Kapchan 1996:49) and Tashelhit, regardless of whether the "you" is the intended addressee. This convention literally enacts Vološinov's enjoinder that "There can be no such thing as an abstract addressee, a man [*sic*] unto himself, so to speak. With such a person, we would indeed have no language in common, literally and figuratively" (1973 [1929]:85).

12 *ad aġ isamḥ ṛbbi*; "May the Lord forgive us," was said in the place of goodbye when people had been speaking frankly, talking about someone not present, or speaking in a way that might have angered the interloctor.

13 *iwa ajjataġ ka ur gignġ ma tnt ifrrun*
immnεa zman ad iga d fllaġ aṛumi
iwa laḥ irgazn daġ isafarn as llan
iwwi daġ waḍu tida urunt tmġarin

14 The bled el-makhzen–bled es-siba distinction was understood slightly differently by rural Ishelhin, on the one hand, and by scholars and French Protectorate officials, on the other. The Anti-Atlas mountains were ruled by the Qayd Tiouti during the Protectorate period. In vernacular usage I encountered, the word siba meant fighting, chaos, and lawlessness; it referred to a period more than a place, a time, as one elderly man explained to me describing the early Protectorate period, when Hayda Mouwis was pasha of Taroudant, "They go to some tamazirt, they surround it, they take their animals, they kill people." It remained unclear whether the "they" referred to Hayda Mouwis's people or just groups of armed men. The absence of a strong central ruler at certain historical moments was sufficient for some insiders to claim that a specific location was in a state of siba. See, for example, the late nineteenth-century letters between the State of Tazerwalt of the saint Sidi Hmed u Musa and the makhzen or central government (Ennaji and Pascon 1988:178, 198).

Chapter 5

1 This kind of romantic discourse about the village, especially in song, is widespread today throughout the Mediterranean. See for instance on Corsica, Jaffe (1999:43), on Greece, Caraveli (1980, 1982, 1985), and on Malta, Sant Cassia (2000).

2 See Hoffman (2002a) for a more detailed structural and spatial analysis of weddings (timġriwin, sing. tamġra) among the Ait Musi of Ida ou Zeddout.

3 See Hoffman (2002a) for a discussion of the moral economy and generational change in women's tizrrarin, and for selected musical notations; Hoffman (2000a) contains an analysis of prosodic and musicological qualities and further song texts. See Rovsing Olsen (1984) for an ethnomusicological analysis of Ida ou Zeddout tizrrarin.

4 See Hoffman (2002b) for a discussion of the conflation in Tashelhit between "to want to" and "to go" that makes it difficult to express the idea of wanting to go somewhere (or do something) but not being able to. Here again, Ishelhin embrace a Herderian philosophy of *Besonnenheit* ("the total economy of his sensuous and cognitive, or his cognitive and volitional nature"), rejecting the separation of reason, will, and emotion so central to Kant's thinking (in Bauman and Briggs 2003:166).

5 Internal to Tashelhit poetry, personal pronouns are commonly interchangeable, so that number and person need not remain consistent within and between lines. Here, first person singular and plural are used. As Gal has commented on the formulaic quality of Abu-Lughod's (1986) Egyptian Bedouin ghinnawas ("little songs"), this strategy "disguise[es] the identities of poet, addressee, and subject. It is fleeting and ambiguous . . ." (Gal 1995b:177).

6 This echoes Hart's reporting of the expression *han aɛrab ur igi g*[w]*mak a ašlḥiy*: "An Arab is not your brother, oh Ashelhi." This became something of a proverb, but was first uttered in the 1960s by a Berber regionalist singer over Radio Maroc, named Muha u-Mazun, who was imprisoned several times. It is not clear whether he was a Tamazight speaker as were the others in Hart's book on the Ait 'Atta of south-central Morocco (Hart 1984).

7 See Kapchan (1996) for a masterful analysis of market women's language and the marketing of female gender in Beni Mellal, Morocco.

8 The liver was the Arab repository of affect as well in early Islamic times, as evidenced in poetry. For the Weweya of Indonesia, lament, sadness, and humility occurs in the liver (Kuipers 1998:60). Among Ishelhin, I often heard it said that the liver (*tasa*) was where one feels love for parents and children, and the heart (galb) was where one feels romantic love. This is a clear example of a lexical borrowing from Arabic into Tashelhit for an introduced concept, marking the difference between types of love in a way that is impossible with a single word in Western languages.

Chapter 8

1 For a discussion of these issues in the orthographic conventions of Amazigh activist print media in Morocco, see Hoffman (2000a:339–59).

2 "Cool" in Tashelhit (*fjijin*) has the two meanings of the same term in English: as slang for "hip" or "great," and as a temperature reading warmer than cold but cooler than warm.

3 Note that this term, pronounced *imsqarn* in some places (since the *g* and *q* are interchangeable in Tashelhit), is the word used by young women in the mountains to describe the young men with whom they sit and talk in pairs.

4 A "translation" of the Quran is something highly contested by many believers who claim that the Quran's original wording cannot be changed lest it lose meaning; there are "interpretations" available in many languages. A Tashelhit version published by Jouhadi in 2003 has been highly controversial and its dissemination was long-delayed.

5 Generational difference in multiple aspects of speech behavior (narrative style, use of fixed forms especially formulaic religious invocations and proverbs, as well as lexicon) characterizes MA-speaking communities across Morocco as well as Tashelhit-speaking groups. In many instances the distinction can be partly explained by the influence of hegemonic Arabic speech styles reinforced in schools. But schooling itself does not explain generational change in speech styles, because there is not a significant difference, if any, between the speech of young women who have attended a few years of primary school in the village and their unschooled peers.

6 Hart (1984) documented the same injunction among Tamazight speakers of the Eastern High Atlas who told someone speaking MA or French, "*sawl s imi nk*!" (lit. "speak with your mouth," meaning "speak your own language").

7 In contrast, few Ishelhin claim to understand Tarifit in the Riff mountains of northern Morocco, and they are not attuned to pick up the phonological differences that distinguish it from Tashelhit, for instance the Riffi /š/ in the place of the Tashelhit /k/. Tashelhit first person singular pronoun "I" is *nkk* or *nkki*, and in Tarifit it is *nš*.

8 See Haeri (2003) for discussion of the development of Egyptian Arabic and Classical Arabic in Egypt to fit contemporary needs.

References

Aatabou, N. 1983. J'en ai marre. *Country Girls and City Women.* Audio recording.

Abu-Lughod, L. 1986. *Veiled Sentiments: Honor and Poetry in a Bedouin Society.* Berkeley, CA: University of California Press.

—— 1991. Writing against Culture. In R.G. Fox (Ed.), *Recapturing Anthropology.* Santa Fe, NM: School of American Research, 137–62.

Adam, A. 1972. Berber Migrants in Casablanca. In E. Gellner and C. Micaud (Eds.), *Arabs and Berbers.* Lexington, MA: Lexington Books, 325–43.

Agnaou, F. 2002. *Gender, Literacy, and Empowerment in Morocco.* Series in Middle East Studies-History, Politics and Law. New York: Routledge.

Alahyane, M. 1990. Le processus de mutation à Lakhsas Anti-Atlas occidental. *La Culture Populaire* 37–48.

Ali, A. 1984. *Al Qur'an: A Contemporary Translation.* Princeton, NJ: Princeton University Press.

Amahan, A. 1998. *Mutations sociales dans le Haut Atlas: Les Ghoujdama.* Rabat: Editions La Porte.

Anderson, B. 1991 [1983]. *Imagined Communities: Reflections on the Origin and Spread of Nationalism.* New York: Verso.

Aouchar, A. 2002. *Colonisation et Campagne Berbère au Maroc.* Casablanca: Afrique Orient.

Appadurai, A. 1996. *Modernity at Large: Global Dimensions of Globalization.* Minneapolis, MN: University of Minnesota Press.

Austin, J.L. 1962. *How to Do Things with Words.* Cambridge, MA: Harvard University Press.

Bakhtin, M.M. 1981 [1934]. *The Dialogic Imagination: Four Essays.* Austin, TX: University of Texas Press.

Balzer, M.M. 1999. *The Tenacity of Ethnicity: A Siberian Saga in Global Perspective.* Princeton, NJ: Princeton University Press.

Barth, F. 1969. Introduction. *Ethnic Groups and Boundaries: The Social Organization of Cultural Difference.* Prospect Heights, IL: Waveland Press.

Basso, K.H. 1996. *Wisdom Sits in Places: Landscape and Language among the Western Apache.* Albuquerque, NM: University of New Mexico Press.

Bauman, R. 1977. *Verbal Art as Performance.* Rowley, MA: Newbury House Publishers.

Bauman, R. and C.L. Briggs. 1990. Poetics and Performance as Critical Perspectives on Language and Social Life. *Annual Review of Anthropology* 19:59–88.

—— 1992. Genre, Intertextuality, and Social Power. *Journal of Linguistic Anthropology* 22:131–72.

—— 2003. *Voices of Modernity. Language Ideologies and the Politics of Inequality.* Cambridge: Cambridge University Press.

Baumann, G. 1987. *National Integration and Local Integrity.* Oxford: Clarendon Press.

Benhlal, M. 1981. Migration interne et stratification sociale au Maroc: le cas des Soussis. *Lamalif* 129:38–50.

Bennani-Chraibi, M. 1994. *Soumis et Rebelles: Les Jeunes au Maroc.* Casablanca: Le Fennec.

—— 2000. Youth in Morocco: An Indicator of a Changing Society. In R. Meijer (Ed.), *Alienation of Integration of Arab Youth: Between Family, State, and Street.* Richmond: Curzon Press.

Bentahila, A. 1983. Motivations for Code-switching among Arabic-French Bilinguals in Morocco. *Language & Communication* 33:233–43.

Berdi, A. 1988. *The Impact of Literary Arabic on Tashelhit Dialect Used in Radio Broadcasts.* Faculty of Letters, Department of English. Rabat: Université Mohammed V.

Berque, J. 1967. *French North Africa: The Maghrib between Two World Wars.* New York: Frederick A. Praeger.

Bidwell, R. 1973. *Morocco under Colonial Rule: French Administration of Tribal Areas 1912–1956.* London: Frank Cass.

Bloch, M. 1975. *Political Language and Oratory in Traditional Society.* London: Academic Press.

Bohlman, P.V. 1988. *The Study of Folk Music in the Modern World.* Bloomington, IN: University of Indiana Press.

Boukous, A. 1977. *Langage et Culture Populaires au Maroc.* Casablanca: Les Imprimeries Dar el Kitab.

—— 1995. *Societé, Langues et Cultures au Maroc.* Casablanca: Annajah Al-Jadida.

Bourdieu, P. 1966. The Sentiment of Honor in Kabyle Society. *Honour and Shame: The Values of Mediterranean Society.* London: Weidenfeld and Nicolson.

—— 1977. *Outline of a Theory of Practice.* Cambridge: Cambridge University Press.

—— 1990. *The Logic of Practice [Le sens pratique].* Stanford, CA: Stanford University Press.

—— 1991. *Language and Symbolic Power [Ce que parler veut dire].* Cambridge, MA: Harvard University Press.

Bourdieu, P. and J.-C. Passeron. 1970. *La Reproduction: éléments pour une théorie du système d'enseignement.* Paris: Les Editions de Minuit.

Boyarin, J. (Ed.) 1993. *The Ethnography of Reading.* Berkeley, CA: University of California Press.

Brel, J. 1961. On n'oublie rien. *Marieke.* Music and lyrics by J. Brel and G. Jouannest. Paris: Philips. Audio recording.

Brett, M. and E. Fentress. 1996. *The Berbers.* Oxford: Blackwell.

Briggs, C.L. 1986. *Learning How to Ask: A Sociolinguistic Appraisal of the Role of the Interview in Social Science Research.* Cambridge: Cambridge University Press.

Burnham, P. 1996. *The Politics of Cultural Difference in Northern Cameroon.* Washington, DC: Smithsonian Institution Press.

Calvet, J.-L. 2000. Users Are Choosers. http://www.unesco.org/courier/2000_04/uk/doss25.htm, accessed October 12, 2005.

Caraveli, A. 1980. Bridge between Worlds: The Greek Women's Lament as Communicative Event. *Journal of American Folklore* 93:129–57.

—— 1982. The Song beyond the Song: Aethetics and Social Interaction in Greek Folksong. *Journal of American Folklore* 95:129–58.

—— 1985. The Symbolic Village: Community Born in Performance. *Journal of American Folklore* 98:259–86.

Casey, E.S. 1996. How to Get from Space to Place in a Fairly Short Stretch of Time. In S. Feld and K. Basso (Eds.), *Senses of Place*. Santa Fe, NM: SAR Press, 13–52.

Caton, S.C. 1990. *"Peaks of Yemen I Summon": Poetry as Cultural Practice in a North Yemeni Tribe*. Berkeley, CA: University of California Press.

CERED. 1995. *L'Exode Rural: Traits d'Evolution, Profils et Rapport avec les Milieux d'Origine*. Direction de la Statistique. Rabat: Editions Guessous.

Chernela, J. 2003. Language Ideology and Women's Speech: Talking Community in the Northwest Amazon. *American Anthropologist* 1054:794–806.

Chtatou, M. 1997. The Influence of the Berber Language on Moroccan Arabic. *International Journal for the Sociology of Language*. Special issue, Berber Sociolinguistics, 101–18.

Clement, C. 1949. *Etude sur la Tribu des Ida ou Zeddout*. Cercle de Taroudannt, Annexe d'Irherm, Bureau des Affaires Indigènes.

Clifford, J. 1988. *The Predicament of Culture: Twentieth-Century Ethnography, Literature, and Art*. Cambridge, MA: Harvard University Press.

—— 1997. *Routes: Travel and Translation in the Late Twentieth Century*. Cambridge, MA: Harvard University Press.

Clifford, J. and G.E. Marcus (Eds.) 1986. *Writing Culture: The Poetics and Politics of Ethnography*. Berkeley, CA: University of California Press.

Colloredo-Mansfeld, R. 1999. *The Native Leisure Class: Consumption and Cultural Creativity in the Andes*. Chicago: University of Chicago Press.

Combs-Schilling, E. 1989. *Sacred Performances: Islam, Sexuality, and Sacrifice*. New York: Columbia University Press.

Coplan, D.B. 1988. Musical Understanding: The Ethnoaesthetics of Migrant Workers' Poetic Song in Lesotho. *Ethnomusicology* 323:337–68.

Crawford, D. 2001. Work and Identity in the Moroccan High Atlas. Ph.D. dissertation, University of California at Santa Barbara.

Crawford, D. and K.E. Hoffman. 2000. Essentially Amazigh: Urban Berbers and the Global Village. In K. Lacey (ed.), *The Arab-Islamic World: Multidisciplinary Approaches*. New York: Peter Lang.

Davies, E. and A. Bentahila. 1989. On Mother Tongue and Other Tongues: The Notion of Possession of a Language. *Lingua* 78:267–93.

Davis, D. and S. Davis. 1989. *Adolescence in a Moroccan Town: Making Social Sense*. New Brunswick, NJ: Rutgers University.

Deshen, S. 1989. *The Mellah Society: Jewish Community Life in Sherifian Morocco*. Chicago: University of Chicago Press.

Di Leonardo, M. 1998. *Exotics at Home: Anthropologies, Others, American Modernity*. Chicago: University of Chicago Press.

Djebar, A. 1993. *Fantasia: An Algerian Cavalcade*. Portsmouth, NH: Heinemann.

Doubleday, V. 1999. The Frame Drum in the Middle East: Women, Musical Instruments and Power. *Ethnomusicology* 431:101–34.
Douglas, M. 1966. *Purity and Danger: An Analysis of Concepts of Pollution and Taboo.* London: Routledge & Kegan Paul.
Duranti, A. 1997. *Linguistic Anthropology.* New York: Cambridge University Press.
Durham, D. 1999. The Predicament of Dress: Polyvalency and the Ironies of Cultural Identity. *American Ethnologist* 262:389–411.
Dwyer, D. 1978. *Images and Self-images: Male and Female in Morocco.* New York: Columbia University Press.
Dwyer, K. 1982. *Moroccan Dialogues: Anthropology in Question.* Baltimore, MD: The Johns Hopkins University Press.
Eagleton, T. 1991. *Ideology: An Introduction.* London: Verso.
—— 2000. *The Idea of Culture.* Oxford: Blackwell.
Eckert, P. and S. McConnell-Ginet. 2003. *Language and Gender.* Cambridge: Cambridge University Press.
Eickelman, D. 1976. *Moroccan Islam: Tradition and Society in a Pilgrimage Center.* Austin, TX: University of Texas Press.
El Aissati, A. 1993. Berber in Morocco and Algeria: Revival or Decay? *Revue de l'AILA* 10.
El Gherbi, E.M. 1993. *Amenagement Linguistique et Enseignement du Francais au Maroc.* Meknes: La Voix.
El Khayari, T. 1985. *Agriculture au Maroc.* Rabat: Editions Okad.
El Moujahid, E.H. 1994. La dimension intérculturelle dans la poésie berbère tachelhit moderne. *L'Interculturel au Maroc: Arts, Langues, Littératures et Traditions Populaires.* Casablanca: Afrique Orient, 109–26.
El Mountassir, A. 1992. La littérature proverbiale chez les Achtoukn Souss – Sud du Maroc. *Dirassat* 6:105–31.
Ennaji, M. and P. Pascon. 1988. *Le Makhzen et le Sous Al-Aqsa: La Correspondance politique de la maison d'Iligh (1821–1894).* Casablanca: Les Editions Toubkal.
Errington, J. 2003. Getting Language Rights: The Rhetorics of Language Endangerment and Loss. *American Anthropologist* 1054:723–32.
Fabian, J. 1983. *Time and the Other: How Anthropology Makes Its Object.* New York: Columbia University Press.
Feld, S. and K.H. Basso. 1996. *Senses of Place.* Santa Fe: School of American Research Press.
Ferguson, C. 1959. Diglossia. *Word* 15:325–40.
Ferguson, J. 1997. Country and City on the Copperbelt. In A. Gupta and J. Ferguson (Eds.), *Culture, Power, Place.* Durham, NC: Duke University Press, 137–54.
—— 1999. *Expectations of Modernity: Myths and Meanings of Urban Life on the Zambian Copperbelt.* Berkeley, CA: University of California Press.
Fernea, E.W. 1976. *A Street in Marrakech: A Personal View of Urban Women in Morocco.* Prospect Heights, IL: Waveland Press.
Fishman, J.A. 1980. Social Theory and Ethnography. In P. Singer (Ed.), *Ethnic Diversity and Conflict in Eastern Europe.* Santa Barbara, CA: ABC-Clio, 84–97.
Foucault, M. 1977. *Discipline and Punish: The Birth of the Prison.* New York: Vintage Books.
——1990 [1978]. *The History of Sexuality: An Introduction.* New York: Vintage Books.
Friedman, J. 1992. The Past in the Future: History and the Politics of Identity. *American Anthropologist* 944:837–59.

—— 2003. Globalizing Languages: Ideologies and Realities of the Contemporary Global System. *American Anthropologist* 105(4):744–52.

Friedrich, P. 1979. Poetic Language and the Imagination: A Radical Reformulation of the Sapir-Whorf Hypothesis. In A.S. Dil (Ed.), *Language, Context, and the Imagination: Essays by Paul Friedrich*. Stanford: Stanford University Press, 441–512.

—— 1989. Language, Ideology and Political Economy. *American Anthropologist* 912:295–312.

Frye, D. 1996. *Indians into Mexicans: History and Identity in a Mexican Town*. Austin, TX: University of Texas Press.

Gal, S. 1989. Language and Political Economy. *Annual Review of Anthropology* 18:345–67.

—— 1995a. Language and the "Arts of Resistance". *Cultural Anthropology* 103:407–24.

—— 1995b. Language, Gender, and Power: An Anthropological Review. In K. Hall and M. Bucholtz (Eds.), *Gender Articulated: Language and the Socially Constructed Self*. New York: Routledge, 169–82.

Galand-Pernet, P. 1987. Littérature orale et représentation du texte: les poèmes berbères traditionnels. *Etudes de littérature ancienne*. Paris: Presses de l'Ecole normale supériere (PENS) 3:107–18.

Galaty, J.G. 1982. Being "Maasai"; Being "People-of-cattle": Ethnic Shifters in East Africa. *American Ethnologist* 9:1–20.

Geertz, C. 1963. The Integrative Revolution. In C. Geertz (Ed.), *Old Societies and New States*. New York: Free Press, 108–13.

—— 1973. *The Interpretation of Cultures*. New York: Basic Books.

—— 1983. *Local Knowledge: Further Essays in Interpretive Anthropology*. New York: Basic Books.

Geertz, C., H. Geertz, and L. Rosen. 1979. *Meaning and Order in Moroccan Society*. Cambridge: Cambridge University Press.

Gilbert, J. 1994. *The Great Fires Poems 1982–1992*. New York: Alfred A. Knopf.

Good, B. 1977. The Heart of What's the Matter: The Semantics of Illness in Iran. *Culture, Medicine, and Psychiatry* 1:25–58.

Goodman, J. 1996. Dancing toward "La Mixité": Berber Associations and Cultural Change in Algeria. *Middle East Report* 263:16–19.

—— 2005. *Berber Culture on the World Stage: From Village to Video*. Bloomington, IN: Indiana University Press.

Goodwin, C. and A. Duranti. 1992. Rethinking Context: An Introduction. In A. Duranti and C. Goodwin (Eds.), *Rethinking Context: Language as an Interactive Phenomenon*. New York: Cambridge University Press, 1–42.

Goodwin, C. and M.H. Goodwin. 1992. Assessments and the Construction of Context. In A. Duranti and C. Goodwin (Eds.), *Rethinking Context: Language as an Interactive Phenomenon*. New York: Cambridge University Press, 147–90.

Goodwin, M. 1990. *He-Said-She-Said: Talk as Social Organization among Black Children*. Bloomington, IN: Indiana University Press.

Guessous, S. 1996. *Au-delà de toute pudeur*. Paris: Eddif.

Guneratne, A. 2002. *Many Tongues, One People: The Making of Tharu Identity in Nepal*. Ithaca, NY: Cornell University Press.

Gupta, A. and J. Ferguson (Eds.) 1997. *Anthropological Locations: Boundaries and Grounds of a Field Science*. Berkeley, CA: University of California Press.

Haeri, N. 2003. *Sacred Language, Ordinary People: Dilemmas of Culture and Politics in Egypt*. New York: Palgrave Macmillan.

Hammoudi, A. 1993. *The Victim and Its Masks: An Essay on Sacrifice*. Chicago: University of Chicago Press.

—— 1997. *Master and Disciple: The Cultural Foundations of Moroccan Authoritarianism*. Chicago: University of Chicago Press.

Hannaoui, A. 1987. *Diglossia, Medial Arabic and Language Policy in Morocco*. Stony Brook, NY: State University of New York.

Hannoum, A. 2001. *Postcolonial Memories: The Legend of the Kahina, a North-African Heroine*. Portsmouth, NH: Heinemann.

Hart, D. 1984. *The Ait 'Atta of Southern Morocco; Daily Life and Recent History*. Cambridge: MENA Press Ltd.

—— 2000. *Tribe and Society in Rural Morocco*. London: Frank Cass.

Harvey, P. 1994. The Presence and Absence of Speech in the Communication of Gender. In P. Burton, K. Kushari Dyson and S. Ardener (Eds.), *Bilingual Women*. Oxford: Berg, 44–64.

Heath, J. 1989. *From Code-Switching to Borrowing: Foreign and Diglossic Mixing in Moroccan Arabic*. London: Kegan Paul International.

Heidegger, M. 1977. Building Dwelling Thinking. In *Martin Heidegger: Basic Writings*. New York: Harper & Row, 319–39.

Hensel, C. 1996. *Telling Our Selves: Ethnicity and Discourse in Southwestern Alaska*. New York: Oxford University Press.

Herzog, G. (Ed.) 1950. Song. In M. Leach (Ed.), *Funk and Wagnall's Dictionary of Folklore, Mythology and Legend*. New York: Funk and Wagnall.

Hill, J. 1985. The Grammar of Consciousness and the Consciousness of Grammar. *American Ethnologist* 124:725–37.

—— 1987. Women's Speech in Modern Mexicano. In S.U. Philips, S. Steele and C. Tanz (Eds.), *Language, Gender and Sex in Comparative Perspective*. New York: Cambridge University Press, 121–60.

—— 2002. "Expert Rhetorics" in Advocacy for Endangered Languages: Who Is Listening, and What Do They Hear? *Journal of Linguistic Anthropology* 122:119–33.

Hill, J. and K. Hill. 1986. *Speaking Mexicano: Dynamics of Syncretic Language in Central Mexico*. Tuscon, AZ: University of Arizona Press.

Hirsch, S.F. 1998. *Pronouncing and Persevering: Gender and the Discourses of Disputing in an African Islamic Court*. Chicago: University of Chicago Press.

Hoffman, B. 1967. *The Structure of Traditional Moroccan Rural Society*. The Hague: Mouton & Co.

Hoffman, K.E. n.d. Colonial Practices and Postnational Preoccupations: Internal Fractures in the Berber – Arab Distinction. *Berbers and others: Redefining Ethnicity in the Contemporary Maghrib*. K.E. Hoffman and S.G. Miller (Eds.).

—— 2000a. The Place of Language: Song, Talk and Land in Southwestern Morocco. Ph.D. dissertation, Columbia University.

—— 2000b. Administering Identities: State Decentralization and Local Identification in Morocco. *Journal of North African Studies* 53:185–200.

—— 2002a. Generational Change in Berber Women's Song of the Anti-Atlas Mountains, Morocco. *Ethnomusicology* 463:510–40.

—— 2002b. Moving and Dwelling: Building the Moroccan Ashelhi Homeland. *American Ethnologist* 294:928–62.

—— 2003. Emigration, Gender, and the Burden of Language Preservation. In J. Blythe and M. Brown (Eds.), *Maintaining the Links: Language, Identity and the Land.* Bath: Foundation for Endangered Languages, 93–100.

—— 2006. Berber Language Ideologies, Maintenance, and Contraction: Gendered Variation in the Indigenous Margins of Morocco. *Language & Communication* 26(2):144–67.

—— Forthcoming 2008. Purity and Contamination: Language Ideologies in French Colonial Native Policy in Morocco. *Contemporary Studies in Society and History* 50.

Hoisington, W. 1984. *The Casablanca Connection: French Colonial Policy, 1936–1943.* Chapel Hill, NC: University of North Carolina Press.

Holt, M. 1994. Algeria: Language, Nation and State. In Y. Suleiman (Ed.), *Arabic Sociolinguistics: Issues and Perspectives.* Richmond: Curzon Press, 25–41.

Hymes, D. 1972. On Communicative Competence. In J.B. Pride and J. Holmes (Eds.), *Sociolinguistics.* New York: Penguin.

—— 1984. Linguistic Problems in Defining the Concept of "Tribe." In J. Baugh and J. Sherzer (Eds.), *Language in Use: Readings in Sociolinguistics.* Englewood Cliffs, NJ: Prentice-Hall.

Ibn Khaldûn. 1967 [1377]. *The Muqaddimah: An Introduction to History.* Princeton, NJ: Princeton University Press.

—— 1968 [1377] *Histoire des Berbères et des dynasties musulmanes de l'Afrique septentrionale.* Paris: P. Geuthner.

Ilahiane, H. 2004. *Ethnicities, Community Making, and Agrarian Change: The Political Ecology of a Moroccan Oasis.* New York: University Press of America.

Irvine, J. 1979. Formality and Informality in Communicative Events. *American Anthropologist* 81:773–90.

—— 1985. Status and Style in Language. *Annual Review of Anthropology* 14:557–81.

—— 1989. When Talk Isn't Cheap: Language and Political Economy. *American Ethnologist* 162:248–67.

Irvine, J. and S. Gal. 2000. Language Ideology and Linguistic Differentiation. In. P.V. Kroskrity, B.B. Schieffelin and K. Woolard (Eds.), *Regimes of Language.* Santa Fe, NM: School of American Research Press, 35–83.

Issawi, C. 1982. *An Economic History of the Middle East and North Africa.* New York: Columbia University Press.

Ivy, M. 1995. *Discourses of the Vanishing: Modernity, Phantasm, Japan.* Chicago: University of Chicago Press.

Jaffe, A. 1999. *Ideologies in Action: Language Politics on Corsica.* New York: Mouton de Gruyter.

Jakobson, R. 1987 [1920]. *Language in Literature.* Cambridge, MA: Harvard University Press.

Jameson, F. 1984. Postmodernism, or the Cultural Logic of Late Imperialism. *New Left Review* 14653–92.

—— 1989. Nostalgia for the Present. *South Atlantic Quarterly* 88(2):517–37.

Jouhadi, H. 2003. *Translation of the Meanings of the Koran [tarjamat ma'ani al qur'an al karim illa llugha al amazighiyya].* Casablanca: An-najah al-Jadida.

Kapchan, D. 1996. *Gender on the Market: Moroccan Women and the Revoicing of Tradition.* Philadelphia: University of Pennsylvania.

Kaye, J. and A. Zoubir. 1990. *The Ambiguous Compromise: Language, Literature and National Identity in Algeria and Morocco.* New York: Routledge.

King, K.A. 2001. *Language Revitalization Processes and Prospects: Quichua in the Ecuadorian Andes*. Buffalo: Multilingual Matters.

Koester, D. 1995. Gender Ideology and Nationalism in the Culture and Politics of Iceland. *American Ethnologist* 223:572–88.

Kosansky, O. 2002. Tourism, Charity, and Profit: The Movement of Money in Moroccan Jewish Pilgrimage. *Cultural Anthropology* 173:359–400.

—— 2003. *All Dear unto God: Saints, Pilgrimage and Textual Practice in Jewish Morocco. Anthropology*. Ann Arbor, MI: University of Michigan Press.

Kroskrity, P.V. 1993. *Language, History, and Identity: Ethnolinguistic Studies of the Arizona Tewa*. Tuscon, AZ: University of Arizona Press.

Kuipers, J.C. 1998. *Language, Identity, and Marginality in Indonesia: The Changing Nature of Ritual Speech on the Island of Sumba*. Cambridge: Cambridge University Press.

Kulick, D. 1992. *Language Shift and Cultural Reproduction: Socialization, Self, and Syncretism in a Papua Guinean Village*. New York: Cambridge University Press.

Kuper, A. 1999. *Culture: The Anthropologists' Account*. Cambridge, MA: Harvard University Press.

Labov, W. 1978. *Women's Role in Linguistic Change*. Annual Meeting of the Linguistic Society of America, Boston, MA, December.

Lafuente, G. 1999. *La Politique Berbère de la France et le Nationalisme Marocain*. Paris: Harmattan.

Lakhsassi, A. 1986. La conception de la poésie Tashelhit. *Lamalif* 183:56–8.

Lee, B. 2001. Introduction. In G. Urban, *Metaculture*. Minneapolis: University of Minnesota Press.

Lefebvre, H. 1991. *The Production of Space*. Oxford: Blackwell.

Levin, S. 1999. *Juifs parmi les Berbères: Photographies d'Elias Harrus*. Paris: Musée d'Art et d' Histoire du Judaïsme.

Levy, A. 1999. Playing for Control of Distance: Card Games between Jews and Muslims on a Casablanca Beach. *American Ethnologist* 263:632–53.

Lorcin, P.M.E. 1999. *Imperial Identities: Stereotyping, Prejudice and Race in Colonial Algeria*. London: I.B. Taurus.

Lortat-Jacob, B. 1981. Community Music as an Obstacle to Professionalism: A Berber Example. *Ethnomusicology* 25.1:87–98.

Lutz, C.A. 1988. *Unnatural Emotions: Everyday Sentiments on a Micronesian Atoll and their Challenge to Western Theory*. Chicago: University of Chicago Press.

McDougall, J. 2004. Myth and Counter-Myth: "The Berber" as National Signifier in Algerian Historiographies. *Radical History Review* 86:66–88.

Maffi, L. 2001. *On Biocultural Diversity*. Washington, DC: Smithsonian Institution Press.

Maggi, W. 2001. *Our Women Are Free: Gender and Ethnicity in the Hindukush*. Ann Arbor, MI: University of Michigan Press.

Malkki, L.H. 1995. *Purity and Exile: Violence, Memory, and National Cosmology among Hutu Refugees in Tanzania*. Chicago: University of Chicago Press.

Manuel, P. 1993. *Cassette Culture: Popular Music and Technology in North India*. Chicago: University of Chicago Press.

Marcus, G.E. 1986. *Anthropology as Cultural Critique: An Experimental Moment in the Human Sciences*. Chicago: University of Chicago Press.

—— 1998. *Ethnography through Thick and Thin*. Princeton, NJ: Princeton University Press.

Marthelot, P. 1973. Ethnie et région: le "phenomène" berbère au Maghreb. M. Galley and D. Marshall (Eds.), *Proceedings of the First Congress on Mediterranean Studies of Arabo-Berber Influence.* Algiers: Société National d'Edition, 465–74.

Masquelier, A. 2002. Road Mythologies: Space, Mobility, and the Historical Imagination in Postcolonial Niger. *American Ethnologist* 294:829–56.

Méraud, M. 1990. *Histoire des A.I., Le service des Affaires Indigènes au Maroc.* Paris: La Koumia – Public-Réalisations.

Messick, B. 1987. Subordinate Discourse: Women, Weaving, and Gender Relations in North Africa. *American Ethnologist* 142:210–25.

Miller, J. 1984. *Imlil: A Moroccan Mountain Community in Change.* New York: Westview Press.

Mills, M.A. 1991. *Rhetorics and Politics in Afghan Traditional Storytelling.* Philadelphia: University of Pennsylvania Press.

Milroy, L. 1987. *Language and Social Networks.* Oxford: Basil Blackwell.

Ministère de la Prevision Economique et du Plan. 1994. Division de la Statistique, Population Rurale par Fraction et Douar. *Recensement générale de la population et de l'habitat du 1994.*

Montagne, R. 1973 [1931]. *The Berbers: Their Social and Political Organisation.* London: Frank Cass.

Nettle, D. and S. Romaine. 2000. *Vanishing Voices: The Extinction of the World's Languages.* Oxford: Oxford University Press.

Niezen, R. 2003. *The Origins of Indigenism: Human Rights and the Politics of Identity.* Berkeley, CA: University of California Press.

Ochs, E. 1979. Transcription as theory. In E. Ochs and B.B. Schieffelin (Eds.), *Developmental Pragmatics.* New York: Academic Press, 43–72.

—— 1992. Indexing gender. In A. Duranti and C. Goodwin (Eds.), *Rethinking Context: Language as an Interactive Phenomenon.* New York: Cambridge University Press, 335–58.

Ossman, S. 1994. *Picturing Casablanca: Portraits of Power in a Modern City.* Berkeley, CA: University of California.

—— 2002. *Three Faces of Beauty: Casablanca, Paris, Cairo.* Durham, NC: Duke University Press.

Ouakrime, M. 2001. Promoting the Maintenance of Endangered Languages through the Internet: The Case of Tamazight. In C. Moseley, N. Ostler, H. Ouzzate (Eds.), *Endangered Languages and the Media: Proceedings of the Fifth FEL Conference, Agadir, Morocco.* Bath: Foundation for Endangered Languages.

Pascon, P. 1986. *Capitalism and Agriculture in the Haouz of Marrakesh.* New York: Routledge & Kegan Paul.

Peets, L. 1988. *Women of Marrakech: Record of a Secret Sharer 1930–1970.* Durham, NC: Duke University Press.

Pleines, J. (Ed.) 1990. *La Linguistique au Maghreb/Maghreb Linguistics.* Rabat: Editions Okad.

Povinelli, E. 1993. *Labor's Lot: The Power, History, and Culture of Aboriginal Action.* Chicago: University of Chicago Press.

—— 2002. *The Cunning of Recognition.* Durham, NC: Duke University Press.

Pratt, M.L. 1987. Linguistic Utopias. In N. Fabb, D. Attridge, A. Durant and C. MacCabe (Eds.), *The Linguistics of Writing: Arguments between Language and Literature.* New York: Methuen, 48–66.

Rabia, Officier Interprète. 1935. *La coutume Ait Tayia.* MAE Série Maroc DAI Carton 454. Nantes: Ministère des Affaires Etrangères.

Rabinow, P. 1977. *Reflections on Fieldwork in Morocco.* Berkeley, CA: University of California Press.

Rindstedt, C. and K. Aronsson. 2001. Growing Up Monolingual in a Bilingual Community: The Quichua Revitalization Paradox. *Language in Society* 315:721–42.

Rosaldo, M.Z. 1980. *Knowledge and Passion: Ilongot Notions of Self and Social Life.* New York: Cambridge University Press.

Rosen, L. 1984. *Bargaining for Reality: The Construction of Social Relations in a Muslim Community.* Chicago: University of Chicago Press.

Rosenberger, B. 1970. Tamdult: cité minière et caravanière présaharienne IX–XIVs. *Hesperis Tamuda* XI:103–40.

Rovsing Olsen, M. 1984. *Chants de mariage dans l'Atlas marocain: Ethnologie.* Paris: Université de Paris X.

—— 1997. *Chants et Danses de l'Atlas Maroc.* Paris: Cité de la Musique/Actes Sud.

Rubin, G. 1975. The Traffic in Women: Notes on the "Political Economy" of Sex. In R.R. Reiter (Ed.), *Toward an Anthropology of Women.* New York: Monthly Review Press.

Sadiqi, F. 2003. *Women, Gender, and Language in Morocco.* Leiden: Brill.

Sant Cassia, P. 2000. Exoticizing Discoveries and Extraordinary Experiences: "Traditional" Music, Modernity, and Nostalgia in Malta and Other Mediterranean Societies. *Ethnomusicology* 442:281–301.

Sapir, E. 1921. The Musical Foundation of Verse. *Journal of English and Germanic Philology* 20:213–28.

—— 1995 [1933]. Language. In B. Blount (Ed.), *Language, Culture, and Society.* Prospect Heights, IL: Waveland Press.

Saroli, A. 2004. Can Quechua Survive? *Cultural Survival Quarterly.* Available at www. cultural survival.org/publications, accessed January 18, 2004.

Schieffelin, B.B. 1990. *The Give and Take of Everyday Life: Language Socialization of Kaluli Children.* Cambridge: Cambridge University Press.

Schieffelin, B.B. and R.C. Doucet. 1994. The "Real" Haitian Creole: Ideology, Metalinguistics, and Orthographic Choice. *American Ethnologist* 211:176–200.

Schieffelin, B.B. and K.A. Woolard. 1994. Language Ideology. *Annual Review of Anthropology* 23:55–82.

Schiffrin, D. 1988. *Discourse Markers.* Cambridge: Cambridge University Press.

Schuyler, P.D. 1979. A Repertory of Ideas: The Music of the "Rwais," Berber Professional Musicians from Southwestern Morocco. Ph.D. dissertation, University of Washington.

Scott, J. 1990. *Domination and the Arts of Resistance: Hidden Transcripts.* New Haven: Yale University Press.

Seeger, A. 1987. *Why Suya Sing: A Musical Anthropology of an Amazonian People.* Cambridge: Cambridge University Press.

Shatzmiller, M. 2000. *The Berbers and the Islamic State: The Marinid Experience in Pre-Protectorate Morocco.* Princeton, NJ: Markus Weiner Publishers.

Sherzer, J. 1987. A Diversity of Voices: Men's and Women's Speech in Ethnographic Perspective. In S. Phillips, S. Steele and C. Tanz (Eds.), *Language, Gender and Sex in Comparative Perspective.* New York: Cambridge University Press, 95–120.

Silverstein, M. 1976. Shifters, Linguistic Categories, and Cultural Description. In K. Basso and H.A. Selby (Eds.), *Meaning in Anthropology*. Albuquerque, NM: University of New Mexico Press.

—— 1979. Language Structure and Linguistic Ideology. In P. Clyne (Ed.), *The Elements: A Parasession on Linguistic Units and Levels*. Chicago: Chicago Linguistic Society, 193–247.

—— 1987. Shifters, Linguistic Categories and Cultural Description. In B. Blount (Ed.), *Language, Culture, and Society*. Prospect Heights, IL: Waveland Press, 187–221.

—— 1998. Monoglot "Standard" in America: Standardization and Metaphors of Linguistic Hegemony. In D. Brenneis and R.H.S. Macaulay (Eds.), *The Matrix of Language*. Boulder, CO: Westview Press, 284–306.

—— 2003. Indexical Order and the Dialectics of Sociolinguistic Life. *Language & Communication* 23:193–229.

Silverstein, P.A. 2004. *Algeria in France: Transpolitics, Race, and Nation*. Bloomington, IN: Indiana University Press.

Silverstein, P.A. and D. Crawford. 2004. Amazigh Activism and the Moroccan State. *Middle East Report* 233:44–8.

Smith, B.H. 1983. Contingencies of Value. *Critical Inquiry* 1:1–35.

Spitulnik, D. 1998. Mediating Unity and Diversity: The Production of Language Ideologies in Zambian Broadcasting. In B.B. Schieffelin, K.A. Woolard and P.V. Kroskrity (Eds.), *Language Ideologies*. New York: Oxford University Press, 163–88.

Spratt, J.E., B. Seckinger and D.A. Wagner. 1991. Functional Literacy in Moroccan School Children. *Reading Research Quarterly* 262:178–95.

Stewart, K. 1996. *A Space on the Side of the Road: Cultural Poetics in an "Other" America*. Princeton, NJ: Princeton University Press.

Stora, B. 2001. *Algeria 1830–2000: A Short History*. Ithaca, NY: Cornell University Press.

Suleiman, Y. 1994. Nationalism and the Arabic Language: An Historical Overview. In Y. Suleiman (Ed.), *Arabic Sociolinguistics: Issues and Perspectives*. Richmond: Curzon Press, 3–24.

—— 2003. *The Arabic Language and National Identity*. Washington, DC: Georgetown University Press.

Swearingen, W.D. 1987. *Moroccan Mirages: Agrarian Dreams and Deceptions, 1912–1986*. London: I.B. Tauris.

Swigart, L. 1992. Two Codes or One? The Insiders' View and the Description of Codeswitching in Dakar. *Journal of Multilingual and Multicultural Development* 131(2):83–102.

—— 1994. Cultural Creolisation and Language Use in Post-colonial Africa: The Case of Senegal. *Africa* 642:175–89.

Taifi, M. 1995. Sentiment d'appartenance linguistique et aspirations sociales: exemples marocains. *Awal* 12:89–98.

Taroudant Province Public Administration. n.d. *Monografia Iqlim Taroudant [Monograph of Taroudant Province]*. Taroudant Walidiya.

Taussig, M. 1992. *The Nervous System*. New York: Routledge.

Tedlock, D. 1983. *The Spoken Word and the Work of Interpretation*. Philadelphia: University of Pennsylvania Press.

Thomas, L. 1918. *Voyage au Goundafa et au Sous*. Paris: Payot.

Tilley, C. 1994. *A Phenomenology of Landscape: Places, Paths and Monuments*. Oxford: Berg.

Tilmatine, M. 1992. A propos de néologie en berbère moderne. *Afrikanistische Arbeitspapiere AAP* 30:155–66.

Trudgill, P. 1983. Sex and Covert Prestige: Linguistic Change in the Urban Dialect of Norwich. In P. Trudgill (Ed.), *On Dialect*. New York: New York University Press and Oxford: Basil Blackwell, 169–85.

Tsing, A.L. 1993. *In the Realm of the Diamond Queen: Marginality in an Out-of-the-Way Place*. Princeton, NJ: Princeton University Press.

Turino, T. 1993. *Moving Away from Silence: Music of the Peruvian Altiplano and the Experience of Urban Migration*. Chicago: University of Chicago Press.

Urban, G. 2001. *Metaculture: How Culture Moves through the World*. Minneapolis, MN: University of Minnesota Press.

Vološinov, V.N. 1973 [1929]. *Marxism and the Philosophy of Language*. Cambridge, MA: Harvard University Press.

Wagner, D. 1993. *Literacy, Culture and Development: Becoming Literate in Morocco*. New York: Cambridge University Press.

Waterbury, J. 1972a. *North for the Trade: The Life and Times of a Berber Merchant*. Berkeley, CA: University of California Press.

Waterbury, J. 1972b. Tribalism, Trade and Politics: The Transformation of the Swasa of Morocco. In E. Gellner and C. Micaud (Eds.), *Arabs and Berbers*. Lexington, MA: Lexington Books, 231–57.

Weber, E. 1976. *Peasants into Frenchmen: The Modernization of Rural France, 1870–1914*. Stanford, CA: Stanford University Press.

Weingrod, A. 1990. Saints and Shrines, Politics, and Culture: A Morocco-Israel Comparison. In D. Eickelman and J. Piscatori (Eds.), *Muslim Travelers: Pilgrimage, Migration, and the Religious Imagination*. Berkeley, CA: University of California Press, 215–35.

Wilce, J. 1998. *Eloquence in Trouble: The Poetics and Politics of Complaint in Rural Bangladesh*. New York: Oxford University Press.

Williams, R. 1973. *The Country and the City*. New York: Oxford University Press.

—— 1977. *Marxism and Literature*. New York: Oxford University Press.

Wolf, E.R. 1982. *Europe and the People without History*. Berkeley, CA: University of California.

—— 1999. *Envisioning Power: Ideologies of Dominance and Crisis*. Berkeley, CA: University of California Press.

Wolf, M. 1992. *A Thrice Told Tale: Feminism, Postmodernism and Ethnographic Responsibility*. Stanford, CA: Stanford University Press.

Woolard, K.A. 1998a. Simultaneity and Bivalency as Strategies in Bilingualism. *Journal of Linguistic Anthropology* 8(1):3–29.

—— 1998b. Introduction: Language Ideology as a Field of Inquiry. In B.B. Schieffelin, K.A. Woolard and P.V. Kroskrity (Eds.), *Language Ideologies: Practice and Theory*. New York: Oxford University Press.

Wright, G. 1991. *The Politics of Design in French Colonial Urbanism*. Chicago: University of Chicago Press.

Yeats, W.B. 1924. *The Collected Works of W.B. Yeats,* Volume I: *The Poems*, edited by R.J. Finneran. London: Macmillan.

Youssi, A. 1990. Lexical Processes in the Berber of the Media in Morocco. In J. Pleines (Ed.), *La Linguistique au Maghreb*. Rabat: Editions Okad, 264–81.

Index

CPSIA information can be obtained at www.ICGtesting.com
Printed in the USA
BVOW061945091012

302587BV00003B/1/P

9 781405 154215